Crimes
Discreetly Veiled

F. J. P. VEALE

Author of
The Man from the Volga: A Life of Lenin
Frederick the Great
Advance to Barbarism

With a Foreword by

THE RT. HON. LORD HANKEY, G.C.B., G.C.M.G., G.C.V.O.

Illustrated

INSTITUTE FOR
HISTORICAL
REVIEW

P.O. BOX 1306 • TORRANCE, CA. 90505 • USA

Illustrations facing pages
32, 48, 80, 96, 160, 176, 208, 224

Cover shows the historic city of Dresden after it was bombed day and night by British and American planes. 135,000 were killed, mostly women and children refugees fleeing from the advancing Red Army. The city held no military significance, and was undefended.

To

ROSEMARY

for

invaluable translating

and research

Publishing history of this title:

1958 1st edition published in London by Cooper Book
      Company
1959 1st USA edition published by Devin-Adair, New York
1979 This edition published by Institute for Historical
      Review. P.O. Box 1306, Torrance, CA 90505.

This title: *The Veale File, Volume 2: Crimes Discreetly Veiled* ISBN: 0-911038-54-X

Companion title: *The Veale File, Volume 1: Advance to Barbarism* ISBN: 0-911038-53-1

CONTENTS

———◆———

FOREWORD

by

the Right Hon. Lord Hankey
G.C.B., G.C.M.G., G.C.V.O.

Thanks to what has come to be known as 'The Iron Curtain of Discreet Silence', at the termination of the Second World War, there was a seemingly unanimous acceptance of the then novel legal proposition that an accuser is a fit person to act as judge of his own charges. After some two years, however, two small books, written concurrently and independently, were published in this country challenging this proposition as contrary to established legal principles and common sense, "Epitaph on Nuremberg" by Montgomery Belgion and "Advance to Barbarism" by the author of the present book, Mr. F. J. P. Veale. Enlarged versions of both books were subsequently published in the United States, Mr. Montgomery Belgion's book under the title "Victor's Justice" in 1949 and Mr. Veale's book under its original title in 1953.

Quite independently, others were working on similar lines and these two books were followed in 1950 by my own book, "Politics: Trials and Errors", and in 1951 by Mr. R. T. Paget's realistic "Manstein" and by Viscount Maugham's weighty book, "U.N.O. and War Crimes" with its balanced criticism and wise counsel for the future.

I was privileged to write a foreword to "Manstein" and a political 'Postcript' to Viscount Maugham's book, and perhaps that is one reason why my services have been requisitioned again, this time by Mr. Veale.

That these books, and others too numerous to mention, published both here and abroad, have contributed to a gradual change in public opinion is suggested by the fact that before the end of June 1957, the last of the German prisoners serving sentence by a British Court as war criminals had been released from Werl, after which the prison was closed down. In Japan also the last prisoner held on British account had been released from Sugama in January 1957, and the last held on Australian account on 4th July 1957. Many of them, of course, had been set free under the normal regulations, but clemency played a large part both in securing relaxation of the original procedures and in individual hard cases which were brought to light by the patient and persistent efforts of individuals, following the publication of many books in many lands, including those mentioned above. To a varying extent most of the N.A.T.O. Powers had *mutatis mutandis,* pursued similar policies.

Even at Spandau, the blackest spot in the picture, where the victims of the Nuremberg International Tribunal were, and are, interned under international guardianship in shameful conditions of humiliation—sufferings which are well described by Mr. Veale in Chapter VII—the numbers held have been reduced to two or three. In their case, release or relief can only be obtained by the agreement of the four responsible Powers, which unfortunately include Soviet Russia. That is a matter to which the fanatical believers in the "international method" should give their attention.

Soviet Russia bulks prominently in "Crimes Discreetly Veiled", which consists of independent sketches of six events in contemporary history. Indeed it is written from the angle that up to now, the facts relating to them have been repressed or distorted in the interests of the Stalin Myth which was adopted during the Second World War for reasons of political expediency.

A good example of this is afforded by the description in Mr. Veale's Chapter II of the very awkward dilemma in which the Nuremberg Tribunal was placed when the Russian Prosecutor insisted on indicting the German prisoners for responsibility for the ghastly Katyn murders. I will not spoil this interesting story by describing how adroitly the dignified British President of the Tribunal side-stepped this notoriously false accusation, but most readers will agree with Mr. Veale's regret that the Tribunal was debarred from a thorough investigation, which must have exposed to the world Soviet Russia's guilt, by the limitation of its jurisdiction imposed by the Charter to crimes "committed in the interest of the European Axis countries". Still we have some compensation for the Tribunal's inability to undertake the task in Mr. Veale's masterly presentation of the evidence in this Chapter, which, to judge by my own experience, will come as a surprise to most readers.

Equally surprising is the description of the death of Mussolini in Chapter III. Although containing no new facts or disclosures, it is of absorbing interest. Most of us have some vague recollection of horrible orgies at Milan *after* the Duce's death, but how many could piece together into a consistent story such episodes as his arrest while leaving the gates of the Royal Palace at Rome after his dismissal by the King; his transfer to a mountain hotel in the Apennines; his daring rescue by German airmen; his attempt at Hitler's instance to raise an army of North Italian partisans to supplement stubborn resistance by the German army; his failure before the relentless advance of the allied armies, and the reaction of those and other allied victories on North Italian public opinion, especially the effect on the many Italian Communist partisans, of the Russian successes on the Eastern Front.

The most thrilling part of the story, however, is the account of the death of Mussolini and his mistress—not by execution, the word used in many important works of reference, which would pre-suppose judicial trial and sentence, but as Mr. Veale shows to be practically certain by an act of sheer murder by Communist partisans—a crime that for political reasons, has never been brought to book. The deed was done after a desperate attempt by the Duce to reach the northern end of Lake Como and escape into Austria, in the beautiful region of Menaggio, which, many readers must have visited, like my wife and myself who visited it during our honeymoon. But it is a tragic and complicated story in which, once more, I will not attempt to anticipate Mr. Veale's vivid account.

In the third tale of these new Arabian Nights Mr. Veale's "hero" (in the sense of "chief man in a story or poem", to quote the dictionary) is not a great politician like Mussolini, or a general or admiral as in later Chapters, but a French doctor, who, for years and years abused his position as a member of one of the most noble and respected professions to extort money, by ingenious devices, even though they involved the death of his patients. The story reaches its climax in the later years of the German occupation of France, when Dr. Petiot devised and carried out a diabolical, but entirely bogus, scheme for extorting large sums of money from "patients" who came to him in the belief that he was in a position to secure their escape from France through one or other of the underground channels that had sprung up. Once their passage money to distant lands, together with a substantial fee to the pretended escape association was handed over, the victims, with their suitcases and valuables, were given a "rendez-vous" in the doctor's house, in a fashionable quarter of Paris, where they vanished forever by methods which I leave for Mr. Veale to describe. As, in any event, it was not until a long time had passed that any message could be received from them, owing to the fact that communications were slow, and the whole business of escape illicit and unreliable, it was long before suspicion was aroused. Consequently, years elapsed before Petiot could be brought to book—which is the most interesting part of the story—but eventually, he was condemned and guillotined.

The moral of the tale, which links it up to the rest of the book, is that in time of war and especially of armed occupation by an enemy, the whole machinery of government, law and justice is bound to become dislocated. Under a regime of partisan activity, it is hard for the police to distinguish between patriotic acts, to which the eyes must be closed, and banditry and crime; and, under the cloak of patriotism, crime flourishes. These conditions are not propitious for the investigation and repression of crime.

But the story traced out in matter-of-fact terms, and covering every detail, is of sustained interest, and Mr. Veale has unearthed a character in real life which Conan Doyle, H. G. Wells, or Monsieur Le Coq might have envied in fiction. As in most of these six tales, truth is shown to be stranger than fiction.

In Chapter V Mr. Veale brings to notice another notable figure, but of a very different type from Dr. Petiot. This time it is a brave and skilful German military leader, Major Walter Reder, whose unit was part of an armoured division that was singled out for special and generous praise in one of Field Marshal Lord Alexander's despatches for skill and fanatical bravery in its resistance. All had gone well with the Major until his unit was withdrawn from the fighting line to deal with a serious threat to the German lines of communication, by a group of Communist Partisans (of whom we last heard in Chapter III). Reder's task was performed with distinction and success, although, owing to a leg injury which lasted for many years, he could take no active part in the operations which he directed by telephone from a hillside some miles away. But, as is apt to happen when dealing with Partisans in civilian dress, a number were killed and years later, after the end of the War, Reder was indicted as a War Criminal and accused of responsibility for horrible crimes, such as the massacre of the civilian population of the little town of Marzabotto—which Mr. Veale suggests, never took place, and for which, as Mr. Veale brings out so well, he could not possibly have been guilty if it had—since he never visited the town in his life. Originally, he was arrested in Austria at the request of the Italian Government by the Americans, who, after a long detention, decided that the charge was baseless, and then, for unknown reasons, handed him over to the British, who, in their turn, found the charges baseless, and, to quote Mr. Veale, "also adopted the Pontius Pilate precedent, and handed him over to the Italians".

There I shall take leave of him and urge my readers to learn from Mr. Veale's skilful account the astonishing story of political complication which, up to the time of writing, has stood in the way of his release. In that story, as usual, the Communists play a sinister part.

The case of General Ramcke, the gallant defender of Brest, who is the hero of Chapter VI, bears some resemblance to that of Major Reder, and is, in a general way, better known in this country. But, once more, by patient investigation, Mr. Veale brings to light every aspect of this story — from the General's chivalrous welcome by the American General to whom he surrendered at Brest, to his final trial by a French Court in political conditions which rendered almost impossible a verdict of "not guilty" and forced the Court to adopt an ingenious verdict worthy only of "Mr. Facing-Both-Ways". None of the Allied Governments came well out of the story, but it had a good ending with the release of the hero.

Coming to the last Chapter, "The Super-Ersatz Crime", the best commentary I can make, bearing on the fine character of Admiral Raeder, the hero of the tale, is to publish, for the first time, the following translation of the generous letter that I received from him in November 1955—shortly after his release from Spandau: —

Erich Raeder
Grossadmiral 2 D.Dr.p.c.

Bad Oeynhausen
14 November 55
Golliwitzer-Meier-Institut.

To Lord Hankey
London
House of Lords

My Lord,

Having been released from Spandau Prison on September 28th, 1955 I am conscious of a sincere urge to express to your Lordship my most heartfelt thanks for your intervention —as just as it has been effective—on behalf of the so-styled German "War Criminals". I know that you have been attacked in the Press on this account—a fact that makes me thank you even more heartily. I should like you to know that your letter of September 21st, 1954, to the *Times*, which we in Spandau Prison read in abbreviated form in the German Press, awoke in us prisoners the confident hope that something was being done to put an early end to our imprisonment. For this, too, our grateful thanks are due to your Lordship.

In sincere Gratitude,

I remain,

Yours sincerely,

Erich Raeder,

Grand-Admiral (Retd.).

One of the most satisfactory features of this generous letter, as I put it in my reply of 19th November, was that:—

"It was a real encouragement to my friends and myself to learn at first hand from your letter that the message in one of my letters to the "*Times*" was able to penetrate the formidable barrier of Spandau, even in a much attenuated form, and that it brought to you and your comrades some spark of hope . . . "

It might interest readers of "Crimes Discreetly Veiled" to recall the terms of that letter, which were as follows:—

WAR CRIMINALS
To the Editor of The Times

Sir,—My letter in the "Times" of August 4, after urging the Western allies to release their remaining war criminals in Germany and Japan before the coming high level talks, ended as follows:—"If the U.S.S.R., where larger numbers are involved did the same (and why not?) the results would be far-reaching."

Now the miracle has happened, and Marshal Bulganin and Dr. Adenauer have stolen a march on the Allies. The results are already appreciable and may become outstanding. Tension between Germany and Russia has been relaxed, Germany hopes for a new era, and, as foreseen in your leading article of September 15, Dr. Adenauer's position at home and the policy he conducts have been strengthened—and he needs every ounce of strength for his coming negotiations.

But the outstanding features of the Moscow talks, which have hardly been noticed, are that the tradition of failure in negotiations between the outside world and the U.S.S.R. has been broken, and that on a great moral issue pressed by Dr. Adenauer for five gruelling days on grounds of sheer humanity, Marshal Bulganin has, subject to a not unreasonable quid pro quo, made a gesture unprecedented in modern times.

It is to be hoped that the western allies will be able to

give a cordial welcome to the Russo-German initiative and to co-operate in a spirit of friendly rivalry. The change in Soviet policy should remove the main obstacle to the release of the ageing inmates of Spandau and their counterparts in in Tokyo. The relatively small remnants serving sentences in Werl, Landsberg, Wittlich, Neuwied, and Sugama should be set free as a matter of course, for it is unthinkable that the Christian Powers should cling to a meticulous insistence on the extreme letter of the law when, on this particular issue, their former Communist ally is applying on a generous scale the principles of mercy and forgiveness on which Christianity is founded.

In short, the Big Four have a golden opportunity this autumn to liquidate a policy which, whatever its merits 10 years ago, is out of tune with the present state of the world.

Yours faithfully,

HANKEY.

House of Lords, Sept. 21, 1955.

That this letter should have brought so much hope as to prompt the Grand-Admiral to mention it shows how drowning men will clutch at a straw. But it evoked several other interesting messages from Germany, including an expression of "sincerest thanks for this generous suggestion" from the Federal Chancellor, Dr. Adenauer, which I especially value. Even more satisfactory was that it was followed by an agreement which included the release by Soviet Russia of some 7,600 German prisoners held as War Criminals, though I do not claim "*post hoc propter hoc*" for that.

I should also like to think that the letter contributed, if only a little, towards the satisfactory figures for releases quoted at the outset of this foreword.

However, this may be, it is my hope and firm belief that the historical research and courage devoted by Mr. Veale to a revelation of the truth in these chapters will result in a rapid clearing up of any outstanding injustices that may remain, and that one obstacle to peace and understanding between the former enemies may thus be cleared away.

HANKEY.

2nd October, 1957

CHAPTER 1.

Introduction:

THE GREAT STALIN MYTH

Among his experiences as a war correspondent in a campaign which has already become half forgotten except as a remote and misty legend, Mr. Ashmead-Bartlett describes to us in his graphic book, "The Uncensored Dardanelles"* how he stood on the bridge of the flagship "Swiftsure" with Admiral Nicholson and other officers and watched the sinking of the battleship "Triumph" off Gaba Tepe on the 25th May, 1915. Hit by a torpedo from a German submarine, the unfortunate battleship, after listing heavily for eight minutes, turned over and after floating bottom upwards for twenty minutes, sank beneath the waves in a cloud of smoke and steam carrying the majority of her crew with her. Admiral Nicholson gazed for a few moments at the spot where she had vanished, then closed his telescope with a snap and turning to his assembled officers, announced, "Gentlemen, the 'Triumph' has gone."

"We had all seen her go," comments Mr. Ashmead-Bartlett, "but I suppose she had not officially sunk until the admiral announced the fact."*

Mr. Ashmead-Bartlett was, of course, merely putting a humorous construction on Admiral Nicholson's observation in an attempt to enliven his description of the latest tragic episode of a campaign which up to then had consisted mainly of disasters and disappointments. He would have been incredulous had he been assured that within a few years it would become a recognised practice of historians to divide facts not open to dispute into those facts which were officially admitted to have happened and those facts which officially were deemed not to have happened.

This practice was first adopted in Soviet Russia and it has been carried further in Soviet Russia than anywhere else. When, after the death of Lenin in 1924 the struggle for power between

---

* "The Uncensored Dardanelles" by Ashmead-Bartlett, (Hutchinson, London), p.110.

Trotsky and Stalin at last ended in the triumph of the latter, it became necessary to efface the undeniable fact that Trotsky had been Lenin's right-hand man during the Russian Revolution in which major political convulsion Stalin had been only a secondary figure. Trotsky's contribution to the Communist revolution of 1917 became to Russian historians a fact which officially was not! Trotsky himself was deemed not to have lived. The gap left in the story of the Communist Revolution by the summary elimination of the first Soviet War Minister was filled by a fictitious person of the same name who, it was said, had throughout been a secret Czarist sympathiser.

Some twenty years later a similar fate overtook a very different person from the brilliant Jewish demagogue. When in July 1945 Phillipe Pétain, Marshal of France, was convicted at a mock trial of having conspired against the security of the State and of having collaborated with the German enemies of France, it became necessary to rewrite the story of the defence of Verdun in 1916, incomparably the most glorious episode in French history since the days of the great Napoleon. So the heroic defender of Verdun was quickly replaced by a fictitious figure, a secret sympathiser with Germany from infancy, in spite of whose treachery the French army at Verdun, presumably leaderless, had repulsed the German onslaught.

After the death of Stalin, his successors at length decided to re-write the official history of Russia and the achievements of Trotsky became officially recognised facts. No doubt ultimately French history will be similarly re-written when the facts of the career of Phillipe Pétain will once again be recognised as facts by official French historians. But this will not happen so long as survive among those in power in France those who not only engineered his condemnation but insisted on keeping him in captivity on a dreary little island off the Atlantic coast until he died there a lonely death at the age of ninety-five.

In the Soviet Union under Stalin, not only were historical facts not deemed officially to have happened, but even certain established facts of science were officially declared invalid. Thus the Central Committee of the Communist Party solemnly proclaimed that Lysenko was politically and therefore scientifically right when he laid down that a changed environment can change heredity and pledged itself "to root out all unpatriotic idealist Weissmannite-Morganist ideology". This repudiation on idealogical grounds, according to Dr. Julian Huxley,* cost the U.S.S.R. hundreds of

* See Dr. Julian Huxley's letter to the "Daily Telegraph" of the 16th April 1956.

million pounds a year—by preventing the improvement of the maize crop by the "bourgeois" genetic methods which have been so successful in the United States. Not until the death of Stalin, was restored to Russian scientists the right to take into account one of the laws of biology.

Even more disastrous, for themselves, was the repudiation by the Nazis of certain of the theories of Professor Einstein, which when adopted as a working hypothesis, suggested research along lines which led ultimately in the United States to the splitting of the atom and the production of the first atom bomb. But Einstein was not only a Jew but a Communist fellow-traveller. Because his political opinions were unacceptable, it was held his scientific theories must be rejected as erroneous. When the Americans took possession of the German laboratories on the occupation of Germany in 1945, they were astonished to find what little progress had been made in Germany during the war years to construct a nuclear weapon. Had they been unhampered by the political fanatics, the German physicists might have been able to supply Hitler with an atom bomb, the mere possession of which by him in 1945 would assuredly have induced his enemies at least to abandon their demand for Germany's unconditional surrender.

Fortunately British scientists have not to date been called on to ignore any of the laws of nature for political reasons. British historians, on the other hand, have not been so fortunate. True, to date, they have not been required to write the story of a historical event leaving out the achievements of the principal participant therein. On the other hand they have long felt themselves compelled to pass over or to minimize certain historical events none of which are open to denial and some of which are unquestionably of far-reaching importance.

Thus, so far as European history is concerned, the outstanding outcome of the Second World War is without question the forced mass-deportation of the bulk of the inhabitants of that vast area extending from the Gulf of Finland in the north to the sources of the Oder in the south. British historians have refrained from studying this appalling subject and disclosing facts which are not open to redress and which few readers would desire to hear. Or, to take another example, no British historian has seen fit to deal with the disclosures of American historians concerning the Japanese attack on Pearl Harbour.* Outside the United States, the reputation of President Roosevelt as an amiable and guileless

---

* The reader is referred to "Back Door to War" by C. C. Tansill, (Regnery, Chicago, 1952) and "The Final Secret of Pearl Harbour" by Rear Admiral Robert A. Theobald.

peacelover remains unshaken.

In totalitarian countries history is recorded with discretion for the simple reason that an indiscreet historian does not long survive an indiscretion. In France there still remains legislation, enacted in 1945, more or less moribund indeed but unrepealed, imposing severe penalties for mentioning facts deemed to traduce 'La Patrie'. Even after the passage of more than a decade a French historian who ventured, for example, to deal objectively with such a subject as the mock-trial of Marshal Pétain would run the risk of being prosecuted for 'traducing', and the result of such a prosecution would still depend mainly on the state of French public opinion at the time of the trial. In Great Britain objective historical research is neither subject to the arbitrary requirements of politicians nor to the restrictions of a penal code. Nevertheless in the years following the Second World War objective research was restricted by a largely subconscious reluctance to acknowledge certain historical happenings because they could not be made to harmonise with an interpretation of contemporary history which had been accepted during the struggle for the sole and sufficient reason that acceptance of it would help the war effort.

This book consists of a collection of studies of six distinct historical subjects. All are or were for upwards of a decade discreetly veiled from public attention. Interesting and historically significant for different reasons, they are linked together by the fact that all of them are or have been until recently relegated to that category of events which by tacit consent are deemed not to have happened. Deemed unworthy of consideration by right-thinking persons, investigation will disclose that all conflict with one or other of the propaganda myths universally accepted during the Second World War.

In the last analysis the discovery will be made that the six historical matters dealt with in this book conflict either directly or indirectly with the Stalin Myth or with some subsidiary myth based on or arising from this paramount myth.

When in June 1941 Hitler doomed all the achievements of his career down to that date by that supreme act of insanity, the invasion of Russia, he drove into the camp of his enemies a state more fundamentally antagonistic to them than he was himself. When in the following autumn President Roosevelt at last succeeded in involving his country in the war, there came into existence what Sir Winston Churchill has subsequently labelled 'The Grand Alliance', a motley jumble of Powers, great and small, separated by conflicting interests and ambitions and the bitterest animosities and suspicions and linked together only by the fact that all were, for a variety of reasons, at war with Hitler. For the successful prosecution of the war some semblance of harmony had somehow to be achieved. This could only be done by burying in oblivion until victory was won the history of the preceding quarter of a century. Temporarily inconvenient but undeniable facts had to be discreetly veiled and convenient fictions for the time being substituted. In Great Britain the most important of these fictions concerned the character of Joe Stalin and his murderous regime.

The will to believe being strong, the Stalin Myth soon won general acceptance. By the time of the Yalta Conference in 1945 its acceptance had indeed become a political necessity. Without faith in this myth, victory would have provided little cause for rejoicing. So the British public gazed with admiration at photographs of the 'Big Three', Churchill, Roosevelt and Stalin, seated comfortably before the palace in which they had just agreed that one-third of Europe should be handed over to the tender mercies of the Red Army and that the border of Asia with Europe should be pushed forward to the Elbe, less than 500 miles from London as the crow—or rather, the jet plane—flies. At the time of course this decision was not disclosed. In lieu thereof stress was laid on the golden future which obviously lay in store for mankind generally and the British Empire in particular. To make this rosy picture credible, it was necessary to attribute to Sir Winston's two colleagues the far-sighted benevolence for which he himself was famed. In regard to President Roosevelt there was not much difficulty about this—everyone knew that he was a guileless peace-lover who had succeeded in involving his country in the war on the side of Britain. It was not then known that in his plans for the future he had no use for the British Empire. Judging from Sir Winston's smiling face, the President had not at the time of the Yalta Conference disclosed to his British allies that the British possessions in Asia, together with the Asiatic possessions of the French and Dutch, must be surrendered to the nationalist parties in those lands as part of the price of victory. At Yalta, Roosevelt's views on 'colonialism' were not known and he radiated upon all his celebrated charm. There was not at that time the least reason to regard him otherwise than as a worthy joint architect of the Brave New World which lay ahead.

But in the case of Joseph Stalin, alias Djugashvilli, scores of incontrovertible and universally known facts existed proving that he was one of those few outstanding figures in history in whose character it was hard to find a redeeming quality. Not only had he caused to be butchered wholesale his political opponents but also his supporters and friends when they ceased to be useful to him. During the Great Purge, 1936 to 1938, on trumped-up charges which he knew to be false, he had sent to their deaths the men who had been Lenin's most trusted colleagues during the Russian Revolution: to terrorise the peasants, he had condemned to death or exile tens of thousands of those who had failed to achieve success for the agrarian schemes of his regime, and in 1940 he had ordered the forced mass-deportation of the inhabitants of the Baltic States. On suspicion of being opposed to his rule, several millions of hapless people were then labouring in the slave camps of Siberia and the Arctic Circle. To present such a man as one of the joint architects of the Brave New World which lay ahead would be like portraying a gallows as the central feature of a picture of the Garden of Eden.

It was thus a political necessity that the real Joe Stalin should disappear from human memory. Just as had happened in the case of the real Leon Trotsky and was destined to happen in the case of the real Marshal Pétain, the void left by his disappearance was filled by a fictitious figure. In place of the real Joe Stalin emerged the bluff, jovial figure of 'Marshal' Stalin, a man of sterling qualities if outwardly a little brusque, a man who, if perhaps a trifle heavy-handed with those who incurred his displeasure, was nevertheless wholeheartedly devoted to British and American political and commercial interests and consequently to the cause of humanity.

It must already seem astonishing that so blatantly fictitious a myth as the Stalin Myth should have won so easily and quickly such widespread and unquestioning acceptance. But during the preceding twenty years the public mind had been unconsciously prepared for its acceptance. In 1917 the Russian Revolution had been almost universally acclaimed as an outstanding landmark in the history of human progress: by many the abolition of Christianity and the establishment of dialectical materialism as the official faith of Russia had been received with approval. Thereafter no happening in Soviet Russia from the Red Terror to the Great Purge lacked ardent defenders or apologists in influential non-Communist circles outside the U.S.S.R. Political progress, it was maintained, was synonymous with movement to the Left. As the party forming the extreme left wing in the struggle against 'reaction', the Communist Party, whatever might be its short-comings and even crimes, was to be preferred by all genuine believers in 'progress' to any party of the Right. Communism was merely Liberalism in a hurry.

In Great Britain and in the United States during the nineteen twenties the younger generation at the universities accepted this view of Communism. The careers of such men as Harry Dexter White and Alger Hiss appear incomprehensible until it is remembered that they merely carried into practice the outlook which in youth they had shared with most of their contemporaries.

When in 1941 Hitler invaded Russia, the view that Communism was only Liberalism in a hurry had long been the accepted view of the English-speaking intelligentsia. When urged to accept this view by the politicians, the man-in-the-street naturally found little difficulty in complying. Once accepted, it was but a short step to agreeing that Stalin was really only a sort of Georgian counterpart of Mr. Gladstone. Like the great English Liberal statesman, Stalin was a crusader for political progress even if his methods might seem to some crude and perhaps deplorably harsh.

The creation of the Stalin Myth necessitated the creation of a whole series of subsidiary myths and the re-writing of much recent history. It was not sufficient to veil discreetly the doings of Stalin himself and those acting directly under his orders, such as Molotov who negotiated with the Nazis for a joint attack on Poland in 1939 and directed Soviet foreign policy throughout the war; Andrei Vyshinsky who acted as prosecutor at the more important mock-trials during the Great Purge and later helped to stage the Nürnberg trials; General Ivan Serov, the M.V.D. chief, who in 1940 supervised the the mass-deportations of the inhabitants of the Baltic states, Lithuania, Latvia and Esthonia, and who after the war supervised the mass-deportations of the inhabitants of East Prussia, Pomerania and Silesia; and Beria, the head of the M.V.D., who after Stalin's death was overthrown by Malenkov and liquidated as a traitor. Since Stalin was the high priest of Communism, the doings of Communists generally throughout the world had to be whitewashed.

Since the outbreak of the 'cold war' between the U.S.A. and the Soviet Union, Communism has again come to be regarded in the United States and Great Britain with suspicion and aversion. The fact has become forgotten that for at least seven years after Hitler invaded Russia in 1941, Communist activity was looked upon with approval, or at least with complacency, since this activity, was in the main directed against the common enemy Fascism. As a result, right-thinking British historians were required to gloss over atrocities committed by Communists, who, rightly regarded, were worthy of all honour and respect as the supporters of that great champion in the crusade against Fascism, the loyal ally and friend of Churchill and Roosevelt, 'Marshal' Stalin.

As an offshoot of the Stalin Myth a carefully constructed

myth was created concerning the activities of the Partisans operating on the Allied side during the Second World War. The reason
for the creation of this myth may not be immediately apparent.
When the first groups of Partisans were formed in France shortly
after France's withdrawal from the war in July 1940, the French
Communists stood sullenly aloof from the activities of these Partisan groups because the High Priest of Communism, Stalin, had
signed a pact of friendship with Hitler and the orthodox Communist view was that the war was a capitalist struggle in which
Communists had no concern. These first groups of Partisans were
composed mostly of youthful members of the upper classes. Their
inspiration was French nationalism and they were bitterly opposed
to Communism, which they regarded as only a shade less obnoxious
than Nazism—the two movements had become allied and were for
practical purposes indistinguishable. The speciality of these
nationalist groups was sabotage, with the assistance of British spies
as a useful sideline. For support, direction and financial aid they
looked to London.

This state of affairs ended abruptly when Hitler invaded the
Soviet Union in June 1941. Groups of Communist Partisans were
at once formed all over France. Their speciality was murder, pre-
ferably of isolated German soldiers caught unawares, but in default of such, of anti-Communist French citizens. From the outset
bitter hostility existed between these two distinct Partisan organisations, the nationalist organisation which looked to London and
the Communist organisation which looked to Moscow. Although
in the struggle against the common foe the two organisations
worked closely together—the Communists never hesitated to
accept British and American arms and money — yet no real co-
operation could exist between them. A similar state of affairs arose
in all the countries of occupied Europe in which partisan movements against the occupying forces later sprang up. The non-
Communist Partisans fought always with the knowledge that victory might give their Communist allies an opportunity to liquidate
them. When as in Jugoslavia, the opportunity occurred, it was
not allowed to slip. Thus immediately the Germans had been
expelled from Jugoslavia, the Communist Partisans under Tito
ruthlessly liquidated the Nationalist Partisans of General Mihailovitch.

It was impossible to disavow the doings of the Communist
Partisans since they were composed of supporters of that great
and good friend of Roosevelt and Churchill, 'Marshal' Stalin. At
the same time it was equally impossible to defend their doings. A
way out of the difficulty was found by treating these two mutually

antagonistic Partisan organisations as one and by focussing all attention on the activities of the nationalist organisations. Right-thinking British historians long continued to endorse this war-time fiction. As a result, in the public mind a Partisan, whether a Frenchman or a Jugo-Slav, an Italian or a Belgian, remains a heroic lover of liberty, a starry-eyed patriot, fighting against the Nazi tyranny, who performed melodramatic exploits which have since served to inspire a succession of best-selling novels and successful films.

Patriotic, non-Communist underground organisations certainly operated in all the occupied countries of Western Europe, but their contribution to the struggle was comparatively unimportant in comparison with the contribution of the much larger, better organised and infinitely more ruthless Communist organisations operating in Western Europe in conjunction with the various Communist organisations operating behind the German lines in the East. Sabotage and spying were mere sidelines for the Communist Partisans whose activities ranged from the murder of isolated soldiers to large scale organised attacks on the rear of the German forces such as that at Marzabotto in Italy in September 1944, carried out by "the Red Star Brigade" referred to later in this book in the chapter on the case of Major Reder. Now that British troops have been the victims of a series of ruthless campaigns in Egypt, Palestine, Cyprus and elsewhere, conducted against them by armed civilian organisations inspired by and using the technique of underground warfare perfected by the Communist underground movement during the Second World War, there is much less disposition than formerly to whitewash Communist methods of waging guerilla warfare. Nevertheless, the tacit agreement still holds that the activities of the Communist underground movement during the Second World War should be discreetly hidden by focussing attention on the spectacular exploits of daring-do, performed by the various nationalist underground movements.

The outbreak of the 'cold war' between the United States and the Soviet Union deprived the Stalin Myth and the various subsidiary myths attaching to it of practical utility. No longer was it politically expedient to profess the belief that Stalin was a statesman inspired by a lofty love for humanity and that his Communist supporters throughout the world were stainless crusaders against 'Fascist' violence and crime. In the United States at least facts concerning Communism were once again frankly recognised. A few years later the threat of Communist aggression made it necessary to enlist the support of the German people for the defence of Europe. It then became necessary to abandon the myth that all the woes of Europe for the past three hundred years were attributable to the inherent passion of the German people to wage wars of aggression against their peaceful neighbours. Even the principal exponents of this interpretation of history, if such it can be called, repudiated it. Thus Lord Vansittart abruptly abandoned his favourite thesis that Germany was the "butcher bird of Europe" and began to clamour with characteristic vehemence for immediate German rearmament as the sole means of protecting Europe from that lust for conquest which he had previously maintained existed only in the German breast*. Nevertheless general astonishment was occasioned throughout the world when in 1956 the Stalin Myth was formally repudiated by Stalin's successor, formerly his most obsequious supporter, Nikita Khrushchev. Thenceforth it was no longer incumbent on loyal Communists to venerate Stalin as the wise and benevolent 'Big Brother'. All along, it appeared, he had been a cruel and ruthless tyrant.

Khrushchev's speech to the 20th Congress of the Communist Party in Moscow on the 20th February 1956 contained nothing not long known by his hearers, but when its contents were at last disclosed outside Russia it came as a paralysing shock to the intelligentsia of the non-Communist world who for three decades had been industriously propagating the fiction that a Communist paradise was flourishing in Russia under Stalin's wise and benevolent, if somewhat strict, paternal guidance.

Speaking as one who had worked in the closest contact with Stalin and whose life had often depended on being able to comply with his slightest whim, Khrushchev described his late master as "capricious, irritable and brutal." He denounced Stalin's "use of the most cruel repression against anyone who disagreed with him, against those who were only suspected of hostile intent." Naively he condemned "mass-terrorism" on the ground that "the exploiting classes had already been liquidated." As head of the new Russian Government, Khrushchev declared that "Lying, slanderous and absurd accusations concerning the preparation of fictitious plots were established by the lavish use of torture." He illustrated his accusations by a number of specific examples of Stalin's mass-terrorism, among them disclosing that out of one hundred and thirty-nine members and candidates of the Party's Central Committee who were elected at the 17th Congress, no less than ninety-eight persons—that is to say 70%—had been arrested and shot, most of them in the years 1937 and 1938.*

* See his article "A Matter of Life or Death" in the Sunday Chronicle of October 25th, 1953, and later similar articles.
* See the report of Khrushchev's speech in the "Times" of June 5th, 1956.

THE GREAT STALIN MYTH

Relying on the authority of Khrushchev, we may therefore have no hesitation in studying the subjects dealt with in this book. Facts need no longer be rejected from consideration because they conflict with the Stalin Myth. And now that this myth has been abandoned even in the Kremlin, the various subsidiary myths created to support it can also be abandoned. Although no doubt Khrushchev would be one of the last to admit it, there is no longer any occasion to attach fictitious virtues to the colleagues and supporters of one now admitted to have been a tyrant without ruth or scruple. When facts are frankly faced difficulties disappear. Thus we can now see that Audisio, the self-confessed murderer of Mussolini, only acted in the way an ardent supporter of Stalin could be expected to act: we need no longer idealise the crimes of the Italian Communist Partisans.

The first chapter of this book deals with the Katyn Forest Massacre, a political crime specially noteworthy for two reasons. Of all the crimes committed during Stalin's regime it is the only crime which aroused world-wide attention and interest. Secondly, the Katyn Forest Massacre is unique in that the facts concerning it were investigated by a neutral international committee within a few months of its discovery and the identity of its perpetrators established beyond any possibility of doubt.

The Katyn Forest Massacre may indeed be cited as a classic example of a crime discreetly veiled. Blazoned forth to the world for propaganda purposes by Dr. Goebbels, the news of the discovery of this crime was received with professed incredulity in Allied countries and by assertions that it could only be an impudent invention designed to cast discredit on the far-famed humanity of the Soviet regime. Needless to say neither side was in the least interested in establishing the actual truth. Needless to say the organisation controlled by Heinrich Himmler would not have hesitated to carry out a similar massacre if such would in any way have helped Germany's war effort, and Dr. Goebbels would have readily justified the crime. Dr. Goebbels was only concerned with establishing the truth because it happened that the truth if established would prevent the Poles from wholeheartedly co-operating with the Soviet Union against Germany. His Allied opponents were only concerned with suppressing the truth because the truth if disclosed would create a breach between Poland and the Soviet Union. Ultimately Mr. Eden's exhortations to the Poles to forget the subject until victory was achieved were substantially successful. The Katyn Forest Massacre became a crime discreetly veiled. It remained discreetly veiled until to the general astonishment the Soviet authorities insisted on charging 'the major German war-

criminals' awaiting trial at Nürnberg on many other charges with having been the perpetrators of this crime also. Why the Soviet authorities adopted this course remains a mystery to this day. Equally mysterious is the fact that they made no effort to support the charge. We are no longer under any obligation to pretend that the Soviet authorities would have hesitated to have established the charge by means of faked documents and forged affidavits had they really desired to obtain a conviction. Had they adopted this course a conviction could easily have been obtained since the Tribunal at Nürnberg was expressly authorised to accept any evidence placed before it at its face value.

The trial at Nürnberg did nothing to remove the veil of discreet silence which had been draped round the Katyn Forest Massacre. The Tribunal heard in silence what the Russian prosecutor had to say on the subject: it prudently decided to omit all reference to the matter when the time for delivering judgement arrived. The days wasted at Nürnburg hearing this impudent charge merely served to bring back to the public mind for a short while a crime which had been carefully buried in oblivion. Some years later, after the outbreak of the 'cold war', the facts were carefully sifted by a committee appointed by the Senate of the United States. The result however merely confirmed the unanimous conclusion reached by the neutral international committee which had investigated the crime a few months after its discovery.

Although veiled from the attention of the general public, the truth concerning the Katyn Forest Massacre must have been known to many of the leading personages taking part in the Nürnburg Trial. The fact that a fictitious charge was solemnly entertained without protest or comment throws a flood of light on the working and attitude of mind of that august body, the so-called International Military Tribunal.

Far more important historically, however, is the fact that the truth concerning the Katyn Forest Massacre had been known to the British and American foreign offices for over a year before Sir Winston Churchill and President Roosevelt met Stalin at the momentous Yalta Conference in February 1945.

As a result of this Conference it was agreed that all eastern Europe up to the Elbe should be handed over to the tender mercies of the Red Army. It is now tacitly admitted that the political judgement of Sir Winston Churchill and President Roosevelt on this occasion went disastrously astray*. But the question is

---

* How disastrously was not realised for over a decade. As a result of the Yalta Agreement the Russians were enabled to seize the German rocket missile research station on the island of Rügen. Thanks to the German

ignored how they came to make a blunder of such magnitude. Can we believe that they had not been advised by their foreign offices of the truth concerning the Katyn Forest Massacre from which could they not have deduced the character of the man with whom they had to deal? Can we believe that they had forgotten that at the Teheran Conference only some months before, Stalin had announced an intention to carry out a super-Katyn massacre in the shape of a massacre of 50,000 German soldiers and technicians? These questions remain hard to answer. By future apologists of Stalin the Katyn Forest Massacre can be dismissed as an unimportant incident. It is quite possible that he only formally sanctioned this massacre as a mere routine proceeding in accordance with the general policy of his regime. But apologists for the leading Western statesmen who took part at the Yalta Conference will have a far harder task. It will be no easy matter to establish that their subservience to the demands of the Red Dictator was the result of guileless innocence and not of callous indifference to the fate of the tens of millions of helpless and innocent people whom they handed over to his mercy.

The second chapter of this book deals with the murder of Benito Mussolini.

At first mention this may appear an event which from its nature was not and could not be discreetly veiled. Immediately it had taken place the news was broadcast all over the world. Within a few days a person who undoubtedly had taken part in the deed proclaimed in the Italian press that he himself had shot Mussolini and published an account of what had taken place which substantially may be accepted as approximately correct. During the last decade several books and innumerable newspaper articles have been written on the subject. In such circumstances how was it possible to veil the truth?

It was indeed impossible to veil the essential facts of this crime since these were at once disclosed by one of those who undoubtedly took part. But no pains and ingenuity were spared to veil the essential nature of the deed. The person who claimed to have shot Mussolini — a professional Communist agitator named Audisio—declared that before shooting him he had read the sentence of death passed upon him. This claim—almost certainly untrue—was seized upon eagerly. Mussolini had been proclaimed Public Enemy No. 2. Was it not common knowledge that he was guilty of innumerable although unspecified crimes? What could

scientists and technicians captured there, the Russians were able in 1957 to astonish the world by winning the lead in the production of intercontinental missile weapons.

be more natural than that when this arch-criminal against humanity fell into the hands of his countrymen, he should be promptly brought before some court having jurisdiction to hear and adjudicate upon the charges brought against him? His manifold crimes being so manifest, the trial would naturally be short and could only end with a sentence of death. What more natural and humane than that this sentence should be promptly carried out? It was perhaps unfortunate that Claretta Petacci should have been executed at the same time, a person against whom no charge or complaint had ever been made. Still as nothing was known generally about her, it might be safely assumed that justice had overtaken her for some unspecified offence.

Thus was created a fiction based not on facts but on the war propaganda myth that Mussolini was a super-criminal and that his political opponents were starry-eyed idealists heroically battling against his cruel tyranny. For a decade after Mussolini's death it was de rigueur to refer to it as an execution, and to the above mentioned Audisio as the executioner of Mussolini. This assertion can be verified by referring to the editions of the standard encyclopaedias and books of reference published within ten years of Mussolini's death. The statement that Mussolini was executed is made without comment as if this were a fact established beyond all question.

But of course it is not a fact that Mussolini was executed. It has been established beyond any possibility of doubt that no court or tribunal of any kind considered any charges against him or passed any sentence on him. The probability seems to be that those who murdered him acted on their own initiative. If they did not act on their own initiative, at the most they relied on instructions from other and more influential members of the Italian Communist Party.

At long last the truth on this issue seems generally to have become recognised. Mussolini was murdered. But although the general outline of the story has become clear much still remains obscure. Quite distinct from this long persisting desire to uphold a wartime propaganda fiction is the urgent need felt by many influential persons in Italy to suppress the facts relating to the disappearance of the treasure which Mussolini was carrying with him on his flight. The murder of Mussolini and the disappearance of this treasure are happenings indissolubly linked. It is a fact that a number of persons who took part in the events which led to the murder of Mussolini and the disappearance of the treasure have mysteriously vanished without trace. One explanation is that these missing persons have fled with the treasure, but the general opinion in Italy is that they have been murdered because they knew too much and that the bulk of the treasure has disappeared into the coffers of the Italian Communist Party.

A veil of secrecy still obscures—and will most probably always obscure—the truth. Roman Dombrowski, after years of careful investigation, in his recently published book, "Mussolini: Twilight and Fall", is driven to the reflection, "In face of the many mysteries, contradictions and ambiguities connected with Mussolini's death, we are driven to query whether there is such a thing as objective historical truth, and to wonder how many lies and distortions be concealed in the pages of history".*

In a nutshell it may be said that outside Italy the veiling of the facts relating to the death of Mussolini resulted from the war-time idealisation of the Partisan movements which arose in the occupied countries during the Second World War. It was felt that as Mussolini was done to death by Partisans in the course of their heroic struggle against tyranny, somehow this act of theirs must be justifiable. To this idealisation can be attributed also the veil of discreet silence which still surrounds the unique career of that opportunist of genius, Dr. Marcel Petiot, which is the subject of the fourth chapter of this book.

Not that there was anything of a political nature in the crimes of Dr. Petiot. On the contrary, the essence of the complaint against him was that all his doings were strictly non-political. If Petiot could have established that one of his numerous victims had been a German general or a leading French collaborator, the fact that he had done to death numerous other persons for his own personal profit would have been regarded indulgently by the court which tried him. If only he could have proved that he was a self-appointed executioner of the enemies of France who, in the course of his duties might in an excess of patriotic zeal have liquidated and despoiled a number of innocent persons, he would have been certain of acquittal. Many self-appointed executioners who had allowed their enthusiasm to run away with their judgment in this way, were after the "liberation" decorated as heroic 'resistance fighters' and kissed on each cheek by General de Gaulle. If only Petiot could have proved that he was a member of one of the murder gangs subsequently officially recognised as having operated for 'La Résistance', he would have been safe. No one would have been so unreasonable as to insist on proof that all his victims had been the enemies of France. At times of national emergency errors of judgment are pardonable. Many others in France at the time had

* "Mussolini: Twilight and Fall" by Roman Dombrowski, Heinemann, London, 1956, Page 236.

committed murder for personal profit but at the same time they had also committed political crimes: Petiot, on the other hand, had operated entirely for his own personal profit. He was sent to the guillotine.

Dr. Marcel Petiot was unquestionably one of the greatest criminals of the 20th century, perhaps of all time. A brilliant opportunist with an amazingly quick perception of all the possibilities of a novel situation, original and daring, with the effrontery of an Horatio Bottomley and the cold-blooded ruthlessness of his contemporaries, Heinrich Himmler and General Ivan Serov, Petiot as a mass-murderer may be said to stand in a class by himself.

One would naturally imagine that criminologists throughout the world would have contended eagerly with each other to produce the most complete biography of Dr. Marcel Petiot with the minutest details of his extraordinary career. Yet after ten years, even in France, not a single book has been written about him. In Great Britain he is remembered vaguely as an imitator of Landru who somehow or other was associated with the French resistance movement. And this, of course, is utterly wrong. As we have said, the complaint against Petiot was that he was *not* associated with the French resistance movement.

The reason why Petiot has been denied the sinister fame to which he is entitled is that his career can only be studied in relation to the conditions of life existing in France during the last years of the German occupation and the years immediately following the Liberation. His crimes were only possible because of these conditions: in fact, the modus operandi of his crimes was simply an application of the existing conditions. By itself the story of Petiot's crimes provides a vivid picture of the conditions prevailing in France during their commission. This picture, based on facts, utterly contradicts the fictional picture popularly accepted of a gallant people joyously expelling its cruel foreign oppressors. It discloses a state of general demoralisation, hard to parallel in the history of any civilized country. Acts of terrorism were in general approved by public opinion partly because they were generally directed against the occupying forces and partly because disapproval was discouraged by acts of terrorism. Petiot carried on his grim trade against a background of murder, secret denunciation, private acts of vengeance, treachery and blackmail.

It is popularly believed that Liberation brought relief in a spontaneous outburst of joy. In fact, conditions became worse. The German occupying forces for their own protection had at least provided some check on the murder gangs: the regime of General de Gaulle for long made no effort to protect life or property. While the French police watched benevolently, thousands of supporters of the Vichy regime were publicly lynched: women accused of association with the Germans were driven naked through the streets to have their hair cut off on platforms for the entertainment of delighted crowds. Mere estimated figures carry little weight: exact statistics are still unobtainable. In the first months after the liberation, according to official American estimates, the number of "summary executions" totalled 80,000. According to M. Adrien Tixier, one of de Gaulle's ministers, between August 1944 and March 1945, 105,000 persons were officially and semi-officially done to death.

Such figures convey little. One incident in the career of Dr. Petiot outweighs volumes of statistics. When the police first entered his house they discovered in the cellar several human heads and the dismembered remains of a score of bodies. Asked to account, the doctor explained quietly that they had come across by accident the execution chamber where a punitive group of 'La Résistance' liquidated the Boches and their collaborators—"the particularly troublesome ones".

In Paris in March 1944 this seemed an entirely adequate explanation to give for a cellar full of human remains. The police saluted politely and permitted Dr. Petiot to take his departure without further objection. No wonder the story of his career of crime has been discreetly veiled.

Dr. Petiot's career of crime was rendered possible by the complete breakdown of law and order as a result of the intensive underground campaign waged in Paris by the Communists against the occupying forces. The Marzabotto Affair, the subject of the chapter following, was the outcome of another phase of Communist activity, in this case waged in the rear of the German armies defending Italy from the Anglo-American invasion.

It may reasonably be maintained that the Marzabotto Affair is not really the story of a crime but is the story of the creation and development of a myth. Or to be more precise, it is the story of the events upon which a myth has been built. In fact nothing in any way noteworthy seems ever to have happened in the small town of Marzabotto since the remote days when the Etruscans first established a settlement on this site some six hundred years before Christ. During the Second World War Marzabotto lay on one of the main German lines of communication and for this reason was frequently both shelled and bombed by the Americans and a number of its inhabitants killed or injured. Ultimately it was evacuated by the Germans without fighting.

The name Marzabotto has been adopted as a convenient title

to label certain happenings which took place in the neighbouring mountains towards the end of the summer of 1944. The main outline of what occurred is not in dispute. Certain bands of Communist Partisans who called themselves "The Red Star Brigade" had been operating behind the German front south . of Bologna, extremely successfully according to their own accounts. At length, General Max Simon, the German commander of this sector, decided that this danger from the rear must at any cost be eliminated. Picked troops were withdrawn from the front line and by a converging movement the Partisans were finally surrounded in a strongly entrenched position in the mountains south of Marzabotto. In a day of fierce fighting the trenches of the Partisans were stormed and all resistance finally broken.

This fighting in which both sides suffered heavy losses has been used as the foundation for the creation of the myth that the hard-pressed German troops on this sector, not content apparently with repulsing repeated attempts to break through by numerically greatly superior American forces, suddenly and for no reason decided to attack a small open town in their own rear and massacre its inoffensive inhabitants. This extraordinary story has won such wide acceptance that it has become customary to refer to Marzabotto as the Italian Oradour.

The Marzabotto Affair may be accepted as a convenient label for an allegedly cruel and purposeless massacre of defenceless and inoffensive men, women and children by brutal soldiery which is said to have taken place in September 1944 on the northern slopes of the Apennines south of Bologna. It will be sufficient here to add that the German officer who directed the main thrust against the "Red Star Brigade", a Major Walter Reder, was charged with responsibility for this alleged massacre. As at his trial his captors performed the joint roles of accusers and judges, the problem of his guilt must still be regarded as a completely open question.

A sketch of the Marzabotto Affair is included in these pages because the so-called trial of Major Reder serves as a good example of what may be termed the Pontius Pilate class of war-trial, a class of war-trial which has been hidden with special care behind the curtain of discreet silence. Major Reder had had a distinguished career on many fronts during the Second World War as a front-line commander. He had been several times wounded and had received the highest military decorations. Some months after the conclusion of hostilities, he was arrested by the American occupying forces in Austria on a complaint being lodged against him by the Italian Government that upon him rested the responsibility for the death of a number of Italian Communist Partisans. After

Churchill, Roosevelt and Stalin at Livadia Palace in Yalta, during their three-power conference in February, 1945. Stalin remained confident and cool in securing his major concessions. Roosevelt was frail and approaching death.

(United Press International)

Stalin continued his one-way achievements for Russia at Potsdam with Churchill [later Attlee] and Truman. (July, 1945.) The division of Germany, agreed upon at Teheran and Yalta, was confirmed here.

a long detention in a concentration camp, the American authorities decided that the Italian complaint was baseless. But the Americans did not, as one might expect, thereupon release him. Following the precedent set long ago by Pontius Pilate, they formally washed their hands of the matter, and, for some unexplained reason, handed him over to the British. The British examined the charges, also found them baseless, also adopted the Pontius Pilate precedent, and in their turn handed him over to the Italians.

Normally this procedure, when adopted, ended with the automatic conviction and death of the accused. The trial of Major Reder which took place at Bologna was treated in Italy as a major political issue: while it proceeded, Communist mobs demonstrated outside the courthouse. Acquittal in the circumstances was politically impossible, but the Italian military court—to its great credit—decided to save Major Reder's life by convicting him and sentencing him to life imprisonment. An appeal to the Supreme Military Court in Rome was dismisssed in March 1954 as regards the sentence, but the ridiculous direction of the lower court that he should be deprived of his rank was quashed. As a consequence Major Reder was detained in prison but was treated as an officer and not as a convicted criminal. He has remained in prison ever since because it was the concern of no one to secure his release. The Americans and the British insist that the case is entirely an Italian domestic matter. Major Reder is technically an Austrian subject because he had been born in Bohemia, in 1915, then part of the Austro-Hungarian Empire, and, as such, the German Government has no right to intervene on his behalf. On the other hand, to the Austrian Government Major Reder is a German officer who had fought loyally for Germany throughout the war. While the question of responsibiliy for his fate is being languidly debated, Major Reder remains in prison.

The fate of the celebrated defender of Brest, General Bernard Ramcke, dealt with in the next chapter, was very similar to that of Major Walter Reder. This case also serves as an example of the Pontius Pilate war-crimes trial. Like Major Reder, General Ramcke had had a distinguished career as a front-line commander: a general of paratroops, he had particularly distinguished himself in the conquest of Crete in 1941. His defence of the great French fortress and naval arsenal of Brest in 1944 against overwhelmingly superior American forces commanded by General Troy H. Middleton, was the outstanding military achievement of his career. When unconditional surrender at last came in 1945, General Ramcke was a prisoner of war in the hands of the Americans. In exactly similar circumstances as in the case of Major Reder, General

Ramcke was handed over by the Americans to the British who at length handed him over to be tried by his accusers, in his case, by the French.

The chief point of difference between the two cases is that whereas specific and serious charges were, right or wrongly, brought against Major Reder, the accusers of General Ramcke never seem to have made up their minds exactly what were the crimes which they considered he had committed. The French Press denounced him vehemently as a super-criminal responsible for the death of many gallant Communist Partisan fighters. But whereas direct evidence of a kind was produced against Major Reder, there was no direct evidence against General Ramcke of any description. Probably he would never have been brought to trial at all but for the chance that after waiting seven years for release owing to lack of evidence, a violent political campaign was launched in France to arouse public opinion against the then recently proposed re-arming of Germany. It happened that General Ramcke was the last remaining prominent German leader who had been detained as a suspected war-criminal and who still remained in French custody. In default of any other well-known German leader against whom a more specific case could be made out, General Ramcke was charged with a hurriedly collected assortment of offences. No attempt was made to hide the fact that the sole purpose of the trial was to re-awaken anti-German feeling in France by dilating on these alleged offences at length during the course of the protracted proceedings. The public prosecutor in his final speech bluntly urged the court to convict as a kind of national testimonial to the heroic fighters of 'La Résistance'. Like the Italian military court at Bologna which tried Major Reder, the French military court which tried General Ramcke steered a discreet middle course. Owing to lack of evidence, conviction was impossible: on the other hand, acquittal would have been regarded by French public opinion as a reflection on 'La Résistance'. General Ramcke was formally convicted and sentenced to five years imprisonment. As he had been in prison five years awaiting trial, this sentence resulted in his immediate release.

Although General Ramcke's accusers denounced him vehemently as a war-criminal of the blackest description, some may feel that his case would be better classified as a political 'stunt' carried out in the form of a trial. It is certainly not open to dispute that his conviction was the result of intense political pressure. But if we dismiss the verdict as amounting to an acquittal and regard General Ramcke as an innocent man falsely accused, his treatment from the time he surrendered to the Americans at Brest in 1944 to the date of his release by the French in 1951 must be regarded as so outrageous as to be nothing short of criminal. According to the dictum of that distinguished Indian jurist, Mr. Justice Rahabinode Pal, the farce of a trial of a leader of the vanquished side by his captors, the victors, is in itself a particularly heinous war-crime. If we accept his dictum, the criminals in this case were not General Ramcke and his two co-defendants in the dock but the cynical French politicians who engineered this trial and who strove to obtain the conviction of an innocent man, in default of evidence, by appealing to political prejudice. And of course if this view be accepted, no further explanation need be sought why the whole subject has been for so long discreetly veiled.

It is always desirable whenever it be possible to end a book on a relatively cheerful note. This is not easy with a book dealing in part with war-crimes, "that dolorous and deplorable subject", as the American historian, Professor Harry Elmer Barnes, has described it. This book begins with an account of the discovery of a mass-grave in which were found some three thousand human bodies, "clotted together by dense putrefaction and deformation due to pressure". With so gruesome a beginning it should be possible to conclude with an ending which in comparison might seem cheerful!

The subject of "The Super-Ersatz Crime" has been chosen as offering at least a possibility of treatment in a not entirely lugubrious vein. At least the matter ended happily with the release of the victim, if only after an ordeal lasting ten years during which he was subjected to a course of treatment expressly designed to inflict on him every possible indignity, deprivation and discomfort. Now that this ordeal is over, one can concentrate on the comic aspects of the matter which, strange to say, are not lacking.

Far from being discreetly veiled, the trial of Admiral Raeder began amid a frantic blaze of propaganda and the dazzling arc-lights of publicity. No effort was spared to make the occasion the subject for a national jollification in the shape of a trial at law: to the public the matter was presented as a sort of glorified "V" Day guaranteed to last for months. At the start the proceedings were reported as voluminously as the then acute paper-shortage permitted: innumerable flashlight photographs were taken of every-one concerned, from Admiral Raeder and the other 20 occupants of the dock to the most obscure member of the team of legal luminaries foregathered together from all over the world to prose-cute these newly created crimes: no detail of the arrangements for the trial escaped notice and praise, from the elaborate loud-speaker equipment with which the court-room was fitted to the hard and uncomfortable seats provided for the prisoners in the dock.

At first the reflex action of the public was most gratifying to the promoters of the Nürnberg Trials. Very quickly, however, interest waned. Long before the inevitable result was reached, everyone had become heartily weary of the whole matter. It was then decided that the sooner the subject was forgotten, the better. The news that Admiral Raeder and the other surviving victims of the trials had been sent to spend the remainder of their lives in Spandau Prison was passed over without comment. No attempt was made to explain what exactly was the crime which he was supposed to have committed. Quickly the whole matter was buried in oblivion.

Both Admiral Raeder's trial at Nürnberg and his subsequent captivity at Spandau took place in an atmosphere of make-believe, delightfully reminiscent of Alice in Wonderland. This atmosphere can only be enjoyed, however, if the grim fact be dismissed from mind that Admiral Raeder was a living person forced to take part in an elaborate and carefully devised political gesture. An effort must be made therefore to regard him merely as a fictional subject of fictional charges just as the three unfortunate gardeners in "Alice in Wonderland" ordered to execution by the Queen were the fictional subjects of a fictional capital sentence. Alice wasted no sympathy on them since, as she later pointed out. "You're all nothing but a pack of cards".

Throughout his experiences at Nürnberg and Spandau, Admiral Raeder's role was strictly impersonal. It happened there was a spare place in the dock at Nürnberg, and as the cynical Whitney R. Harris puts it, "Admiral Raeder as former Chief of the German Navy was a not illogical defendant-counterpart of Field Marshal Keitel".* Thus he found himself numbered among "the major war-criminals", not as an individual, but as a symbol. In the role of a "not illogical naval counterpart" to the head of the German Army, he suffered the fate which one of his judges, General Nikitchenko declared, had already been agreed upon at the Yalta Conference.

In his famous story, Lewis Carroll does not give names to the gardeners whom the Queen ordered to summary execution. For his purpose it was sufficient to tell us that there were three of them. For our purpose, neither the character nor the career of Admiral Raeder is of importance. Having been "a not illogical defendant-counterpart" symbol at Nürnberg, he became simply Prisoner No. 4 in Spandau Prison.

* "Tyranny on Trial" by Whitney R. Harris, page 29.

THE GREAT STALIN MYTH

If the Nürnberg-Spandau episode be read with the label Prisoner No. 4. substituted for the name of Erich Raeder, it will be found one of the most diverting episodes in history.

Chapter II

THE KATYN MASS MURDER

What remains the most celebrated and widely-known crime committed during the Second World War came to light in February 1943 following a report by some Polish civilian workers to the German military authorities in Smolensk that in the neighbouring Katyn Forest were several artificial mounds or hillocks on which small pine trees, obviously recently planted, were growing. Enquiries among the local peasantry established that various vague and sinister rumours were in circulation concerning the unloading of numerous prisoners in Polish uniform at the local station of Gniezdovo and their immediate transport by lorries to an unknown destination in the forest nearby. Preliminary digging, carried out in spite of the frost, revealed several bodies and indicated that these mounds were huge graves. Systematic digging began on the 29th March, 1943, with the result that the Berlin Broadcasting Station on the 12th April, 1943, was able to announce the discovery of a huge pit 28 metres long and 16 metres wide filled with twelve layers of bodies, dressed in Polish uniforms. All had been murdered by a bullet fired at the back of the head. "The clotting together of the bodies by dense putrefaction and deformation due to pressure", made counting difficult but the number of bodies was estimated provisionally at 3,000. Other mounds in the neighbourhood were being investigated.

The historians vainly searched their records for an atrocity of comparable magnitude committed in modern times, but at first the man in the street remain unimpressed. If the First World War had made any permanent impression on his mind, it was to instil it with an ineradicable suspicion of all atrocity stories. In 1914 he had accepted at their face value all he had been told of the Belgian atrocities: he had thrilled with horror at the story of the Crucified Canadian and had been filled with disgust at the Corpse Factory story. A few years later he had been blandly informed that these stories were fabrications invented for his benefit in order to inspire him to fight more energetically. While he approved the result, the man in the street was filled with a subconscious resolve not to be made a fool of a second time. He took little interest, in consequence, in the stories which were told him of the atrocities committed by the Bolsheviks after the Russian Revolution. No doubt most of these stories were true, but having been caught once, he was not going to attempt to guess what percentage were lies. Later, during the Civil War in Spain, he heard with languid interest how the Communist supporters of the Republican Government were accustomed to burn monks and nuns alive, and how Fascist planes had cruelly bombed Guernica without regard to the safety of the inhabitants simply because a defeated horde of Communist warriors were in flight through the town. When he heard reports of the oppression of the German-speaking inhabitants of the Sudetenland by the Czechs, he dismissed the subject as Nazi propaganda: similarly, when he was told of the treatment of prisoners in Hitler's concentration camps, he dismissed the matter as Jewish propaganda. It is true that after the outbreak of war in 1939, he dutifully accepted the propaganda stories served out to him by the Ministry of Information, but he did so only as a patriotic duty, in a spirit very different from the naive enthusiasm of 1914.

Naturally, therefore, when the news of the Katyn Forest Massacre arrived, it was at first dismissed as war propaganda. Three thousand corpses indeed!—everyone knew Dr. Goebbels would not hesitate to claim the discovery of thirty thousand corpses —or three hundred thousand corpses for that matter—in some inaccessible part of Russia if he thought such a claim would have the slightest propaganda value!

Opinion changed rapidly, however, when it became known that the Germans were issuing pressing invitations to representatives of all the neutral countries to visit the site of the crime and see for themselves what had taken place. Most certainly when the Corpse Factory myth had been put forward in 1917 no invitations had been issued to neutral investigators to examine the forged diaries and other documents which General Charteris had produced in its support. Finally, it was learned that the Germans were asking the International Red Cross to send a commission to investigate, a request which had the hearty support of the exiled Polish Government in London. Clearly the Katyn Forest Massacre was not just another example of war propaganda. A ghastly crime had clearly taken place, and when it was learned that the Soviet Government had given an emphatic refusal to consent to an investigation by the International Red Cross, any possible doubt vanished as to the identity of those responsible. The report of the neutral commission headed by the Swiss Professor, Dr. Naville, that the victims were Polish prisoners of war in Russian captivity who had been massacred by their captors merely confirmed what had previously been universally accepted as the truth.

From the day of its discovery, no real mystery attached to the Katyn Forest Mass-Murder: when the report of the neutral commission was published, any possible doubt concerning the details of the crime or the identity of the criminals disappeared. It might have passed into history as one of the number of blots on European civilisation which had occurred during the Second World War, chiefly remarkable because its details had been established beyond all question. Two years later, however, a mystery was gratuitously attached to the crime, a mystery concerning which it is at present only possible to speculate.

Before dealing with this mystery, a brief outline of the crime must be given.

In August 1939 Herr von Ribbentrop and Mr. Molotov came to an agreement to divide Poland between Germany and Soviet Russia along a line popularly known as "the Ribbentrop-Molotov Line", and in accordance with this agreement, German troops invaded Poland on the 1st September. In little over a fortnight the resistance of the Poles had been shattered and on 17th September, the Red Army proceeded to occupy Eastern Poland. This military operation was carried out with little resistance since the bulk of the Polish Army was in the West striving to hold up the German advance and many of the Polish units in the East surrendered without resistance, believing the assurances of the Moscow radio that the Red Army had come to rescue them from the Germans. Where resistance was offered, it was quickly overcome. Brest-Litovsk was shelled into surrender by the combined fire of Nazi and Communist artillery: General Langner, Commander of the Lemberg garrison, surrendered on terms to the Red Army which were shamelessly broken once his troops laid down their arms. The balance of the Polish Army, including those in flight eastward and the eastern frontier garrisons, amounting in all to some 227,454 men, according to the official Soviet figures, passed into Russian captivity.

We are not concerned here with the fate of the rank and file. All were transported to prisoner of war camps in the interior of Russia. Many no doubt died of the hardships they suffered. The majority ultimately returned to Poland after the war.

The officers and the members of such picked units as the Frontier Guards and the Military Police were less fortunate. They numbered about 15,000 men of which 3,920 were sent to a camp at Starobielsk, 4,500 were sent to a camp at Kozielsk and the remainder, numbering 6,567 to a camp at Ostashkov. Later, a few hundred of these prisoners were selected for special training in

Communism at a small camp near Griazoviec. Here they remained, receiving excellent treatment, until after the outbreak of war between Germany and Russia. In this way they escaped the fate of their comrades.

On the 22nd June 1941, the existing situation was transformed by the German invasion of Russia. Soviet Russia and Poland found themselves allies against the common enemy, Germany. Immediately the problem arose of making use of the thousands of Polish prisoners of war in Russian captivity. By an Agreement between the Soviet Government and the exiled Polish Government in London, dated the 30th July 1941, it was arranged that all Polish citizens in Russia should be released, and shortly afterwards by a military agreement, it was decided the released prisoners of war should be formed into a Polish army to fight under Russian command.

Gradually the released Polish prisoners of war began to arrive at the assembly centres from all over the vast territories of the U.S.S.R. for training and arming. Very soon it became apparent that their officers were missing. For over a year the Polish authorities had been receiving complaints that the relatives in Poland of these officers had received no communication from them of any kind later than the spring of the previous year. The Soviet authorities were polite and reassuring. Transport and administration had been disorganised by the German advance: of course the missing men would turn up very shortly. Among those approached by the anxious Poles was Beria, who, it will be remembered, was to become, after the death of Stalin in 1953, the most powerful man in Russia until overthrown after a few weeks by Malenkov and summarily liquidated. In 1941 Beria was ahead of the Political Police, then known as the N.K.V.D., formerly the G.P.U., and before that, the Cheka. In view of his official position it is probable he personally made the arrangements for the liquidation of the missing Polish officers. He, of course, professed to know nothing of what had become of them. Equally without result was an appeal to Vyshinsky, the notorious Public Prosecutor at the mock-trials held during the Great Purge of 1936-37. The Polish Ambassador in Moscow then had an interview with Molotov who could only assure him that the search for the missing 15,000 men was diligently proceeding. In despair, the Ambassador applied for and obtained an interview with Stalin himself. The interview took place in the Kremlin in the presence of Molotov on the 14th November 1941. Stalin professed surprise when he was assured that all the Polish prisoners had not been released in accordance with the Russo-Polish agreement of the previous July. He himself telephoned, or pretended to telephone, the headquarters of the N.K.V.D. for information. He did not disclose what he was told, however, and the interview ended with a repetition of the usual assurances that the search was going on.

On the 1st December 1941 the Polish authorities sent General Sikorski to the Kremlin provided with a list of the names of all the prisoners who had been at the camps at Starobielsk, Kozielsk and Ostashkov. He was seen by Stalin himself in the presence of Molotov. Stalin suggested the missing men might have escaped over the frontier into Manchuria! But, he declared, the search should go on regardless of trouble and expense. On the 18th March 1942 Stalin was seen by the Polish Commander-in-Chief, General Anders: Stalin declared that the search had now been extended to Francis Joseph Land in the Arctic Circle. It was still proceeding.

As early as the 3rd November 1941, the Polish Government had appealed to the British Government to ask the Soviet Government to find the missing officers, so urgently needed for the training of the new Polish Army. This date is important since it shows that as early as this, the British Government knew officially that 15,000 Polish officers were missing, and as from this date were kept fully informed of the various excuses put forward by the Kremlin, continued throughout the whole of 1942, why they could not be produced. In other words, eighteen months before the discovery of the mass-graves in the Katyn Forest, official circles in Whitehall had every reason to suspect that a horrible crime on an enormous scale had been committed.* The discovery announced over the German wireless on the 12th April 1943 merely confirmed this suspicion.

The proposal of the German Government that the mass-graves at Katyn should be investigated by the International Red Cross, a proposal strongly supported by the Polish Government, was particularly embarrassing to the British Government. With the knowledge of the facts already possessed, no one in Whitehall could doubt what the result of such an investigation must be.* Certainly no one in the Kremlin entertained any doubt. The Soviet Government curtly rejected the application of the International Red Cross for its consent to investigate the matter. The International Red Cross refused to act without the consent of all parties concerned and when the indignant Poles persisted, Molotov handed the Polish

* In fairness to Sir Anthony Eden it should be pointed out that it was no part of his duties as H.M. Foreign Secretary to appoint himself a sort of unofficial coroner on the discovery of a number of human bodies reported to have been discovered in a wood in a remote part of Russia. With the knowledge in his possession he could hardly help forming an opinion, but until fully investigated by the local authorities the matter was officially sub judice.

Ambassador a note breaking off diplomatic relations between the Soviet Union and Poland, a drastic step which Mr. Anthony Eden informed the House of Commons on the 4th May 1943 had filled His Majesty's Government with regret.

In fact, as Mr. Joseph Mackiewicz says in his book, *"The Katyn Wood Murders"*,* "Katyn had ceased to be a crime; it had become a political problem". The paramount political aim of the Western Allies was to retain the support of the Soviet Union, which the folly of Hitler and Ribbentrop had presented to them. At whatever cost there must be no breach with the Soviet Union. From a practical point of view, the support of Poland mattered little. If necessary, Poland must be abandoned to Russia—as in fact was done a couple of years later. At the moment, however, all that was necessary was to urge the Polish Government not to make any more fuss and to forget the subject. General Sikorski, indeed, remained obdurate. Fortunately, he was shortly afterwards killed in a mysterious air crash when flying back from Egypt to lay his unwelcome views before the British Government. Other matters distracted public attention and gradually the view became accepted—except among the Poles—that the Katyn Forest Massacre had best be forgotten. As Mr. Arthur Bliss Lane, former United States Ambassador to Poland, delicately puts it in the preface which he contributed to Mr. Mackiewicz's book above mentioned, "For reasons of war censorship many facts regarding the crime were concealed from the public at the time. Unfortunately, it must now be admitted, the fear of Soviet displeasure prevented the United States and British Governments from assuming a stronger stand in protecting the interests of their other ally, Poland".

Owing to the refusal by the Soviet Union, to consent to an investigation the International Red Cross refused to investigate the crime. As the only available alternative, the Germans organised a commission of medical-legal experts from the universities of twelve neutral countries to visit Katyn and to report what they found. This neutral commission and the numerous neutral citizens who visited the site, among them the Polish author, Mr. Mackiewicz, established beyond question the main details of the crime, in particular the approximate date when it was committed. As Mr. Mackiewicz points out in his books, the question *who* committed the crime is answered beyond all possible doubt by the proof of the *time* when it was committed. The victims became prisoners of the Russians in September 1939: as stated above, they ceased to correspond with their relations in Poland in April 1940; the neutral investigators found

* "The Katyn Wood Murders" by Joseph Mackiewicz, Hollis and Carter, London, 1951.

numerous letters, diaries, notebooks and other documents in the pockets of the victims. None of these bear a later date than April 1940. In the graves, among the bodies, a number of old newspapers were found, in particular copies of the Soviet propaganda newspaper, printed in Polish, "Voice of the Union". Most of these newspapers were dated March or April 1940; none bore a later date.

The reader is reminded that the war between Germany and the Soviet Union started on June 22nd 1941. These Polish prisoners could not, therefore, have fallen into German hands until after July 17th, when the city of Smolensk and the Katyn Forest district nearby was occupied by the Germans, by which time, of course, the murdered men had been in their graves over fourteen months!

It has been frequently stated that 15,000 Polish officers were murdered in the Katyn Forest. This is probably incorrect. Some 15,000 Polish prisoners, of whom 8,000 were officers disappeared without trace not later than April 1940. The bodies of not more than 4,500 of these men were found buried three years later in the Katyn Forest. All of them had been imprisoned at the camp at Kozielsk. The fate of the remaining 10,000 prisoners who had been imprisoned in the other two camps, Starobielsk and Ostashkov, remains unknown. That they were murdered also, round about the same time, there can be no doubt whatever. They may also have been murdered in another part of the Katyn Forest where they now lie in undiscovered graves. Or they may have been taken away for 'liquidation' to another and more remote part of Russia. Only one thing can be said with certainty concerning them and that is that, like their comrades whose bodies were found in the Katyn Forest, they are dead.

The evidence at Katyn points to the massacre there having been carried out systematically and methodically. Usually the method adopted at a Communist mass liquidation is to turn machine guns on the victims until all are dead. At Katyn the skull of each victim was pierced by a hole made by a small calibre revolver fired at the back of the head. Mr. Mackiewicz suggests that three assassins dealt with each prisoner individually, two, one on each side, holding the victim's arms, and the third firing from behind. Probably this took place at the edge of the open grave, the victim falling forward on to the bodies of his already liquidated comrades.

The instant the news was broadcast over the German wireless on the 12th April 1943 that the bodies of the missing Poles had been discovered in the Katyn Forest, the Kremlin authorities announced that it possessed full information as to what had happened to them. For the previous eighteen months they had been assuring the Polish authorities that they had not the faintest idea of what had become of the missing men: that they were searching frantically for them even (according to Mr. Stalin himself) among the icebergs of Francis Joseph Land. But now it appeared that they possessed full and exact information: there was no mystery as to their fate whatever. In July 1941 the prisoner of war camp in which they had been confined had been captured with all its inmates by the German invaders. The missing Poles had therefore passed from Russian to German custody. Obviously the Germans had murdered them with the villainous intention of later bringing a false charge against the Soviet Government in the hope of damaging the far-famed reputation of the Soviet Union for humanity and rectitude.

It is unnecessary to comment here on this explanation. Something obviously had to be said and it is hard to suggest any other explanation which would have sounded more plausible. The situation which arose as a result of the finding of the bodies in the Katyn Forest is unique in political history but extremely common in the criminal annals of all countries. Thus it has frequently happened that a wife has disappeared suddenly and anxious relatives have at length induced the police to make enquiries. From the husband of the missing lady a variety of explanations is obtained—she has gone away to friends, or she has eloped, or has emigrated to some remote country. Enquiries prove fruitless: the husband professes to be as much puzzled as anyone. Sometimes, as a result of some clue, the body of the missing lady is found—generally somewhere in the premises of the husband; in the Crippen case, for example, buried in the cellar. The husband is then asked if he would like to put forward a new explanation.

The present writer cannot recall a case in which, in these trying circumstances, an explanation, later accepted by the jury, was put forward. Possibly as good as another would be the explanation that the lady had gone to live with a neighbour with a grudge against the husband who in order to revenge himself on the husband, murdered her and then buried the body in the husband's house so that a false charge could be brought against that innocent man.

Anyway, it was along these lines Mr. Stalin's advisers advised him to deal with a very awkward situation. No doubt Mr. Molotov assured him that the Western allies would gladly accept what was told them and Mr. Beria assured him there were no eye-witnesses, and that the killers of the N.K.V.D. could be relied upon from long experience to carry out their duties thoroughly and with all proper precautions.

45

THE KATYN MASS MURDER

No eye-witness has indeed recorded these ghastly doings at Katyn but the truth concerning them is established with a far greater certainty by circumstantial evidence all of which points in the same direction. In political crimes particularly, the evidence of persons professing to have been eye-witnesses is often open to the gravest suspicion. Patriotism, prejudice and duress lead readily to perjury.

The standard legal text book, "Wills on Evidence", analyses circumstantial evidence under ten headings, of which *Motive, Opportunity* and *Means* are held to constitute a prima facie case.

With regard to *Motive*, the victims of the Katyn Massacre were all members of the anti-Communist classes, supporters of the "reactionary Polish state" which, ever since the defeat of the Soviet invasion of 1920, had been hostile to the Soviet Union. In a speech of the 31st October 1939, Molotov had proclaimed "the annihilation of the miserable product of the Treaty of Versailles which was the Poland built on the oppression of her minorities". As early as this, therefore, the Kremlin had decided to turn Poland into a Communist buffer state under Soviet control, a policy which was duly carried out some five years later in 1945. The Polish land-owning, military and professional classes could not have been assimilated by the new Communist society which the Kremlin was determined to establish in Poland. Classes which are unassimilable can only be dealt with by liquidation. In Marxian legal jargon, the "objective characteristics" of the Polish officers who had become Soviet prisoners in September 1939 clearly justified "the supreme measure of social security"—that is to say, liquidation. Although in special cases—such as the one under consideration—a Marxian Communist might find it expedient to deny that a liquidation had in fact been carried out, yet regarded theoretically from the Marxian standpoint, the Katyn Liquidation would be regarded as fully justifiable.

With regard to *Opportunity*, all the victims were admittedly in the custody of the Soviet authorities from the time of their surrender in September 1939, and with regard to *Means* they were obviously entirely at the mercy of their captors as from the date of their surrender.

This prima facie case is confirmed under two other of Mr. Wills' headings. *Guilty Consciousness* is shown by the pretended search for the missing prisoners which was supposed to have begun in July 1941 and lasted until the discovery of the bodies in the Katyn Forest in April 1943. If it was the truth that the prison camp containing the Polish prisoners later found at Katyn had been captured with its inmates by the advancing Germans in July 1941, why did not Beria, Vishinsky, Molotov and Stalin give this simple explanation to the Polish authorities? Why did they pretend at repeated interviews that they did not know what had become of the missing men? Why this pretended search? Why all these absurd enquiries on the orders of Stalin himself in the Arctic Circle and Francis Joseph Land?

The bogus charge relating to the Katyn Forest Massacre brought against the German "major war criminals" at Nürnberg by the Soviet Government may be regarded as an example of Mr. Wills' heading *Fabrication of Evidence*.

The inclusion of a charge concerning the Katyn Forest Massacre against the German "major war criminals" attached to the crime an element of mystery which until then had been completely lacking. This development was totally unexpected. After the Soviet Government had successfully prevented an investigation of the crime by the International Red Cross, the matter passed gradually into oblivion. The unfortunate Poles were urged not to hamper the war effort by fussing over past wrongs—when victory was achieved they could rely upon everything being forgiven and forgotten.

Only six months had passed, however, after Mr. Eden had expressed the deep regret of the British Government over the refusal of the Soviet Government to agree to the investigation of the Katyn Massacre by the International Red Cross, when those with full knowledge of the facts received an embarrassing reminder. In November 1943, at an official banquet during the Teheran Conference, Mr. Stalin proposed a toast in which he declared that when victory was achieved "50,000 German officers and technicians should be rounded up and shot". To most of those present, the reference to the Katyn Massacre, so recently hushed up, must have been clear: obviously Stalin was proposing a similar massacre for the same political purpose but on an even more gigantic scale. All were filled with surprise by the old Bolshevik's indiscretion: Sir Winston Churchill alone was filled with anger. "The British people", he declared, "will never stand for mass-murder!" Mr. Roosevelt, however, clearly felt the indignation of his British colleague unwarranted, while Stalin seemed "hugely tickled". Mr. Roosevelt suggested carelessly that perhaps a compromise could be reached by agreeing that the number to be massacred should be reduced from 50,000 to 49,500. Apologists for the American President have since suggested that he made this proposal in jest, but it has now been disclosed that at the Yalta Conference in 1945 he expressed a hope that Stalin would propose another toast to a massacre of 50,000 Germans. Like Sir Winston, Roosevelt must have realised that Stalin had the massacre of Katyn in mind. His reaction, however, was very different to that of the British Prime Minister. "Churchill was furious and no fooling", Elliott Roosevelt, the President's son, records. Thanks mainly to Mr. Eden's efforts, however, general amiability was at length restored. By tacit agreement the subject of Katyn was placed upon the index of forbidden topics.

In July 1945, therefore, it was with surprise and consternation that it was learned in London and Washington that at the final meeting of the prosecution staffs preparing for the Nürnberg trials of the German "major war criminals", the Soviet representatives had suddenly announced that they intended to bring a charge that the defendants were responsible for "the killing of 11,000 Polish officers in the Katyn Forest near Smolensk in September 1941". The British and American representatives opposed vigorously but in vain. This charge was included, therefore, in the indictment.

Why the Soviet Government decided to bring this charge was and still remains a complete mystery.

But at the trial itself an even more mysterious question arose. By Article 19 of the so-called Charter creating it, the International Military Tribunal was authorised to disregard all rules of evidence and to accept any evidence placed before it which it might deem to have "probative value". Relying on this article, the Tribunal accepted at its face value, hearsay and other evidence which would have been rejected as inadmissible or worthless by any normally functioning court of law. In particular the Tribunal readily accepted evidence by affidavits and refused to require the persons swearing these affidavits to attend court so that they could be cross-examined on behalf of the defendants.

With all the usual legal safeguards against perjury removed, it would have been easy for the Soviet prosecutor to have proved the guilt of the defendants for the Katyn Massacre to the satisfaction of the Tribunal. The Soviet Political Police could have supplied as many affidavits by eye-witnesses of the crime as the Tribunal would have had the patience to read. If so desired, affidavits could have been laid before the court duly sworn by persons who after a visit to the torture chambers of the N.K.V.D. could remember having seen Field Marshal Goering himself carrying out the massacre with his own revolver.

But instead of producing a case which on the face of it was irrefutable and which the Tribunal by the terms of its Charter would have been bound to accept at its face value, the Soviet prosecutor produced what amounted to no evidence at all! First of all, he submitted to the Tribunal the report of a Soviet State

A partially uncovered mass grave in Katyn Forest near Smolensk, Russia. One of the pictures supplied to the investigating committee by Col. John H. Van Vliet when he testified that the Russians, not the Germans, were responsible for the massacre.

To prove Russian guilt, the Germans uncovered the bodies of 4,500 Polish officers massacred in the Katyn Forest. Over 15,000 Polish prisoners disappeared, altogether.

Commission which had purported to have examined the facts. At best this could be described as third-hand evidence. Next he called as a witness an elderly professor of Sofia University, a Dr. Markov, who had been a member of the neutral commission headed by the Swiss professor, Dr. Naville, which had investigated the crime. Bulgaria was now in Russian occupation and Dr. Markov's life was forfeited for having signed the report setting out the facts proving Soviet guilt. He had been brought all the way from Sofia in order to retract what he had then said. The Tribunal heard him with compassion. It was a pitiful exhibition.

What possible purpose did the Soviet Government hope to serve by bringing this charge? And having been so imprudent as to bring this charge, why were not proper arrangements made to produce evidence upon which the Tribunal would have been compelled by the terms of its Charter to record a conviction?

The object could not have been to establish the cruelty of the German administration on the Eastern front, since this could be easily proved by genuine evidence in support of other counts on the indictment. And the object could not have been to absolve the Soviet Government in the eyes of the Polish people for responsibility for the crime because, in that event, care would have been taken to secure a conviction.

The only possible explanation is that the charge was directed not at the defendants—whose fate was already assured—but at the capitalist allies of the Soviet Government. Hostility between them had always been latent, but it had been firmly repressed so long as the common foe existed. Perhaps historians will point to the belated inclusion of a charge relating to the Katyn Massacre on the charge sheet at Nürnberg as the first undisguised sign of that ill-will from which, in a few years, would develop that state of open hostility known as 'the cold war'.

Still if this view of the matter be accepted, it remains hard to suggest what exactly was the political object the rulers in the Kremlin hoped to achieve by embarrassing their capitalist allies. Probably if any such political object existed, it formed no part of any carefully planned and thought-out scheme. From the very first the Soviet authorities had hardly troubled to disguise their opinion that the war-trials upon which their capitalist allies insisted were nothing but a pompous and hypocritical substitute for the simple method of disposing of captured enemies proposed by Stalin at the Teheran Conference, "despatching them before a firing squad as fast as we capture them". In the passage which the reader will find quoted in the last chapter of this book, the Soviet judge,

THE KATYN MASS MURDER

General Nikitchenko, explained very frankly to his colleagues preparing for the Nürnberg trials what were his own and the views of his government on these proceedings.* The defendants, he declared, had already been found guilty by the representatives of the governments attending the Moscow and Yalta conferences. The only duty of the Tribunal, therefore, was to decide and impose their punishment. If the reader will try for an instant to regard the trial through the eyes of General Nikitchenko, he will realise what an absurd farce this trial, dragging on for over ten months, must have appeared to the Soviet representatives taking part in it.

It is possible, also, a sense of humour may be a factor which has had greater influence on the course of history than some historians have been willing to allow. The gravity with which the representatives of the Western Powers regarded themselves and each other must have appeared in Marxian eyes extremely funny. General Nikitchenko had declared that at the trial "there could be no question of a judge having the character of an impartial person". The judges appointed by the Western Powers seemed unconscious of any difficulty in this respect and throughout purported to act as impartial persons. The solemnity with which they debated points of law and considered minute details of the evidence must to a Marxist have appeared simply ludicrous.

If the inclusion of a charge relating to the Katyn Massacre be attributed to Stalin's untimely sense of humour, no wider aim need be attributed to him than a malicious desire to embarrass the Tribunal. The joke, if such was intended, certainly miscarried completely, although for a time it put the Tribunal in a most worrying dilemma.

If, on the one hand, the Tribunal decided to convict the defendants on this charge unsupported by a shred of real evidence in open disregard of what to common knowledge was the truth, discredit would be thrown on the entire proceedings at Nürnberg. To convict in such circumstances would amount to admitting that the contention of General Nikitchenko was right when he declared that the sole function of the Tribunal was to decide the punishment to be imposed on already condemned persons.

On the other hand, if the Tribunal formally dismissed the charge against the German defendants, this would amount to an implied conviction of the Russian Government. Indisputably a crime had been committed—obviously these unfortunate Poles could not have committed suicide and then buried themselves. If the Germans were innocent, then this crime must have been committed by the Russian captors of the victims. The result of such a decision by the Tribunal would have been an international crisis of the first

* See page 214.

50

magnitude. Probably the Soviet Government would have withdrawn their representatives from Nürnberg and refused to take any further part in the proceedings. The already shaky 'Grand Alliance' would have been in danger of collapse.

It is satisfactory to record that the Tribunal rose grandly to the occasion: the dignity of its president, Lord Justice Lawrence, remained unshaken. Having heard with admirable patience what the Soviet prosecutor had to say about the Katyn Massacre, the Tribunal passed without comment to the consideration of other matters. No later comment on the subject was made at Nürnberg. The judgment of the Tribunal when delivered was found to contain no reference to the Katyn Massacre.

Admittedly this solution of the difficulty was in defiance of the elementary principle of criminal law that the onus of proving a charge rests on the prosecution, which if undischarged by the prosecution entitles the accused as of right to a verdict of acquittal. But the Tribunal had been placed by the Charter creating it above such elementary considerations: by leaving the charge undecided, the Tribunal was complying with the limitation of its jurisdiction imposed by the Charter to crimes "committed in the interests of the European Axis countries". If the Germans were guilty, the crime of Katyn had been committed in the interests of an Axis country, namely Germany, and the Tribunal had jurisdiction to punish it. But if the Germans were innocent, the Russians were guilty, in which case the jurisdiction of the Tribunal to discuss the matter, much less to come to any decision about it, instantly ceased.

It is unfortunately true that as a result of this solution of the difficulty, mankind was deprived of the benefit of hearing what the International Military Tribunal thought about the Katyn Massacre. Still, in view of the Tribunal's decisions on other matters, perhaps the loss to mankind may not be so very great.

Chapter III

THE MURDER OF BENITO MUSSOLINI

On the 10th May 1945 an elderly English gentleman received a photograph which he tells us profoundly shocked him. On the preceding 29th April he had read in the "Daily Express" a brief description of the event, the final scene of which was illustrated by this photograph. The editorial comment had been that the story could "cause no vestige of sorrow, no pang of revulsion". But in regard to one distinguished reader at least this editorial comment was wrong. The "pang of revulsion" felt by this elderly gentleman was spurred to indignant action when a few days later he read a report of an interview given by a then unnamed individual to the Milanese Communist newspaper "L'Unita" reproduced in the same English newspaper. The elderly gentleman had a mastery of forcible English unequalled by any of his contemporaries. To the chief representative of Britain in the area where this event had taken place he sent a telegram in which he referred to this event as "murder" and described it as "treacherous and cowardly". As usual, he experienced no difficulty in finding at once exactly the right words to express his meaning.

The text of the telegram sent by Sir Winston Churchill to Field Marshal Lord Alexander is as follows: —

"The man who murdered Mussolini made a confession, published in the 'Daily Express', gloating over the treacherous and cowardly method of his action. In particular he said that he shot Mussolini's mistress. Was she on the list of war criminals? Had he authority from anybody to shoot this woman? It seems to me the cleansing hand of British military power should make enquiries on these points".

It is regrettably true that there is no record that "the cleansing hand of British military power" was able to carry out the much needed cleansing work which Sir Winston evidently had in mind. Commenting on the subject in his book on the Second World War, "Triumph and Tragedy", written in 1954, Sir Winston consoles himself with the reflection that the murder of the Italian dictator, cowardly, treacherous and unpunished as it was, "at least spared the world an Italian Nürnberg". And there is certainly consolation in this reflection, except, of course, for those who like Sir Hartley Shawcross still profess to believe that 'the German Nürnberg' conferred incalculable blessings on the world.

Full particulars of this double murder were published in the Press throughout the world within a few days of its commission. There was no need to institute a search for the criminal or criminals. Immediately after it had been committed, a person came forward to claim that he had played the leading part in the crime. This claim has been generally accepted, although the claimant is a self-confessed liar who has, to date, given the Italian Press three separate and conflicting accounts of what occurred. In particular, in his first account he proudly claimed the guilt of both of the murder of Mussolini and of the murder of Mussolini's mistress, Claretta Petacci. In his subsequent versions of the story he sought to renounce the credit for the murder of Claretta by suggesting that she was killed by him accidentally. Nevertheless, the essence of his story remains generally accepted, namely that he personally murdered Mussolini with several shots from a sub-machine gun on the afternoon of April 28th 1945 at the entrance to the Villa Belmonte on the Western shores of Lake Como. The Italian Communist Party accepted him as a genuine murderer: entirely on his reputation as such, he was elected a Communist member of the Italian Chamber of Deputies.

The opinion of Sir Winston Churchill on the murder of Mussolini, as evidenced by his telegram to Field Marshal Lord Alexander, was probably shared by a considerable inarticulate section of his countrymen, but it was very quickly realised that whether or not it was possible to feel "a pang of revulsion" at the crime, political expediency required that such a pang should find no public expression. All recollection of the atrocities and crimes for which the Russian dictator, Stalin, had been responsible had been obliterated by the victory of Stalingrad, and now that the triumph of the Red Army had been crowned by the occupation of Berlin, he was regarded by the British and American publics with veneration and awe, more than slightly tinged, perhaps, with apprehension. What had been said in the past about Communist atrocities could not unfortunately be unsaid, but at least a blind eye could be turned on the orgy of Communist atrocities then going on in the eastern parts of Europe occupied by the Red Army in accordance with the Yalta Agreement. Although Communist crimes being committed west of the Iron Curtain could not be altogether ignored, at least they could be referred to in terms which would not wound the Russian dictator's susceptibilities. By tacit agreement it was decided that

THE MURDER OF BENITO MUSSOLINI

the murder of Mussolini must be referred to as an execution. On no account must the word "murder" be used in connection with it.

The practice of referring to this crime as an execution became so firmly established by long use that it was followed long after the reason for its adoption had entirely passed away. Thus the 1947 edition of the Encyclopaedia Britannica writes, "Mussolini and his party were apprehended outside Dongo by Italian partisans, where after trial, they were executed". Both Everyman's Encyclopaedia (1949) and Chambers Encyclopaedia (1950) refer dutifully to Mussolini's death as an execution. As late as April 1955 an article on the crime in the New York Times Magazine was illustrated by a portrait with the caption, "Mussolini's executioner, Colonel Valerio".*

The dictionary defines the word execution as the carrying out of a sentence of death imposed by a court of law. No possible interpretation of the admitted facts of Mussolini's death could justify the use of this word. Whatever his offences and desserts may have been, it is quite certain that no court of law ever adjudicated on any charge brought against him: there was never a conviction or a sentence. Clearly, therefore, he was murdered unless it can be established that he was killed in action during fighting in a civil war, or that, having been made prisoner, he was shot during an attempt to escape. No suggestion has ever been put forward that any such circumstances occurred in his case.

Crimes in any way connected with politics are always difficult to investigate since the facts are obscured by preconceived prejudices. This is particularly so in the case of Mussolini. It is a curious fact that although he played a leading role on the European political stage for nearly a quarter of a century, up to the very end Mussolini remained for his contemporaries a figure of propaganda rather than a living human being of flesh and blood. His enemies denied him any credit for his really outstanding achievements: his admirers often picked out for praise those of his actions which were least to his credit. To many of his fellow-countrymen he was slandered as a cruel tyrant, while to the British public he was for the greater part of his career a figure of fun, an absurd foreigner addicted to making theatrical gestures which on no account could be taken seriously by sensible people. In days when the sinister Stalin was a mere name and long before anyone outside Germany had heard of an ex-corporal named Hitler, Mussolini had been promoted to that small and ever changing group of celebrities, generally consisting of a few royalties (native and foreign), a number of professional cricketers, footballers and boxers, a few native politicians and foreign cinema stars, an odd jockey and an actress

* See Postscript at the end of this chapter on Page 94.

or two, known collectively to the British man-in-the-street as Public Figures. He received the rare honour of having a universally known nickname bestowed on him, and for nearly twenty years maintained his position in this select and rapidly changing group, not, of course, as the foreign statesman who had raised his country from apathy and anarchy to the apparent position of a first-class Power, but as 'Musso' the beloved of the cartoonists.

Now, after more than ten years have passed since his death, it still remains difficult to regard Mussolini otherwise than as a lay figure round which his admirers and detractors spun propaganda myths and slanders. Throughout his long political career, he remained for the British public a synthetic creation of propaganda. As long before as 1914, he first emerged obscurely in the pages of the British Press in the role of the Misguided Socialist who owing to his theoretical objections to war, had become a spokesman of those benighted Italian Socialists who were raising opposition to Italy joining in the crusade recently undertaken by the British and Russian Empires to preserve the liberty of small nations. Suddenly it was learned with gratification that Mussolini had changed this role to that of Patriotic Idealist—to the disgust of his former Socialist comrades, he was now loudly demanding that Italy should attack her ally, Austria, in order to be able to annex the Austrian Tyrol and Trieste. Needless to say, all right-thinking people in Britain at the time loyally repudiated the base suggestion that this sudden volte-face was the result of a bribe by the British Secret Service.

From the celebrated March on Rome in 1922 which made him master of Italy down to as late as the Abyssinian War in 1935, Mussolini was held up to the admiration of the British public in the role of the Benevolent Dictator—the Man-who-got-things-Done. True, a small but extremely articulate group of British Leftists never wearied of denouncing him as a "Sawdust Caesar" who had deprived the Italian people of their liberty and, worse still, had deprived various more or less worthy Liberal and Socialist professional politicians of the chance of making a living at the game of party politics. For long it was almost an article of faith in devout Leftist circles that Mussolini was somehow responsible for the death of Matteotti,* a chatterbox Socialist who had taken a

* Matteotti would now be forgotten as a mere peddler of various Socialist nostrums but for the fact that after the Second World War streets all over Italy were named after him, not in memory of either his undistinguished career or ignominious death, but in the rather childish belief that this somehow would be a slur on the memory of Il Duce. The baseless allegation that Mussolini was in any way personally responsible for Matteotti's death has long since been abandoned.

leading part in the campaign to sabotage the work of reconstruction and who had met his death when being kidnapped by a party of irresponsible Blackshirts. To the vast majority of the British public, however, Mussolini was the honoured colleague of a succession of British statesmen at various international conferences: to the politicians he was the man who could be trusted to mount guard over the Brenner Pass: to British tourists he was the man who had succeeded in making the Italian railways run to time.

From the time of the Abyssinian War and particularly after the outbreak of the Spanish Civil War, down to the Fall of France in 1940, Mussolini gradually ceased to hold the role of Benevolent Dictator and assumed the role of the Enigmatic Figure. Until it was clear which side in the coming war he was going to support, it was impossible either to praise or to condemn him. If he backed Hitler, then he would become automatically Public Enemy No. 2. But if he sided against Hitler then he would become a statesman whose career from its commencement had been utterly above criticism, much less reproach. No one knew what Mussolini was going to do—probably he did not know himself.

After long hesitation, Mussolini decided to keep his word to Hitler in spite of all the blandishments of Mr. Sumner Welles, specially sent over by President Roosevelt to keep Italy out of the war. So history repeated itself: taking advantage of her victim's hour of need, Italy stabbed France in the back just as she had stabbed Austria in the back in 1915. From that moment Mussolini became Public Enemy No. 2, a man whose previous career from the day of his birth had been an unbroken succession of perfidies and crimes. He retained this role until the day of his death five years later.

Not one of the varied and conflicting propaganda roles which Mussolini was presented as playing during his life is more incredible than the role conferred upon him after his death in the pages of Paolo Monelli's recent biography, *"Mussolini: an Intimate Study"*.* According to this biographer, Mussolini was neither evil nor great but was simply a fantastic personage who washed infrequently, was only persuaded to change his shirts with difficulty, wore ridiculous clothes, never learned to shave himself, had the manners of a peasant (although he was not a peasant), was fundamentally irreligious but childishly superstitious, was vain, envious, spiteful, bombastic and although he had served gallantly in the trenches during the First World War, was such a coward that when

* "Mussolini: An Intimate Life" by Paolo Monelli, Thames and Hudson, London, 1953.

he visited North Africa in 1942 he refused to go within hundreds of miles of the front line. On every subject, according to Monelli, he was profoundly ignorant from Art to Military Strategy: when he had to show Hitler during an official visit through the Uffizi Galleries he could not disguise his boredom, and during the Abyssinian Campaign his absurd directions seriously embarrassed his generals.

As if to give his readers no excuse for accepting this portrait as anything but an absurd caricature, Monelli records naively in the historical note at the head of Chapter 9 of his book, "Mussolini follows a policy of internal pacification and reconstruction. Calm and prosperity return to Italy". He offers no explanation how, what he calls "this apparently miraculous cessation of riots, strikes and acts of violence" had been brought about by this grotesque individual, as devoid of gifts as of virtues.

It is true that at the present time a visitor to Italy has to search long and diligently to find an Italian who will admit that Mussolini or his regime possessed a single redeeming virtue. Yet everywhere in Italy he will find what are grudgingly admitted to be enduring monuments to Mussolini's memory in the shape of such public works as splendid arterial roads, new bridges, magnificent public buildings, harbours, reconstructed railways and drained swamps. It has indeed been found impossible to efface all traces of his maxim, 'Credere, Obbedire, Combattere!', although the Empire which he created has utterly vanished away.

The chief interest of the above mentioned biography by Paolo Monelli will be found in the particulars which it gives concerning the relationship of Mussolini with Claretta Petacci whose murder in his arms on the 28th April 1945 by the shores of Lake Como so particularly aroused Sir Winston Churchill's indignant disgust. Monelli portrays Mussolini as a coarse sensualist who from the age of sixteen until his death never lacked one, more or less established, mistress and who in addition after he became dictator adopted the practice of varying the monotony of affairs of state by entertaining a selected woman in the afternoon in his office in the Palazzo Venezia. Further, he alleges, that Mussolini's interviews with ladies having the honour of audiences with him in his official capacity frequently ended in the same way. For these alleged details of what he calls Mussolini's intimate life, Monelli relies on the published memoirs of Navarra who was Mussolini's personal attendant. While it may be readily agreed that from the position he held, Navarra was in a position to record the truth on this subject, some may recall the saying that no man is a hero to his valet and reflect that to his valet a fallen hero may be merely a subject for highly profitable slanders. Be this as it may, it cannot be questioned that Mussolini's relationship with Claretta Petacci was of an altogether different nature. She idealised him as the hero of her dreams, while he at least responded for many years to her entirely selfless passion. Even Monelli is compelled to admit grudgingly that for a time at any rate Mussolini's passion for Claretta Petacci was sincere—"a real passion, very different from his other love affairs". Against this "romantic young woman" as he calls her, Monelli has no venom to throw, and he admits, "Of Claretta herself, no one had anything very bad to say, not even the Duce's son-in-law, Ciano, and his wife, the Duce's daughter, Edda, who were her fiercest enemies". The facts of her death are sufficient proof of the sincerity of Claretta's love for the man who was destined to be labelled Public Enemy No. 2.

To what extent, if at all, can Mussolini be said to have deserved the title of Public Enemy No. 2? From a strictly legal point of view, it is impossible to deny that he was murdered. On the other hand, if it can be shown that his character and conduct had been such as to justify his enemies labelling him Public Enemy No. 2, then can it not be said that although the manner in which he was done to death was technically criminal, yet he richly deserved his fate?

Benito Mussolini was born at Dovia in the Romagna in 1883. His father was a blacksmith and an ardent Socialist. His early associations gave him a natural bias towards Socialism and an introduction to local Socialist circles. After early struggles with poverty and a sojourn in Switzerland, where he was regarded as a dangerous revolutionary, he took up journalism, and by 1910, he had so far succeeded that we find him publishing and editing a small political newspaper of his own, the character of which is sufficiently indicated by its name, 'La Lotta di Classe' (The Class Struggle).

In 1911 Italy declared war on Turkey. In 1946 the International Military Tribunal at Nürnberg was to proclaim through its president, Lord Justice Lawrence, that "the initiation of a war of aggression is the supreme international crime, containing within itself the accumulated evil of all other crimes". We have since been assured, in particular by Mr. Whitney R. Harris, the American prosecutor at Nürnberg, that the concept of aggressive war is impossible to define, and it is indeed a fact that several committees of legal experts had struggled vainly for months to find a definition. But if these experts had undertaken a brief study of Italian history during the preceding thirty-four years, they would have discovered four striking examples of aggressive war from which they could have readily propounded the simple and satisfactory definition

"An aggressive war is an armed attack by one state upon another without provocation or excuse".

The first of these four examples was the Turko-Italian War of 1911, when Italy attacked Turkey in order to annex the Turkish province of Tripoli. There was no excuse for the attack and the only reason it was made was that Turkey was too weak to defend this distant province from conquest by a Power possessing superior sea-power such as Italy.

Mussolini in the pages of his 'La Lotta di Classe' denounced the war as imperialist in terms which we may be sure would have gladdened the heart of Lord Justice Lawrence. It did not, however, gladden the hearts of the Italian Government. Mussolini was sent to prison for nine months.

From his attitude in this matter, except among his Socialist compatriots, Mussolini received neither praise nor fame. The world in general remained blissfully unconscious that the supreme international crime—or for that matter, any crime at all—had been committed. When, however, the political career of Mussolini comes to be considered on the Day of Judgment, assuming that the same view is there taken of aggressive war as was taken by the International Military Tribunal at Nürnberg, we may be sure that Mussolini will receive a substantial award on the credit side of his account which will do something to counterbalance the grave entries which, it is to be feared, will be found later recorded on the debit side.

The second of the four examples of aggressive war provided by recent Italian history occurred in 1915. When the First World War began in the previous year, Italy was a member of the Triple Alliance and as such, bound to support her ally, Austria. Italy refused, however, on an assortment of specious pretexts, to honour her pledges. Like most European Socialists, at its outset, Mussolini denounced the war as a capitalist struggle. He had recently become the editor of the influential national Socialist newspaper 'Avanti', and for the first time his views were read all over Italy. He emphatically demanded complete neutrality. "Down with the War! We must remain neutral", he wrote in his newspaper in August 1914.

But in the following October his expressed views underwent a complete change. From that time he began to urge that Italy should intervene in the war against her hard-pressed allies. As a consequence he was expelled from the Socialist Party. His Socialist colleagues entertained no doubt as to the reason for this betrayal, asking only one question, 'chi paga?'—'who pays?' Strong evidence has since been produced indicating that he had received a substantial payment of French gold to change his views.

Apart from the financial inducement which he almost certainly received, it may be conceded that Mussolini's natural inclinations were all against a policy so drab and unspectacular as strict neutrality. Fifteen years later the German author, Emil Ludwig, greatly daring, ventured to ask him his reasons in 1914 for changing his mind. Mussolini replied with admirable frankness, "Nobody loves a neutral" and went on to point out that if Italy's allies of the Triple Alliance had won, they would never have forgiven her for leaving them in the lurch, while if the Entente Powers had won, Italy would have been contemptuously shut out by them from any share in drafting the treaty of peace. It is certainly greatly to Mussolini's credit that he made no hypocritical pretence of having been influenced by admiration for the ideals for which the Entente Powers professed to be fighting.

By the Spring of 1915 a series of military defeats inflicted by the Czar's armies on the Austrians satisfied the Italian Government that it would be safe to stab Italy's ally in the back. So on the 23rd May 1915, Italy, for the second time in the space of four years, initiated a war of aggression by declaring war on her ally, Austria, or in other words, committed the supreme international crime. In his above mentioned conversation with Emil Ludwig, Mussolini proudly claimed a third share of the responsibility. "There were three of us who worked towards its fulfilment: D'Annunzio, Corridoni and myself. D'Annunzio spread the fire of militant nationalism among Italian youth: Corridoni organised the working masses in his syndicalist movement: I transformed the Socialist Party".

On his own admission, therefore, Mussolini was guilty of having, in 1915, committed the supreme international crime. This crime was not indeed created until 1945, but according to what Sir Hartley Shawcross so frequently refers to as "the principles laid down at Nürnberg", guilt for this particular crime can be incurred retrospectively. Had what Sir Winston Churchill calls "an Italian Nürnberg" taken place, no doubt Mussolini would have been charged with having committed the supreme international crime by initiating an aggressive war against France on the 10th June 1940. If indeed it be possible to commit this crime retrospectively six years before it was declared to be a crime, there is no logical reason why it should not also be possible to commit it retrospectively thirty years before. According to this reasoning, therefore, it is possible to maintain that when Mussolini met his fate in 1945, he had been bearing a burden of guilt, meriting the severest punishment for upwards of thirty years!

THE MURDER OF BENITO MUSSOLINI

Not, of course, that anyone in 1915 realized that the supreme international crime, or any crime at all, had been committed by Italy when she declared war on her ally Austria. On the contrary, the action of Italy produced an ecstatic outburst of praise and admiration. The conduct of the Italian Government was acclaimed in the British Press as exhibiting a lofty idealism unparalleled in history. It was not until the Versailles Conference met to dictate the terms of peace to the vanquished that it was disclosed that by the secret Treaty of London Italy had been bribed to enter the war by a promise that she should be allowed to annex the Austrian Tyrol up to the Brenner Pass; Istria, including Trieste; the Dalmatian coast and islands; Saseno and the town of Valona in Albania and the Greek island of Rhodes—territories inhabited by 350,000 Germans, over a million Slavs and tens of thousands of Greeks, Albanians and Turks. "This treaty", pronounces the Encyclopaedia Britannica, solemnly, "violated every principle of nationality". Truly its disclosure was embarrassing to victors who had just won a war professedly fought to establish the right of self-determination!

Enough has already been written concerning Italy's attack on Abyssinia in 1935, the third of the four examples of aggressive war undertaken by Italy within the space of thirty years. It is sufficient here to say that it was as utterly indefensible as the attack by Soviet Russia on Finland in 1939. The best that can be said in extenuation is that neither Mussolini nor the vast majority of his countrymen were conscious that they were committing an international crime: they regarded themselves as merely taking a belated part in the profitable game of 'African-grab' at which most of the leading European powers had played during the latter half of the 19th century.

The fourth of the four examples of aggressive war provided by recent Italian history occurred in 1940. It resembled in every respect the aggressive war of 1915 except that in this case the victim was not an ally of Italy. For some time previously Mussolini had decided to commit "the supreme international crime", but for long he had been unable to make up his mind whom to select as the victim. Should he betray his ally, Hitler, and attack Germany? The German victories in Norway and France caused him to dismiss the idea. As in 1914, neutrality was contrary to his inclinations. Had he declared war on France immediately after the German break-through at Sedan, his intervention might have had decisive results since it would have enabled the German High Command to disregard the still powerful French forces reforming behind the Weygand line and to turn their whole attention on the

B.E.F. retreating to Dunkirk. Had Mussolini at that critical moment distracted the attention of the French for only a few weeks, the B.E.F. would probably have been wiped out, in which case it is likely that an invasion of England would have followed. Had this invasion taken place, its success or failure would have had a decisive effect not only on the war but on world history. But Mussolini hesitated until he could strike with what appeared to be absolute safety. When at last it came, his intervention was an empty gesture. The allies that he so hesitatingly selected had no cause to feel for him unbounded gratitude, although on the other hand his intended victims had little ground to feel towards him implacable hatred.

Had the Italian people real cause for complaint against their former idol, Benito Mussolini? That he committed the supreme international crime in 1940 gave them no cause whatever to complain since three times in the preceding thirty years the Italian people had joined with enthusiasm in the commission of this crime and in each case had joyfully accepted the spoils thereof. In essence, their complaint against him was that in 1940 he had made the mistake of joining what was to prove to be the weaker side, contrary to the guiding principle of Italian foreign policy since the days of Count Cavour. This, from their point of view, was an unpardonable mistake. Further, it can hardly be denied that Mussolini displayed an irresponsibility hardly short of criminal in subjecting the Italian armed forces to the test of war. Did he not know, or should he not have known, that the might of the costly Italian war machine which he had so carefully built up existed only on paper? Should he not have realised when he boasted of the exploits which his soldiers and sailors would perform at any moment at his command, that he was in the position of a man flourishing a cardboard sword?

Besotted by his own propaganda, by a single act of folly Mussolini undid all that he had achieved during two decades. One military disaster quickly followed another: the Italian people had become accustomed to regard war as an easy method of winning glory and of conquering territory either in conflict with weaker peoples, such as the Turks or the Abyssinians, or, as in the First World War, with the support of powerful allies upon whom the burden of the struggle fell. They were appalled at the unexpected prospect of a life and death struggle with determined and ruthless opponents possessing enormous material resources. As hopes of a swift and easy victory vanished away, a frantic desire to remedy Mussolini's mistake by changing sides in the struggle gradually became overwhelming. A small group of senior officers who had always hated him began to plot against him with the enthusiastic support of King Victor Emanuel. At length on the 24th July 1943 even the Fascist Grand Council turned against him. Count Grandi, who had been an ardent supporter for over twenty years, moved a resolution that he be deposed. Nineteen members of the Council out of the twenty-eight present, including General De Bono and Mussolini's son-in-law, Count Ciano, voted in favour of the resolution. On the afternoon of the following day Mussolini kept an appointment with the King who in the meantime had made secret arrangements for his arrest. As he left the Palace he was unceremoniously jostled into a waiting ambulance van and driven off to some near-by barracks to the disgust of Queen Elena who told her husband that he had violated the rules of royal hospitality by having a guest arrested on his doorstep. General Badoglio, the conqueror of Abyssinia, was appointed by the King to be head of the new Italian Government.

Placed under arrest by Badoglio, Mussolini was rescued from his place of confinement in a clinic on the Campo Imperatore, near Aquila in the Abruzzi Mountains, by German paratroops led by S.S. Captain Skorzeny, in what was perhaps the most daring individual exploit of the Second World War. Installed by Hitler as head of the Italian Social Republic with headquarters at Gargnano on Lake Garda, Mussolini watched with growing despair as the Allied armies to quote Sir Winston Churchill "dragged the hot rake of war up the length of the Italian peninsula". While up to the very last Field Marshal Kesselring succeeded in foiling repeated break-through attempts, he was unable for long to hold up the Allied advance. Not only were his men faced with a numerically superior enemy, possessing enormously superior material resources and undisputed command of the air, but they were subjected to continual harassing attacks from the rear by armed bands of Italian civilians, popularly known as Partisans.

As Mussolini was destined to suffer death at the hands of one of these bands of Partisans, a few words concerning them must be said. Originally they consisted of small disconnected groups composed of opponents of the Fascist regime, deserters from both the Italian and German armies, escaped prisoners of war, fugitives from justice and pure bandits—the latter always present in the remoter parts of Italy. Living, as they did, by robbing neighbouring villages, they were a subject for concern to the local police but had little or no political significance. Their status altered after the Allied landing in Italy when General Badoglio began his broadcasts from the safety of Brindisi appealing to the Italian people to murder without mercy every German within reach, however, whenever, and wherever possible.

General Badoglio was certainly one of the most unattractive of the minor characters of the Second World War. A professional soldier who had served not without some credit in the First World War, he had succeeded in ingratiating himself with Mussolini by professions of ardent loyalty to Fascism. As a reward he had been given command by Mussolini in the Abyssinian Campaign, for his services in which he had been made Duke of Addis Ababa. But this gaudy title was to become merely a source of much embarrassment and worry to him when in 1943 he fled from Rome and surrendered to the Allied forces recently landed in Italy. He found that the Allies were quite willing to make use of him but that they declined to give him any pledges as to his ultimate fate. Badoglio knew, of course, that he was on the list of war criminals, in particular, on account of his use of mustard gas in the Abyssinian Campaign. The Abyssinian authorities were demanding his surrender and he well knew what was the first deprivation suffered by a prisoner of war in Abyssinian hands. Badoglio's fears were well founded. After the unconditional surrender of Germany in 1945, scores of honourable soldiers were arrested in Germany at the request of various allies, notorious for their barbaric treatment of prisoners of war, on the hypocritical pretence that they were going to be sent for trial. The fate of these men at the hands of the Czechs, Poles, Serbs, and Greeks was not less certain or less gruesome than would have been the fate of Badoglio had he been handed over for 'trial' by the Abyssinians.

The only way in which Badoglio could hope to escape some dreadful fate was by atoning for his past by making himself outstandingly useful to his captors. Hence the frantic zeal with which he urged a campaign of extermination against the German troops who had entered Italy in the first place at the invitation of the Italian Government and who were now defending Italian soil from invasion, a task from which he and most of Italy's professional defenders had ingloriously and abruptly retired.

At first Badoglio's appeals achieved little beyond inspiring disconnected acts of sabotage behind the German lines, a sentry stabbed here, a train derailed there, a factory or a bridge blown up. But as the German armies in Italy were slowly driven northward and when the course of the struggle in the other theatres of war put the final outcome beyond all doubt, the civilian population began to join with real enthusiasm the winning side. Foremost in the so-called Resistance Movement were Badoglio's bitter political opponents, the Communists, who not only strove to emulate the exploits of Stalin's Communist commandoes on the Eastern

Front, but seized the opportunity to wage a savage vendetta against those of their fellow-countrymen who supported, or had once supported, the Fascist regime. Waiting to be paid off in blood were innumerable private grudges accumulated during twenty years of dictatorship. An orgy of assassination by the Communists and of savage reprisals by the Fascist Militia developed with ever increasing violence behind the German front, while on the other side of the front raged an equally sanguinary but one-sided orgy since as Dr. Luigi Villari points out "the Allied commands, although they would allow the Partisans no political authority, gave them a free hand to rob, murder and rape as they would".*

From the time of his rescue by Skorzeny and his German paratroops in September 1943 until his murder by the shores of Lake Como in April 1945, Mussolini resided for the most part at the Villa Feltrinelli at Gargnano, his official residence as President of the Italian Republic. With him were his wife and family: Claretta and her parents had at first been put in prison by the Badoglio regime but on their release by the Germans, she took up her residence in a villa not far from Gargnano. Mussolini's health during this period was bad and his state of mind was in general gloomy which is hardly surprising since the news from the various theatres of war grew steadily more and more grave. At times however he enjoyed transient spells of optimism, especially after a visit to Hitler who greatly impressed him by his confident references to the "secret weapons" being prepared in Germany which would completely transform the situation. The last pale triumph of Mussolini's life was the 17th December 1944 when he visited Milan and was received with rapturous enthusiasm by the population. It is certainly hard to account for "the storm of wild hysterical cheering", as Monelli calls it, which greeted his arrival. No doubt this demonstration of loyalty and affection was as lacking any rational basis as the frenzy of bestial hatred into which these same people were to lash themselves as they raged around his corpse only four months later!

Utterly without meaning or significance as no doubt this demonstration was, nevertheless it was destined to have important consequences as the first link in the chain of events which led to his murder. The quite unexpected enthusiasm with which he was received confirmed Mussolini in the delusion that he could rely upon the loyalty of at least a substantial fraction of his countrymen. As a consequence, when in the following April the military situation had obviously become desperate, he decided in spite of

* "Italian Foreign Policy Under Mussolini" by Luigi Villari, Devin Adair Company, New York, 1956, Page 363.

the protests of General Wolff, his German adviser, again to visit Milan, with the intention, apparently of rallying his supporters for some last fantastic resistance in the foothills of the Alps.

This decision to visit Milan was a fatal mistake. At Gargnano he would have been safe. Reference to a map will show that Gargnano lay in the path of the German armies retreating from Italy to the Austrian frontier. Among the main German columns there would have been no reason for him to trouble about Partisan bands. But in Milan, away to the West, were only isolated German units with no other courses open to them but to surrender or to retreat into Switzerland.

This time Mussolini found no enthusiastic supporters in Milan, but only a few desperate adherents and a population waiting anxiously for the signal to join the winning side. Utterly downcast, Mussolini remained in Milan for a few days in a state of helpless indecision. On the 21st April the news arrived that the armies of Field Marshal Lord Alexander had at last occupied Bologna and were advancing into the Po Valley. The final collapse was clearly now only a matter of days.

Escape to neutral territory would probably only offer a temporary respite—as Pierre Laval was later to discover—but if he remained in Italy, his fate would depend upon whose prisoner he became. There were three possibilities.

If he fell into the hands of the adherents of the Italian Government which had surrendered to the Allies, he would probably be put on trial for treason against King Victor Emmanuel. This danger was not very serious as the King and his supporters were mere stooges of the Allies, hopelessly divided among themselves and deprived of all political power. It was unlikely in any event that they would be permitted to have any say in his fate.

Secondly, he might fall into the hands of the Partisans who were dominated by the leaders of the Italian Communist Party. The latter enjoyed the patronage of the High Priest of Communism himself, the mighty Stalin who had recently at the Yalta Conference imposed his views upon his awe-struck allies. By the Italian Communists Mussolini would certainly be shot summarily as a leading Anti-Communist in accordance with principles laid down by Stalin for the disposal of opponents of Communism, as long before as the Teheran Conference. With such backing, his liquidation could be carried out with contemptuous disregard of the British and American military authorities in Italy since the latter were under strict orders from their governments on no account to do anything which might cause offence in the Kremlin.

The third course open to Mussolini was to surrender to the

British and American forces as soon as he could make contact with them. There are reasons for thinking that at one time Mussolini had made up his mind—so far as he was at that time capable of making up his mind about anything—to adopt this course. He knew of course that the Allies had labelled him a war criminal and professed the intention of putting him on trial, but probably he did not regard this threat very seriously. The only act which could be alleged against him was that he had joined the losing side, and under international law as it then existed it was not a crime to be on the losing side in a war. The worst that could be charged against him was that he had repeated in June 1940 what the Italian Government had done in May 1915. What had then merited lavish praise and rich rewards could not suddenly have become criminal. On the face of it, such a charge would be too absurd to be persisted in.

With the Allied armies now rapidly approaching Milan, on the 25th April Mussolini arranged an interview with Cardinal Schuster, the Archbishop of Milan, who had been busying himself with secret negotiations with the various Italian political factions, unofficial representatives of the Allies and the German military authorities with a view to reaching an agreement by which the transfer of power from the Italian Social Republic to the new masters of Italy would take place with as little bloodshed and damage to property as possible. The Cardinal received Mussolini as a sinner come to repent his misdoings and "with pastoral charity" offered him a room in the episcopal palace in which he hoped that he would be safe from his political enemies until the arrival of the Allied troops. What Mussolini thought of this optimistic hope we do not know. He told the Cardinal that in default of an agreement with the Committee of Liberation it was his intention to withdraw to the Val Tellina at the head of Lake Como with three thousand still faithful Blackshirts, there to offer a last desperate resistance. When the Cardinal expressed the opinion that he would find for such a venture the number of his loyal followers were nearer three hundred than three thousand Mussolini replied gloomily, "A few more than three hundred perhaps but not many".

At 6.0 p.m. the Committee of Liberation arrived at the episcopal palace headed by General Raffaele Cadorna, ("unworthy son of an eminent father", Dr. Luigi Villari calls him) and a lawyer politician named Marazza. At first the negotiations proceeded smoothly. Cadorna insisted that surrender must be unconditional, but offered a guarantee that the military forces of the Social Republic should be treated as prisoners of war in accordance with the provisions of the Geneva convention. Marshal Graziani, the commander of the Fascist forces, unfortunately then raised the objection that a surrender on these terms would be an act of disloyalty to the German forces then still fighting gallantly in defence of Italy. Someone incautiously disposed of this objection by disclosing that for some days the Germans had been carrying on secret negotiations for an armistice without reference to their Italian allies.

Asked the pointblank question by Mussolini whether he knew of these negotiations, Cardinal Schuster maintained an embarrassed silence. He had in fact been the principal intermediary, and had deliberately refrained from mentioning this vital fact in his conversation with Mussolini.

Realisation of the completeness of the coming collapse apparently came as a terrific shock to Mussolini. Overcome by a wave of petulant resentment against the Cardinal for his suppression of the truth and against the German generals for carrying on negotiations behind the backs of their Italian allies, Mussolini declared that this information altered the whole situation. In spite of the efforts of the Cardinal and General Graziani to calm him, he insisted on returning to his headquarters at the Milan Prefecture. He promised to return to the episcopal palace in an hour with his final decision.

At the Prefecture a hurried conference was held by the Fascist leaders. During those last days Mussolini had fallen much under the influence of Alessandro Pavolini, the last Secretary-General of the Italian Fascist Party, a political fanatic filled with a determination to provide, at least, an inspiration for the future by a last heroic stand against overwhelming odds. His enthusiasm and confidence quickly overcame his leader's waves of irresolution and despair. Mussolini agreed to leave Milan at once without further discussion and to establish in the mountains to the North a last centre of resistance. Hurried preparations for departure were made. While the Cardinal and the Committee still sat in the episcopal palace awaiting his decision, Mussolini and his leading supporters set forth in a fleet of cars from Milan in the gathering darkness and driving rain along the famous autostrado to Como.

The movements of Mussolini during the last three remaining days of his life can be easily followed by a motorist setting out from Milan in the course of an afternoon or by a pedestrian using public service vehicles and lake steamers in the course of a day. The problems which faced Mussolini were partly geographical and they can therefore be best considered during a visit to the locality. The little town of Como at the southern end of Lake Como is less than

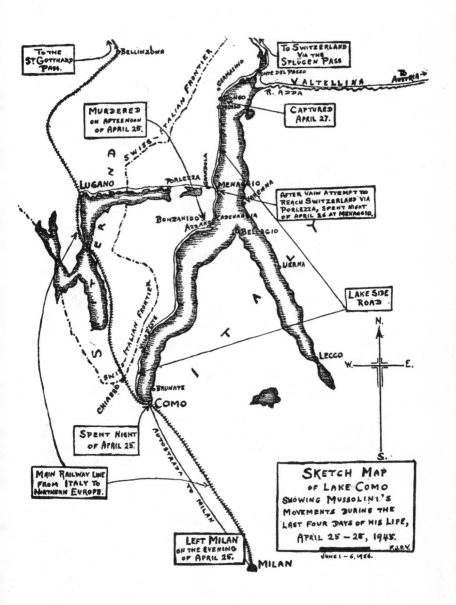

To the
St. Gotthard
Pass.

Bellinzona

To Switzerland
via the
Splügen Pass

Monte del Passo

Valtellina

To Austria →

R. Adda

Murdered
on afternoon
of April 28.

Gravedona

Dongo
Musso

Captured
April 27.

A

Z

Swiss

Lugano

Porlezza

Menaggio

Valenna

After vain attempt to
reach Switzerland via
Porlezza, spent night
of April 26 at Menaggio.

Bonzanigo
Azzano

Cadenabbia

Bellagio

Y

E

Italian Frontier

Varenna

Lake Side
Road.

N

R

Swiss
Italian Frontier
Villa d'Este

I

T

Lecco

W. ———— E.

S

Chiasso

Brunate

Como

Spent Night
of April 25.

Autostrada to Milan

Main Railway Line
from Italy to
Northern Europe.

Sketch Map
of Lake Como
showing Mussolini's
movements during the
last four days of his life,
April 25 - 28, 1945.

F.H.B.V.

June 1 - 6, 1956.

Left Milan
on the evening
of April 25.

Milan

30 miles from Milan to which it is joined by the straight, wide trunk road, the above mentioned autostrada, which Mussolini himself had had constructed. Long after his political mistakes have been forgotten, this trunk road will survive to preserve his memory. The average speed of cars on this road is 60 m.p.h. and consequently, Como itself, less than half an hour's journey away, offered him no place of refuge from his enemies in Milan.

The main road out of Como—a continuation of Mussolini's autostrada from Milan — runs north west to the Swiss frontier at Chiasso, less than four miles from Como. From here the road continues to Lugano and so over the Alps, via the St. Gotthard Pass, to Basle. It is one of the main highways of Europe.

A visit to this short stretch of road from Como to the Swiss frontier at Chiasso will convince anyone how ill-advised Mussolini was to halt at Como at all. Why did he not continue his flight to Switzerland only four miles away? It is true that the presence of Partisan bands is said to have been reported along this road and that the Italian frontier guards were on the point of going over to the winning side. But it surely would not have been impossible for a party of well-armed and desperate men to have fought their way through to safety. Time and labour would have been required to render this stretch of road impassable: no organised opposition by the Partisans was to be expected: the Partisans had never displayed any taste for hard fighting against determined opponents.

No doubt the explanation is that when he arrived at Como on the evening of the 25th April, Mussolini was obsessed by the delusions implanted in his mind by Pavolini. Scorning to find safety along an open road only four miles away, he decided to stop at Como for the night. He stayed at the Prefecture, a 19th century mansion near the Memorial Tower to the inventor, Volta. Further discussions with his followers led to no result. Mussolini wrote a final letter of farewell to his wife whom he had directed to seek refuge in a villa in the neighbourhood and then went to bed for a few hours.

At daybreak Mussolini gave orders that the journey should be continued, not along the main road to Chiasso, which no doubt still lay open, but along the road running northward along the western shores of Lake Como. Pavolini had gone on ahead to contact the column of Blackshirt Militia which he declared was waiting to rally to the Duce's defence. Mussolini hoped to find Pavolini and this column awaiting him at Menaggio, the popular lakeside resort on the western shore of Lake Como. But Marshal Graziani clearly entertained no such delusion. He informed Mussolini that he had decided to remain in Como — a wise decision which undoubtedly saved his life. While his leader continued his journey northward along the lakeside road, the Marshal secluded himself in Como for a couple of days and then gave himself up to the Americans.

At Menaggio there was no sign of Pavolini or of his column of ardent Blackshirts. Mussolini decided to wait at Menaggio for their arrival—another fatal decision since it is possible, although not probable, that if he and his party had pressed on at once they would have reached the Swiss frontier at the Splügen Pass, some 50 miles away, without being molested.

After a few hours waiting there arrived in Menaggio a luxurious car flying the Spanish flag. The occupants carried diplomatic passports purporting to show that they belonged to the Spanish embassy. The occupants were Claretta Petacci and her brother Marcello. Her appearance at this critical juncture filled Mussolini with surprise and exasperation. He had no idea that she had left the villa where she had been living in comparative safety near Gargnano far away to the eastward in order to follow him. At first he refused to see her. "Is she so anxious to die as all that!" he demanded. Claretta refused to go away. At last he agreed to see her. He tried vainly to persuade her to leave at once. Only in his company was she in any personal danger: to achieve perfect safety all she had to do was to avoid attracting attention to herself for a few days until the arrival of the Anglo-American forces. Claretta, however, absolutely declined to leave him, declaring that she was determined to share his fate whatever it might be.

As by mid-day Pavolini and his column of Blackshirts had not arrived at Menaggio, Mussolini decided to attempt to reach Switzerland by the direct secondary road running due west through a gap in the mountain range overlooking the western shores of Lake Como via Grandola to the eastern arm of Lake Lugano and so to the Swiss frontier. A day and a half having been wasted, this decision, which may be attributed to the common sense of Claretta, showed some returning comprehension of the realities of the situation. True, the direct road from Menaggio to Switzerland was a much longer and more difficult road than the short main road from Como via Chiasso to Switzerland. It is a narrow, winding road, passing at several places through tunnels cut in the rock of the mountain sides. But it was clearly unlikely after this delay that the lakeside road by which the party had come from Como would still be unobstructed. Only by this lakeside road could the main road running through Como to Chiasso be reached.

THE MURDER OF BENITO MUSSOLINI

According to one account, Mussolini wasted further time by stopping for lunch at the little hotel at Grandola. In the hotel garden there was further discussion as to what should be done. Finally it was decided that one of the three cars carrying the fugitives should be sent on ahead towards Porlezza to find out if the road to the frontier was clear. Very shortly some members of this advance party returned on foot to say that they had been attacked by Partisans and the car and their leader, Castelli, had been captured.

The plan to reach Switzerland by the Grandola road was immediately abandoned and the refugees returned to Menaggio. They found that Pavolini had at last arrived. Mussolini asked eagerly how many men he had managed to collect—fifteen hundred?—a thousand?

"Twelve", replied Pavolini, "the rats are leaving the sinking ship".

The situation had clearly become desperate. The secondary road westward via Grandola to Switzerland had been found to be blocked. It was certain that the lakeside road running southward to Como by which the party had come early that morning was by this time occupied by Partisans: no doubt Como itself was by this time in the hands of the Partisan units coming from Milan. The only remaining means of escape was to continue the journey northward along the lakeside road from Menaggio via Dongo to the Ponte del Passo at the head of Lake Como. At this point the party would have the choice of proceeding to Switzerland by the steep mountain road to the Splügen Pass or of turning eastward and travelling to Austria by the Val Tellina, the mountain valley in which Pavolini had planned to offer a last desperate stand with his imaginary column of faithful Blackshirts.

How dim was this possibility of escape can only be realised by travelling along this lakeside road running northward from Menaggio. At a dozen places both north and south of Menaggio this road which everywhere winds along the edge of the lake, with water on one side and steep mountain slopes on the other, passes through tunnels cut in the solid rock similar to those of the famous Axenstrasse running along the shore of Lake Lucerne to the St. Gotthard Pass. An easier road to block, it is impossible to conceive. Not only can it be rendered utterly impassable merely by blowing up one of these tunnels but practically anywhere along its length it can easily be blocked by barricades not easy to overcome if resolutely defended.

Shortly after Mussolini's return to Menaggio the news arrived that early the following morning a German motorised transport

72

column would be passing through Menaggio from Como on the way to the Ponte del Passo and thence, via the Val Tellina, to the Austrian frontier. Here indeed was a genuine ray of hope. The Partisans had never shown themselves resolute fighters. No doubt Mussolini recalled how eighteen months before S.S. Captain Skorzeny and a score of paratroopers had without firing a shot rescued him from his confinement on the Campo Imperatore in spite of the fact he was guarded by hundreds of heavily-armed Carabinieri. If he and his party joined this German transport column, they should be able to travel in safety.

Completely out of touch with the course of recent events, Mussolini did not take into account the utter demoralisation which had overtaken so many of the German troops who for so long and so heroically had been defending Italian soil from invasion. The commander of the German motor transport column proved to have only one thought in his mind and that was to return to Germany as soon and with as little difficulty as possible. Probably from painful personal experiences he was indifferent to the fate of any Italian: to him Italy was a land of unreliable allies and treacherous enemies. With an ill grace he said that Mussolini and his surviving Fascist supporters could travel with his transport column if they wanted to do so.

At dawn the following morning, April 27th, the German column of transport lorries and the fleet of cars carrying the Fascist refugees left Menaggio by the lakeside road leading northward. It was headed by an old Italian armoured car, the sole product of Pavolini's efforts to mobilize a last heroic resistance. Then followed some forty German lorries. The Italian cars carrying the Fascist refugees brought up the rear. At first Mussolini travelled in one of these cars but later left it to travel in Pavolini's armoured car. Claretta rode in the car driven by her brother, Marcello.

A number of tunnels cut in the mountain side north of Menaggio were found unobstructed but at a spot only ten miles from the head of the lake the road was blocked by a barricade defended by a force of Partisans in a strong position on the steep, thinly wooded slope alongside the road. Ironically enough this spot was known as Musso, being overlooked by the towering Rocca di Musso, from a stronghold on which the celebrated robber Gian Giacomo Medici in the 16th century had been wont to plunder travellers entering Italy from the Splügen Pass.

Only a few months before, the German soldiers guarding the convoy would have quickly cleared a passage, but now their only desire was to leave Italy for ever and return to their homes. After only a few shots had been fired the German commander left the convoy under a flag of truce and approached the barricade. He was taken to the Partisan leader, Count Bellini delle Stelle, who passed in the resistance movement under the name of 'Pedro'. The Count was only too pleased to accept the suggestion that this column of German lorries should be allowed to return to Germany without fighting. The actual force at his disposal to defend the barricade was small and the result of a fight with disciplined German soldiers would be doubtful. Anyway the war was won so what purpose could bloodshed serve. He made only one stipulation —that the Partisans should be allowed to search the convoy in order to satisfy themselves it contained no Italians. The German commander readily agreed—the fate of a few Italians was of no interest to him.

While this discussion was proceeding — purposely spun out by the Count to give time for as many Partisans as possible living in the locality to rally to his support — Mussolini had slipped unobserved from the armoured car and entered one of the Wehrmacht lorries. When at last the German commander returned from the parley and the signal was given for the convoy to proceed, Pavolini and the other Fascists in the armoured car suddenly realised that the Germans were only concerned with obtaining a free passage for themselves. An attempt was made to turn round the armoured car but it became wedged on the narrow road. The Partisans opened fire from the slope overlooking the road. For a few minutes there was a fierce exchange of fire. Then the Fascists abandoned the armoured car and made a hopeless attempt to escape along the edge of the lake. All were quickly captured, including Pavolini, badly wounded by a shot-gun.

The convoy then proceeded without further incident for about half-a-mile to the small town of Dongo. Here a halt was made in the little square opposite the Prefecture so that a search for Fascist refugees could be made. All the Italians in the convoy were made prisoner, including the bogus Spanish diplomat, Marcello Petacci, and his sister Claretta. Crouched in the driver's cabin of one of the Wehrmacht lorries was a man wearing a German military overcoat and a helmet. According to Audisio's story, Mussolini was recognised and denounced by an ex-sailor named Negri. This, however, is contradicted by the story of a certain Partisan passing under the name of 'Renzo', who later published a detailed account of what took place. According to 'Renzo', he and the political commissar, Lazzaro Urbano, alias 'Bill', searched the German lorries and he himself was the first to recognise Mussolini. The point is, however, unimportant. Mussolini was recognised by someone: he offered no resistance and was taken a prisoner to the Dongo Prefecture.

Mussolini remained in Dongo until the evening when he was taken to the frontier guards' barracks at Germisano. After some hours, however, he was put in a car in the charge of a Captain Neri, one of the Partisan leaders, and driven southward with the intention of taking him to Brunate on the other side of Lake Como, presumably considered a safer place for his detention. To reach Brunate it was necessary to pass through Como. On the way they met a car in which was Claretta who had revealed her identity and had asked to be allowed to join him. The two cars proceeded together in pouring rain towards Como until it was learned that the Americans were approaching the town. It was then decided to turn back to prevent Mussolini falling into American hands.

Ultimately, Neri decided to leave his prisoner in a peasant's cottage near Bonzanigo, a tiny village on the hillside behind the lakeside village of Azzano, a few miles south of Menaggio. Here Mussolini and Claretta spent the remainder of the night guarded by two young Partisans named Sandrino and Lino. It has been suggested that with a little enterprise they could have escaped— the Swiss frontier was only 15 miles away. Perhaps this was what Captain Neri intended when he left his prisoners so insecurely guarded. But Mussolini made no attempt to escape and slept peacefully until 11.0 a.m. the following morning.

After Mussolini had left Milan on the evening of the 25th April, the situation had developed with headlong speed. The administration of the Italian Social Republic ceased to exist that day and the German garrison in Milan withdrew to its barracks. The long delayed signal was given by the Allies to the anti-Fascist factions in North Italy to revolt when, as Dr. Luigi Villari remarks sarcastically, "there was no longer anyone or anything to revolt against". Despite the fact that military resistance had virtually ceased, the Allied troops suspended their occupation of Milan and the other cities lying open to them for several days. The reason for this pause in the advance has never been explained. Dr. Luigi Villari attributes it to the Allied deference to the wishes of Stalin who insisted the Partisans should be given an opportunity to liquidate as many Italians as possible who might stand in the way of the establishment of a Communist dictatorship in Italy. The result of this pause—for which certainly no military motive can be ascribed—was an orgy of murder throughout Northern Italy. For several days the Partisans had a free hand to hunt down and liquidate their opponents.

The news that Mussolini had been taken prisoner was communicated by the Dongo Partisans to their headquarters at Milan

immediately after his capture on the morning of April 27th. It is not clear to whom the anti-Fascist headquarters passed on the news, whether Allied military headquarters were informed, and, if so, what steps were taken by the Allied authorities to ensure the prisoner's safety. Dr. Luigi Villari writes, "There is every reason to believe that the Allies were none too eager to save Mussolini's life, for if he had survived and been put on trial, he might have made revelations extremely awkward for the leading statesmen of the enemy Powers".*

With his intimate knowledge of European 'Power Politics' since 1922, Mussolini would truly have been a most embarrassing figure in the witness box. Presumably the main charge against him would have been that he had initiated and waged an aggressive war against France in 1940. But on such a charge even a War Crimes Tribunal could hardly have ruled out as inadmissible his account of his secret negotiations with President Roosevelt between 1936 and 1940 to attack his ally Hitler.

It is significant that when first made prisoner, Mussolini should have been particularly concerned about the safety of a leather brief-case which he was carrying. He told his captors it contained "secret documents of great historical importance". No doubt these documents were a selection of highly confidential communications which he had received during the troubled years prior to June 1940 which he planned to produce in evidence in the event of his being put on trial as a war-criminal. It is hardly necessary to add that nothing further has been seen or heard of this brief-case after it was taken from him by the Partisans.

The news of Mussolini's capture certainly reached a certain Partisan leader, a Communist bookkeeper named Walter Audisio who in the underground movement was known as 'Colonel' Valerio. This man subsequently claimed that he had an order from the C.L.N.A.I. (the Comitati di Liberazione Nationale Alta Italia— Committee of National Liberation) to take possession of Mussolini and put him to death. But the committee of National Liberation derived such authority as it can be said to have had from the King who had bound himself by the terms of the armistice to hand over Mussolini alive to the Allies. In any event, the Committee of National Liberation had given no such order. Later Audisio was to explain that the order he received came to him from the C.V.L. (Liberation Command of Volunteers). But once again it is clear Audisio lied. This body—a sort of unofficial general staff of the Partisans — had no authority to give any such order and in fact

* See "Italian Foreign Policy under Mussolini" by Dr. Luigi Villari, (Devin-Adair, New York, 1956). Page 367.

never gave one.

The question what authority (if any) this man Audisio had to proceed to where Mussolini was being kept in custody and to put him to death will probably never be cleared up. Two facts, however, appear absolutely clear. One is that no court of law or any body having judicial authority ever passed any sentence of death on Mussolini. The other is that Audisio never received any *written* order from anyone to put Mussolini to death. Audisio was a fanatical Communist who is said to have served in the International Brigade during the Spanish Civil War. It is possible he acted mainly on his own initiative. More probably he acted on the verbal promptings of various leading Italian Communists who assured him that if he acted as a good Communist should he could look to them for support. If this be so, Audisio has not looked for support in vain. The Communist Party approved and still approves his conduct. In 1947 Palmiro Togliatti, the head of the Italian Communist Party, published a statement in the Communist paper, "Unita" that he, Togliatti, had issued an order "as head of the Communist Party and as Vice-Premier of Italy" that Mussolini and all his ministers were to be shot on capture. This order, he declared, was issued by him two days before Mussolini's capture. He does not, however, mention to whom he issued this order. Bonomi, the Italian Premier at the time of Mussolini's death, retorted that this was the first that he had heard of any such order and various non-Communist members of the Committee of National Liberation declared that no such order had ever been disclosed to the Committee. Possibly this alleged order, if not an invention of Togliatti, was communicated by him privately to the various leading Italian Communists.

It should at this point be stressed that the Committee of National Liberation was composed of two distinct groups, Communists and non-Communists, bound together only by a common opposition to Fascism. Their respective aims were quite irreconcilable. The non-Communist group was split into several sections with conflicting aims: some desired to restore the Kingdom of Italy, some to establish a liberal republic and some to create some form of socialist state. The Communist group, on the other hand, was pledged to work heart and soul towards the establishment of an Italian Soviet Republic. It was their intention, if political events outside Italy took a favourable course, to liquidate their non-Communist colleagues just as the Jugo-Slav Communists, led by Broz Josip Tito, had then recently liquidated with murderous efficiency their non-Communist colleagues led by General Mihailovitch.

THE MURDER OF BENITO MUSSOLINI

Togliatti and his Communist supporters never troubled to disguise the fact that their alliance with the other anti-Fascist parties was a mere temporary expedient which would end when Fascism in Italy was overthrown. For the furtherance of Communist aims, they never hesitated to act independently of their non-Communist colleagues. This being their attitude generally, it was perfectly natural that they should deal with such a problem as the disposal of Mussolini without troubling to consult the views of Premier Bonomi or any other non-Communist. The proved facts confirm that they did what they might be expected to do. When the news of Mussolini's capture at Dongo reached the Committee of National Liberation in Milan certain Communist members of the Committee decided privately to send Walter Audisio, alias 'Colonel' Valerio, a ruthless and fanatical Communist fighter, with verbal instructions to liquidate the captured Fascist dictator. With him was sent a Communist member of the Committee named Lampredi, whose alias was 'Guido'.

Lacking any written documents from anyone in authority authorising them to take charge of the matter, Audisio and Lampredi found their task a difficult one. They were coldly received by the local Partisan leaders when they arrived at Como early on the morning of April 28th. As a result of various hitches, and possibly wilful obstruction, they did not reach Dongo until about 2.30 p.m. that afternoon. The Partisan leaders at Dongo were openly suspicious and hostile. Count Bellini delle Stelle at first refused to see Audisio, saying that he was too busy. But in the end an interview took place. Audisio tells us that he spoke "very frankly" with the Count. It is not known what was said. Presumably a "frank talk" was a substitute for written credentials. Audisio's bluff succeeded. The Count's hesitation was at last overcome. Audisio was informed that in the early hours of that morning Mussolini and Claretta Petacci had been taken by Captain Neri to a peasant's cottage on the hillside overlooking Azzano. Perhaps the comforting thought occurred to the Count that the prisoners had taken advantage of the very inadequate arrangements made by Captain Neri to prevent their escape?

Audisio wasted no further time. He set forth at once by car from Dongo back along the lakeside road to Azzano, taking with him Lampredi, alias 'Guido' and the political Commissar of the district, Lazzaro Urbano, alias 'Bill'.

It is difficult, perhaps an impossible task, to put together a complete and unhesitating account of the ensuing course of events. The full truth was known to half a dozen persons: at least a score knew the salient facts. Yet as the last biographer of Mussolini,

THE MURDER OF BENITO MUSSOLINI

Roman Dombrowski, observes, "There are so many mysteries, contradictions and ambiguities connected with Mussolini's death, that we are driven at last to query whether there is such a thing as objective, historical truth".*

Many of the persons who took (or claimed to have taken) leading or secondary parts in the story have described what they did, what they saw or what they learned at the time. Not one of them can be said to have been in the least interested in objective truth. Most of the accounts given are clearly intended either to glorify the Communist Party or to represent the deed as the lawful execution of a Fascist criminal. Two persons at least claim the honour of having fired the fatal shots and nearly everyone connected, however remotely, with the matter is mainly concerned to distort the facts in order to exaggerate the importance of the particular part which he personally played or claimed to have played. All the persons concerned were hitherto obscure individuals and all of them passed under one alias or several. Sometimes they are referred to in the accounts by their real names and sometimes by one alias or another. Inevitably confusion and obscurity has arisen.

Some of those who played leading roles have maintained a rigid silence concerning what they knew. Thus the political Commissar, Lampredi, alias 'Guido', who unquestionably was one of those present when Mussolini was done to death, has neither confirmed nor corrected any of the conflicting accounts which his accomplice, Audisio, has published concerning the deed. Some who have published accounts have disappeared completely so that even their identity has now become uncertain. The most noteworthy example of this phenomenon is supplied by the case of the man who under the pseudonym of 'Renzo' contributed to a Rome newspaper a voluminous account of the events at Dongo at the time of and following the capture of Mussolini. 'Renzo' displays such intimate knowledge of details that some have accepted him as an eye-witness and have identified him with a certain Sauro Gnesi, known to have been at the time a member of Count Bellini delle Stelle's Partisan unit. His account, however, conflicts with so many important points which appear well established, that some have doubted whether he took any personal part at all in the events which he describes and have suggested that he only compiled his account from what he was told by persons who were present. The Partisan, Sauro Gnesi, with whom 'Renzo' has been identified, has vanished without trace. Even more remarkable is the case of

---

* "Mussolini: Twilight and Fall" by Roman Dombrowski, (Heinemann, London, 1956). Page 236.

the man, Michele Moretti, alias Pietro Gatti. He not only claimed to have been present at the killing of Mussolini, but claimed that he himself fired the fatal bullets. Paulo Monelli in his *"Mussolini: An Intimate Life"*,* accepts both claims and writes, "It seems that Mussolini was really killed by Moretti, although the Communist Party built up Audisio as the official hero, and in fact Audisio was elected to Parliament on no other merit." Roman Dombrowski, on the other hand, does not even mention Moretti having been present at the crime. He only mentions Moretti as the Partisan who was sent to Como in a lorry with a quantity of gold bullion found in the Fascist convoy at Dongo and who mysteriously disappeared during the journey together with the bullion.

All these mysteries, contradictions and obscurities are of no real importance. The outstanding fact established beyond any question is that Mussolini was murdered by a group of Communist Partisans. The identity of the various obscure individuals who took part and the exact role each one respectively played is no more important than the names of the professional killers of the N.K.V.D. who carried out the orders of Stalin and Beria to liquidate the Polish prisoners in the Katyn Forest. That crime would be in no way illuminated were it discovered that the names of those who carried it out were 'Ivan' this or 'Nikolas' that. Only two of those who took part in the events leading to Mussolini's death are in any way noteworthy. One is the fanatical Communist agitator, Walter Audisio, alias 'Colonel' Valerio, a man who, if the course of political events outside Italy had taken a different turn, clearly possessed all the qualities which would have fitted him to play, as chief of the political police of the Italian Soviet Republic, the role played in Russia by Dzarzhinsky, Yagoda and Beria. The other is Count Bellini delle Stelle, a young aristocrat whose mind had become so befuddled with Leftist political theories that he joined with enthusiasm a movement which, if successful, would have led to the speedy liquidation of himself and the entire class to which he belonged.

Having explained the difficulties in the way of ascertaining the truth, we may now return to the early afternoon of the fatal day, April 28th, 1945. Since the early hours of that morning Mussolini and Claretta Petacci had been in the charge of the two peasant lads, Sandrino and Lino, in the cottage on the hillside behind Azzano. Audisio, alias 'Colonel' Valerio, Lampredi and the political Commissar, Urbano, alias 'Bill', were speeding south-

* "Mussolini: An Intimate Life" by Paulo Monelli (Thames & Hudson, London, 1953), Page 291.

(Milton Bracker, in The New York Times Magazine)

Walter Audisio, the Communist who directed the murder of Mussolini and his mistress, Claretta Petacci, at the Villa Belmonte, on Lake Como, April 28, 1945. Audisio later in the day had all members of Mussolini's party shot at Dongo, partly to conceal the Communist theft of the public treasure which was being removed to a place of safety. **Audisio was later elected as a Communist member of the Italian Parliament.**

Claretta Petacci, faithful mistress of Mussolini, who was murdered with him by Communist partisans under the direction of Walter Audisio at Villa Belmonte on Lake Como, April 28, 1945. She was killed to help conceal the Communist theft of the "Dongo Treasure." Picture shows her on the eve of the fatal flight from Milan.

ward in a car from Dongo, without any written mandate or authority but filled with murderous intent to carry out the liquidation without a moment's further delay. An American mechanised unit had reached Como: at any time some non-Communist might disclose the whereabouts of the prisoners to the Americans only a half-hour's drive along the lakeside road.

The first account of the liquidation given by Audisio to the Communist daily newspaper 'L'Unita', and reproduced in the "Daily Express" of April 30th, although in many details mendacious, has a certain historical importance since it was accepted throughout the world for many years as the truth. It can still be regarded as the orthodox version. Professional historians with Leftist leanings who insist on regarding the matter as "an execution" rely on this story of Audisio for the faith that is in them.

According to this, the first version of his story, the gallant 'Colonel' walked fearlessly into Mussolini's room, "holding my submachine gun at the ready". In reply to Mussolini's question the 'Colonel' replied, "I have come to liberate you. Hurry! We haven't much time". He gave this answer he explains, because he had already picked on a spot suitable for the commission of his intended crime which was a quarter of a mile or so away—"to get him there I had to resort to stratagem".

Mussolini readily agreed to go with his liberator, and in fact became impatient when Claretta wasted time collecting her belongings. He left the cottage with Audisio but Claretta caught them up before they had gone far down the track which led from the cottage to the road where Audisio had left his car. In her haste she left behind her handbag. During the walk to the road, Audisio says that Mussolini "gave me a grateful look". For no other purpose apparently than to add an artistic embellishment to his treachery, Audisio whispered, "I have also liberated your son, Vittorio". Mussonlini replied, "I thank you from the bottom of my heart".

The two prisoners were put in the back seat of the saloon car with the political commissar 'Bill'. The Liberation Committeeman Lampredi, alias 'Guido', seated himself beside the driver whose identity has not been disclosed. The 'Colonel' perched himself on the running board. The two youths, Sandrino and Lino, who had guarded the prisoners during the night, followed at a trot on foot. The car proceeded slowly since the road leading downhill to the main lakeside road running south to Como and north to Dongo was rough and unmade. At the point where this unmade road joins the lakeside road another road joins it from the right. This road leads back up the hillside to the little church of Saint

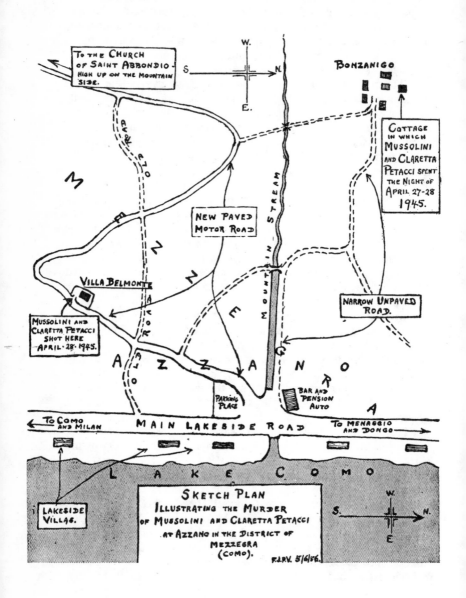

To the CHURCH
of SAINT ABBONDIO.
HIGH UP ON THE MOUNTAIN
SIDE.

W.

S. N.

E.

BONZANIGO

COTTAGE
IN WHICH
MUSSOLINI
AND CLARETTA
PETACCI SPENT
THE NIGHT OF
APRIL 27-28
1945.

OLD ROAD

MOUNTAIN STREAM

NEW PAVED
MOTOR ROAD

M

A
R
I
A

Z

Z

E

VILLA BELMONTE

NARROW UNPAVED
ROAD.

MUSSOLINI AND
CLARETTA PETACCI
SHOT HERE
APRIL 28 1945.

MAIN
ROAD

A

Z

Z

A

N

O

A

PARKING
PLACE

BAR AND
PENSION
AUTO

To COMO
AND MILAN   MAIN LAKESIDE ROAD   To MENAGGIO
AND DONGO

LAKE COMO

LAKESIDE
VILLAS.

SKETCH PLAN
ILLUSTRATING THE MURDER
OF MUSSOLINI AND CLARETTA PETACCI
AT AZZANO IN THE DISTRICT OF
MEZZEGRA
(COMO).

W.

S. N.

E.

F.I.P.V. 5/6/56.

82

Abbondio splendidly situated with a commanding view over Lake
Como to Bellagio on its promontory with the snow-capped mountains on the eastern shore beyond. For the sake probably of motorists
desiring to enjoy the view from the terrace in front of the church
this road has been made up. Fronting this steeply rising road are
a number of private villas facing the lake. One of these, the Villa
Belmonte, had been selected as a suitable spot for the crime. The
Villa itself, an unpretentious, two-storied building, lies well back
from the road in a small garden surrounded by a wall of rough stone
about four feet high with a thick hedge rising above it. The entrance
leading to the house is provided with a gate of galvanised iron between
tall stone pillars.

Just before reaching the entrance of the Villa Belmonte,
Audisio ordered the car to halt. He got out remarking, "I heard
a noise. I am going to investigate". After a pretended investigation
he returned and told the two prisoners to alight. For the first time,
Audisio tells us, doubts as to his intentions seemed to have entered
Mussolini's mind. But he and Claretta alighted and walked towards
the entrance of the Villa Belmonte as directed by their captors.
The gate being closed, they turned and paused for it to be opened.
Mussolini stood just to the left of the left-hand gate post with
Claretta on his right. The exact spot where they stood is now
indicated by two black crosses painted on the wall with the words
"REQUIEM AETERNAM" written in rough Latin capitals to
the left.

Audisio says that he then recited the following incantation.
"By order of the General Committee of the Liberation Volunteer
Corps I am entrusted with rendering justice to the Italian people".

The last paragraph of Audisio's statement reads, "Mussolini
was terror-stricken. Claretta threw her arms around his shoulders
and screamed 'Non deve morire' (He must not die). I said, "Get
back in your place if you don't want to die *first*". (In later versions
Audisio amended this to: "If you don't want to die *also*".) The
woman jumped back in her place. From three paces I shot five
bursts into Mussolini. He slumped to his knees with his head
slightly bent. Then it was Claretta Petacci's turn".

It is noteworthy that in his first account of what occurred,
Audisio makes no reference to any other person having been
present. The liquidation is described as having been carried out
by himself, alone, fearlessly, expeditiously and efficiently. Also he
makes it clear that he was as much resolved to murder Claretta
as he was resolved to murder Mussolini. In later versions he makes
a half-hearted attempt to suggest that Claretta was only killed
because she got in the way of the bullets. He also in later versions

embellishes his story by describing at length how first his sub-machine gun and then his revolver failed to work and how finally he carried out the liquidation with a sub-machine gun which he borrowed from the political commissar 'Guido'.

These details, whether fictional or not, are of little interest or importance. In the opinion of the present writer what probably occurred was very much simpler and less formal. It is not difficult to picture what most likely occurred. When the car drew up outside the entrance of the Villa Belmonte, the two unarmed passengers were ordered to alight by the other four passengers, all heavily armed. They obeyed and began to walk towards the entrance, covered by the weapons of their captors. Then at a signal — probably given by Audisio — fire is opened on them before they have taken half a dozen paces. There was never any question of sparing Claretta — it was just as important for reasons which will be considered later to silence her as it was to silence Mussolini. The gang continued firing until both victims were dead.

It is an ironical fact that Benito Mussolini who had during his life expended so much effort and so much eloquence on con-vincing his countrymen that they were descendants of the ancient Romans whose valour and virtues they had inherited, should at his death so conclusively have demonstrated that the real spiritual home of so many of his countrymen was not the Rome of the Caesars but the contemporary Chicago underworld of Al Capone.

Loyalty to the death has never been a common virtue at any time or in any place. Loyalty of any kind was an exceedingly rare virtue in Italy during the last stages of the Second World War. Paolo Monelli's book, quoted above, has indeed done nothing to help us to an understanding of Benito Mussolini. On the other hand, it has done something to rehabilitate the memory of Claretta Petacci. Had she given a thought to her own safety she would have remained quietly in her villa in eastern Lombardy where it is most unlikely anyone would have attempted to molest her, since, as Monelli stresses, no one had any personal grudge against her. Instead, she insisted on being with her lover at the time of the final catastrophe for no other reason than to give him her support when everyone else had deserted him. To Monelli's credit it should be added that he records—if only grudgingly in a footnote—"The only thing which is clear from all the various versions of the killing is that Claretta sought no mercy for herself".

But from the moment Claretta joined Mussolini at Menaggio her doom was sealed. From one point of view the murder outside the Villa Belmonte was essentially a political crime: it was a

Communist liquidation similar in intention to the Katyn Forest massacre. But quite another factor, human greed, entered also into the crime at the entrance of the Villa Belmonte. When the Partisans searched the cars of Mussolini and his supporters at Dongo they found that he was taking with him a quantity of gold being the funds of the various ministries of the Italian Social Republic, balances of taxes collected, customs receipts etc., and money and valuables belonging to him and to his companions. To this day the value of this treaesure—known as the Dongo Treasure from the fact that it was last seen in the possession of the Partisans at Dongo—remains unknown, but undoubtedly it was very substantial. A recent estimate places its total value at "a dozen milliards of lire at 1945 value". According to 'Renzo's' story, in the car driven by Marcello Petacci was found 35 kilogrammes of bar gold: in another car 18,000,000 Swiss francs. At the trial at Padua in the summer of 1957 of Dante Gorrieri and thirty five other deefendants on charges of murder, robbery and receiving stolen property following the capture of Mussolini twelve years before, evidence was given by the chief cashier of the Finance Ministry that in February 1945 he had been ordered by Pellegrini, the Finance Minister, to take to Mussolini's office currency consisting of 2,150 sovereigns, £2,675 in notes, 278,000 Swiss francs, 149,000 dollars and 18,000,000 French francs. Packed in five or six suit-cases, this currency was placed by Pellegrini in the safe in Mussolini's office. Presumably it was taken by Mussolini with him on his flight and formed a substantial part of the treasure captured by the Partisans two months later at Dongo.

It cannot be doubted that the discovery of treasure was reported to the Communist headquarters at the same time as the news of Mussolini's capture. From a practical point of view it was of far greater importance. With regard to Mussolini, Stalin could be trusted to see that he was liquidated — whether summarily or after a formal trial à la Nürnberg was of no practical importance from the Communist standpoint. But it was of the first importance that this treasure should not be allowed to fall into the hands of either the Allies or of the Italian Government. If it went into the coffers of the Communist Party, there would be no need for some time to trouble the paternal heart of Comrade Stalin for Russian subsidies.

The fate of Mussolini was in fact decided by two decisions of his own. The first was his decision to move from Gargnano, where he was safe among the retreating Germans, to Milan: the second was his decision to take with him all the available cash of the Social Republic to provide a fund for the new centre of resistance which he planned to establish among the Italian Alps. The latter decision sealed his fate since it made it imperative to avoid a trial which would inevitably have included an investigation concerning the disappearance of the treasure. At all costs his voice had to be silenced.

When he first heard of the crime, Sir Winston Churchill expressed surprise that Claretta also should have been murdered. "Was she on the list of war criminals?" he enquired indignantly of Field Marshal Lord Alexander. But, of course, Sir Winston did not then know of the existence of the treeasure, the existence of which made it just as necessary to liquidate Claretta as Mussolinni. In addition, all those who knew of its existence and who could not be absolutely trusted had to be silenced. Mussolini and Claretta Petacci were dealt with first of all. In the months which followed a dozen others were to suffer the same fate and for the same reason.

Having duly liquidated Mussolini and Claretta, the murderers left the two bodies lying in the road at the entrance of the Villa Belmonte, guarded by the two youths, Sandrino and Lino, and hurried back to Dongo to complete their self-appointed task by liquidating the fifteen Fascist leaders who had been captured with Mussolini. Among these fifteen prisoners were Alessandro Pavolini, the last Secretary-General of the Fascist Party: Francesco Barracu; Air Captain Casalinuovo, Mussolini's A.D.C.; Professor Coppola, President of the University of Bologna; Luigi Gatti, Mussolini's secretary; and Claretta's brother, Marcello Petacci. All were summarily liquidated by shooting in the little square in front of the Dongo Prefecture. The victims were lined up facing the lake with their backs to the firing squad. The first misdirected volley left many of them only wounded. Thereupon all the Partisans gathered together in the square to enjoy the spectacle, opened fire in a frenzy of excitement. Wild shooting continued for several minutes during which one of the firing squad was wounded. Audisio tells us that he had no idea how he escaped with his life. No doubt judged by the standard of Stalin's experienced killers at Katyn, the Dongo liquidation was conducted in a very haphazard manner but the desired result was duly achieved.

The liquidation of the whole party captured at Dongo left much necessary work still to be done. From the very start, the previously mentioned Captain Neri of the 52nd Partisan Brigade had made himself difficult. When the prisoners had been brought to the Town Hall at Dongo the Partisans had begun by robbing them of their money, watches and rings. Neri protested vigorously and demanded that nothing in the vehicles should be touched until an inventory had been made of their contentts. Later he insisted on accompanying the vehicles carrying the captured property to the Partisan headquarters at Como and there personally handing everything over to Dante Gorrieri, the secretary of the Communist federation, in exchange for signed receipts. Shortly afterwards Captain Neri, with of course his receipts, disappeared without trace. His body has never been found.

The summary liquidation of Captain Neri, however, did not dispose of the difficulties resulting from his unaccommodating attitude in regard to the treasure. His fiancée, a female Partisan known in the resistance movement as Gianna, had accompanied him on the journey from Dongo to Como and had been present when the captured property had been handed over by him to Dante Gorrieri. In spite of stern warnings to forget the whole subject she started to make enquiries concerning her lover's disappearance and more serious still, concerning what was being done with the treasure. Afraid to visit Como herself, she sent her brother, Caesare Tuissi, to interview Gorrieri who told him in brief to mind his own business as all property captured from Fascists belonged to the Communist Party. Tuissi gave evidence twelve years later of this interview with Gorrieri to the court at Padua and his evidence was corroborated by a female witness who was present at the interview. In June 1945 Gianna disappeared without trace. Shortly afterwards Anna Maria Bianchi, an intimate friend of Gianna, was forcibly abducted by two unidentified Partisans in a motor cycle combination. She was never seen alive again and in July her dead body was found in the lake. From marks on the body it appeared that the unfortunate girl had been tortured before death.

Most significant of all perhaps was the disappearance a little later of her father, Michale Bianchi, who when informed that his daughter's body had been found, told the police that he knew who was responsible for the crime and would avenge her. He left home next day saying that he was going to Como to see Dante Gorrieri. His body has never been discovered.

Not only persons connected directly or indirectly with Captain Neri but many other Dongo Partisans who had taken part in the capture of Mussolini disappeared mysteriously immediately after his murder, among them the above mentioned Michele Moretti*

---

* All accounts agree there was a fourth, unidentified man present at the crime, namely the driver of the car. Is it possible Moretti was the driver? The truth will never be known since Moretti is now either living in luxury in foreign parts on his share of the Dongo loot or is lying at the bottom of Lake Como with a Communist bullet in the back of his head.

(alias Pietro Gatti) who boasted afterwards that he was present at the crime and is believed by some to have fired the fatal shots, and the youth Sandrino who was also present at the crime in the role of a look-out. The other look-out, the youth Lino, was killed a few days after the crime, it was said, in a fight with a comrade. He may have been killed in a private quarrel, but it is more probable that he was 'bumped off' as they would have called it in contemporary Chicago.

The above mentioned disappearances and the disappearance of many others which followed the murder of Mussolini, are open to explanation in one of two ways. It is probable that most of those Partisans who mysteriously disappeared were murdered in order to ensure their silence in regard to the disposal of the Dongo treasure, the bulk of which no doubt disappeared into the coffers of the Italian Communnist Party. This view of the matter is widely held in Italy where the Party headquarters in Rome are still popularly known as the 'Palazzo Dongo'. At the same time it is possible that much of the treasure was stolen by individual Partisans, each one of whom came independently to the prudent resolve to disappear in order to avoid the curiosity of the police. There is no doubt that some of the private captured property and valuables was stolen by individuals. Commissar Moretti is credited with having disappeared with a substantial share of the treasure itself. The Petacci family has instituted proceedings against the Communist leader Luigi Longo for being in possession of a gold cigarette case belonging to Claretta, but little progress to date has been made in the action owing to the immunity enjoyed by the defendant as a Deputy which can only be raised with the authority of the Chamber. For the same reason Audisio has to date escaped prosecution for his crimes. Less fortunate has been the fate of the leading Communist Partisan Dante Gorrieri who in April 1957 with thirty five other persons was at last brought to trial at the assize court at Padua on a wide assortment of charges ranging from murder and robbery to receiving stolen property.

This belated trial at Padua took place as a result of the slowly dawning realization by the Italian public that so long as they remained screened from investigation by political intrigue, the facts relating to the murder of Mussolini and the robbery of the Dongo treasure would be a reproach to Italian justice and to democratic government. For twelve years a sinister shadow overhung Italian political life. With the intention of goading the Communist leaders into taking the matter to court by bringing actions for libel, the anti-Communist press never ceased to publish charges of their guilt and kept the subject continually in the public mind by the publication of new and sensational details of their crimes. Thus, for example, in its noteworthy issue of April 1955 in a challenging article entitled "Dongo ut Des",* the "*Pace e Libertà*" announced that at last it had obtained sworn evidence that Captain Neri and the female Partisan, Anna Maria Bianchi, had been murdered in the summer of 1945 by a Communnist gunman named Bernasconi, whose alias was 'Mirko', at the instigation of Dante Gorrieri who at the time of the crimes had been secretary to the Communist federation at Como and who had since been elected a Deputy to the Chamber. "The thieves and murderers should at last pay the penalty and not sit happily in Parliament sheltered by their immunity as deputies", declared the "*Pace e Libertà*" indignantly. But Gorrieri and the other Communist leaders were not to be lured to their own destruction by such charges. Unlike Oscar Wilde in Victorian times and Alger Hiss in our own day, they steadfastly declined to be goaded into bringing proceedings for libel which might only result in providing evidence for a criminal prosecution. To the exasperation of their opponents they maintainted in face of these charges the Marxian equivalent for an attitude of Christian resignation. But under ever growing pressure from public opinion, the authorities at last felt compelled to initiate a prosecution: the Supreme Court declared that the Partisans were not members of the armed forces and were not therefore entitled to be tried by military courts: the Chamber gave the necessary permission for Dante Gorrieri to be put on trial. And so after an elapse of twelve years Gorrieri and thirty five other members of the Italian Resistance Movement, nearly all of them members of the Communist Party, found themselves in the dock at the assize court at Padua on the 29th April 1957.

It cannot unfortunately be said that any noteworthy facts were brought to light at this belated trial concerning the murder of Mussolini and Claretta Petacci. Most certainly the very careful sifting by the Court of the voluminous evidence placed before it led to the discovery of no clue at all likely to lead to the recovery of the smallest fraction of the missing treasure. But the proceedings at least served to dispel any lingering illusions concerning the character of Mussolini's opponents and the nature and methods

---

* "Dongo ut Des" is a play on the words "Do ut Des". It summarises the attitude of the Anti-Communist parties to their opponents as in effect saying "Unless thou doest (Ut des) what we want, very well, then, "Dongo!" — We shall bring up that painful subject!" Whenever a political crisis arose the anti-Communist parties always brought the Communists to heel by threatening to investigate the disappearance of the Dongo treasure.

of the resistance movement in Italy during the last years of the Second World War. Throughout Italy a reign of terror raged after the collapse of Mussolini's regime but nowhere with greater violence than in the Como area. "A man's life was not worth 5 lire in those days," declared Signor Camori, the chairman of the special commission appointed by the Italian Government to trace the missing treasure immediately after its disappearance. The commission entirely failed in its mission, Signor Camori told the Padua assize court, "because all those we questioned were too much afraid to answer."

The leading Communist politician Luigi Longo, who in 1945 had been deputy leader of the Committee of National Liberation, was called as a witness for the defence. Longo declared that the funds supplied by the Allies to support the partisan movement were totally inadequate and in consequence the Partisans had been forced to be practically self-supporting. The resistance fighters had been authorised—presumably by themselves—to requisition booty captured from the Fascists for current expenses. The orders were that such booty should be handed over to the local partisan head-quarters. Asked by the president of the court whether receipts for such booty were given and accounts kept, Longo replied that it was the invariable rule in a resistance movement never to keep any records in writing as these would provide incriminating evidence in the case of arrest.

A most illuminating answer was given by one of the defendants, a certain Partisan named Vergani, alias 'Fabio', to the president's question how he accounted for the disappearance of Captain Neri. Vergani replied simply that no doubt Captain Neri had been sentenced to death *in absentia* as a traitor by some secret partisan tribunal. He could not of course name the tribunal which had sentenced Captain Neri since the identity of these tribunals was always kept as a closely guarded secret. Its sentence would be verbal and would be carried out by someone acting on verbal instructions. It would be futile to enquire into the matter since of course no written records would exist. The same simple and adequate explanation would account for the death of Gianna, Neri's fiancée.

In view of the evidence given at the assize court at Padua, can there be any reason to repeat the question of Sir Winston Churchill why Claretta Petacci was murdered? The answer so obviously is that she was murdered because she knew the full facts relating to the treasure. Would it have been reasonable to spare Claretta's life if it was really necessary to murder the harmless old peasant Michale Bianchi merely because he had resented the

murder of his daughter Anna Maria Bianchi who had been murdered merely because she was an intimate friend of Captain Neri's
fiancée, Gianna, from whom it was feared she might have obtained
information concerning the fate of the missing treasure?

It only remains to record the final episode of the murder of
Benito Mussolini. For some hours his body and that of Claretta
lay in the road at the entrance to the Villa Belmonte. Having
carried out the massacre of the other Fascist prisoners at Dongo,
as above described, the bodies of the murdered men were put in a
lorry and driven to Milan, the bodies of Mussolini and Claretta
being collected on the way. Milan was reached in triumph about
10.45 p.m. (April 28th) and the bodies dumped for public exhibition
in the Piazzale Loreto in a north-eastern district of the city.

On the morning of the following day, Sunday, April 29th,
the Piazzle Loreto was visited by Milton Bracker of the staff of
'The Times', then chief of 'The Times' office in Rome.* He was
permitted to approach within a few feet of the corpses which were
guarded by a band of Partisans from a raging mob consisting of
the scum of the slums of Milan and, it is to be feared, of other
parts of the city as well, anxious to demonstrate its enthusiasm
for the winning side. When he arrived, Milton Bracker tells us,
"The body of Mussolini retained a vestige of dignity. His close-
shaven head was propped on the ruffled white blouse of his
mistress, Claretta Petacci, still beautiful even in death. His jaw was
as firm as when he had jutted it over the Romans packing the
Piazzi di Venezia. I saw that a bullet had emerged behind the
right ear in a sickening protusion of brains and bone".

An hour or so after Milton Bracker's arrival, two young men
managed to break through the cordon of Partisans and reach the
heap of corpses. Each aimed a kick at the dictator's tempting skull.
"The first kick glanced off. But the other landed full on the right
jaw and there was a hideous crunch . . . Before my eyes it destroyed
the facial contour of Mussolini that the world had known. From
then on, the jawline was gone and the head had to be backed with a
rifle butt to be photographed".

One can imagine the forcible language with which Sir Winston
Churchill would have described these proceedings had he been an
eye-witness. It is satisfactory to find Milton Bracker at least condemned them even if he does so in terms which a maiden aunt
might use when deploring that a favourite niece had returned home
rather late after an evening visit to the cinema. "What happened
in the Piazzle Loreto", he writes primly, "was nothing for the

See the article entitled "Last Days of Mussolini" by Milton Bracker in
The New York Times Magazine of April 24, 1955.

citizens of Milan to be proud of".

It would indeed be hard to parallel this comment as a master-piece of understatement. Milton Bracker then proceeds to argue that Mussolini's fate was inevitable, "for the simple reason he had ruined his country. He was doomed from the moment of the 'stab in the back'—June 10, 1940".

Certainly by "initiating a war of aggression"—'the supreme international crime'—on this date, Mussolini was responsible for the loss by his country of the fruits of two previous wars of aggression, namely the war of aggression against Abyssinia in 1935 and the war of aggression against Turkey in 1911. But the victors in the Second World War did not deprive Italy of the fruits of the war of aggression against Austria in 1915: on the contrary, Italy was confirmed in her possession of the German-speaking Tyrol and of Trieste. This express condonation of the 'stab in the back' of May 23rd 1915 surely precludes any profession of moral indignation concerning 'the stab in the back' of June 10, 1940.

After the above described exploit of the two youthful enthus-iasts for the winning side, the mob in the Piazzale Loreto became completely out of hand. "More bullets were fired into Mussolini's corpse, more people managed to curse and defile it". At last about mid-day someone suggested that the bodies should be hung up somewhere so that everyone in the square should have an unobstructed view of them. The proposal was adopted with enthus-iasm and soon the bodies of Mussolini, Claretta Petacci and three others were strung up by their heels with ropes from the girder of an unfinished petrol station.

An unwilling witness of this emphatic demonstration of loyalty and affection for the winning side was Achille Starace, former secretary-general of the Fascist Party. He was made to stand in an open lorry with his hands raised above his head while the corpses were being hoisted up: he was then dragged to a wall nearby, riddled with bullets and his body hung by the heels beside them.

It was a photograph of this final scene which so aroused Sir Winston Churchill's indignant disgust and caused him to send to Field Marshal Lord Alexander the telegram quoted at the begin-ning of this chapter. Few now will not regret that it was found inexpedient to adopt his suggestion that "the cleansing hand of British military power" might at least have undertaken the task of investigating the authority of these self-styled executioners of Claretta Petacci. If, as Mr. Bracker delicately puts it, the story of Mussolini's end was "nothing to be proud of", the pretence so long maintained by Leftist historians and publicists throughout the world that the crime was a duly authorised and legally carried out execution is even less a subject for pride. It would be easy to recompile a copious record of contemporary and subsequent comments on the crime but the result would be nauseating rather than illuminating.

It is now claimed that this long maintained pretence was actuated by a kindly desire to avoid wounding Communist susceptibilities. If this be true, one can only observe that much skill was wasted to no purpose in suppressing, distorting and misrepresenting the facts. From the Communist point of view the shooting of Benito Mussolini and all those in any way associated with him was entirely justified. All were executed as opponents of Communism. All for this reason deserved their fate just as, for example, Admiral Raeder deserved life imprisonment in Spandau and the victims of the Katyn Forest Massacre deserved to be butchered.

The helm of state is not popularly regarded as a post of danger. It is remarkable, however, how surprisingly high has been the mortality from violence among statesmen during the last hundred years. Mussolini's name is but one addition to a long list beginning with that of President Lincoln shot in 1865 and Czar Alexander the Liberator killed by a bomb in 1881. As we have seen, the exact manner of Mussolini's death remains uncertain, but unquestionably it more nearly resembled the death of Walter Rathenau in 1922 on the one hand than the death of the Archduke Maximilian in 1867 on the other. Mussolini certainly was not unique among modern Europe statesmen for having made mistakes—even of the variety once flippantly referred to by a revered British statesman as "backing the wrong horse". The present condition of Europe bears witness to the limitless capacity of European statesmen during the last fifty years to commit every kind of mistake, blunder and folly. Some of them paid for their follies by suffering a violent death. Only in the treatment accorded to his body after death was the fate of Mussolini unique in modern times.

An account of the murder of Mussolini may therefore fittingly conclude with a description of the final scene in the Piazzale Loreto. Paolo Monelli in his previously quoted book writes: "The bodies were already rigid and the arms contorted in various attitudes—Claretta's as though embracing a partner in a dance. The wind swung the bodies to and fro in a sort of grotesque ballet. The clothes hung down loosely and the faces took on an air of dissolution. Mussolini's face became more and more despairing. Only Claretta's face, seen from far off, looked calm and beautiful. Her eyes were shut and the shadow of a resigned smile could be seen round her mouth".*

Postscript to page 54.

In the introduction to the first instalments of Rachele Mussolini's memoirs of her husband published in the "Sunday Express" of the 4th May 1958 occurred the following passage:—

"A car took them (Mussolini and Claretta Petacci) to the place of execution. It was a small square formed by brick fences. (sic). The executioner pronounced sentence in these terms: 'By order of the General Command of the Liberty Volunteer Corps I am entrusted with rendering justice to the Italian people.'

He shot them. From a distance of three paces he fired five bursts with a machine gun at Mussolini. Then it was the woman Petacci's turn."

The "historical background" to these memoirs having been provided by A. J. P. Taylor, the Oxford historian and Leftist publicist, the present author asked him to state the place and date of trial and the charges upon which the accused were respectively convicted and sentenced.

Mr. Taylor replied airily by letter admitting that no trial had in fact taken place. "They were killed," he wrote, "simply because they fell into the hands of the Resistance, but I cannot regard the killing of Mussolini as a crime. Petacci is a different matter. Her presence was an embarrassment."

Nevertheless the reference to "the place of execution" and to "the executioner pronouncing sentence" in the text clearly suggests that some sort of a trial had previously taken place.

"Mussolini"—An Intimate Life by Paolo Monelli, Thames & Hudson, London, 1953. Page 271.

CHAPTER IV

AN OPPORTUNIST OF GENIUS

(Dr. Marcel Petiot)

By the general public, criminology is regarded primarily as the study of the crime of murder. The most commonplace and crudest murder arouses greater popular interest than any other variety of crime, however original in conception the latter may be and however skilfully it may be carried out. In the annals of English crime, the only name that has become a household word is that of an unfortunate little man who after living a blameless life for nearly fifty years, was driven to desperation by unhappy domestic circumstances. It is even open to question whether Crippin's conviction for murder was justified: it is possible that he was, in fact, only guilty of manslaughter. Neither the man nor his crime was in any way remarkable.

In all civilized countries, murder has always been considered the gravest of crimes: premeditated murder has always been regarded as the gravest variety of murder. Premeditated murder may be sub-divided into those cases in which the criminal's aim was limited to the death of a particular victim and those cases in which the criminal had adopted murder as a means of livelihood.

Cases in which the criminal may be labelled as a professional murderer, are, fortunately, rare. Quite distinct, of course, from this class of case, is the relatively numerous class in which the murderer kills for the pleasure which he derives from killing. The sadistic murderer is an abnormal individual, more or less mad, although he may not be deemed mad in the legal sense as Christie and Heath found to their cost. The professional murderer, on the other hand, is entirely sane, or at any rate his motives are entirely sane. He selects killing as a means of livelihood in the same spirit as another man adopts dentistry or the sale of vacuum cleaners.

If murder be regarded as the gravest and therefore the most interesting variety of crime and if premeditated wholesale murder be regarded as the gravest and therefore the most interesting variety of murder, then the professional murderer must be regarded as the worst and therefore the most interesting variety of criminal.

From the criminals of Europe during the present century, the following outstanding examples of the professional murderer may be selected, George Joseph Smith (Brides-in-the-Bath-Smith) in England, Henri Désiré Landru in France and Fritz Haarmann in Germany. Perhaps the latter is hardly entitled to be included in this group since apparently murder was only a sideline to his legitimate business—he was a meat hawker—and his mental state was such that he was probably partly driven by a sadistic urge. But Smith and Landru were essentially self-controlled, practical businessmen, entirely sane from a medical and from a legal point of view. Both indeed made money from time to time by legitimate means, but if either had made a full and correct return of his income for income tax purposes, an inspector of taxes would, without hesitation, have put the word "murder" under the heading "Principal source of income".

Both George Joseph Smith and Henri Désiré Landru were certainly remarkable criminals and their doings have been described and studied in numerous books and articles. But, although the former was hanged as long ago as 1915 and the latter went to the guillotine in 1922, these two cases remain the only widely known examples of this rare type of crime.

Yet in 1946 took place in Paris the trial of a professional wholesale murderer who was, from every point of view, a far more remarkable criminal than either Smith or Landru. More than ten years have now passed since Dr. Marcel Petiot was led to the guillotine. Nevertheless, although his name is vaguely familiar to most people interested in crime, it still remains hard to find out exact particulars concerning his crimes and still harder to find any reliable information concerning the man himself. In England, he is remembered as a mass-murderer who somehow or other was connected with 'La Résistance'. In France, naturally, his case is better known, but, extraordinary as it may seem, no book has yet been written about his career and no verbatim report of his trial has been published.

Judging from the intense interest which the trial of the 'Monster of Gambais' aroused, one would have expected that French criminologists would have vied with each other in collecting and elucidating every fact remotely bearing on the Petiot case.

The exact opposite has occurred, however, in regard to 'The Monster of the Rue Lesueur'—that iron curtain of discreet silence used to cloak unwelcome military and political happenings has been draw around his career. Yet the career of Dr. Marcel

(*Wide World*)

Dr. Marcel Petiot, on trial in Paris, for the murder of an estimated 63 persons, speaks, poses and gestures during a session of his trial.

Petiot smiles as he stands, hands on hips, answering the questions of members of the court, at the scene of his crime, the cellar of No. 21 Rue Le Sueur.

Petiot has no military or political significance whatsoever. It is true that when as a recently qualified doctor he started in medical practice in a small provincial town, he took part as a Socialist in local politics, becoming at length a Councillor and finally Mayor. But it is probably no injustice to his memory to suggest that in his political career he was actuated more by a desire to increase his clientele by becoming a leading figure in his district than by any deep-rooted political convictions. In fact, at his trial in 1946, the essence of the complaint against him was that he had remained completely detached from the political problems concerning which his countrymen were lashing themselves into a state of frenzy. Dr. Petiot, throughout his career, was essentially an individualist: whatever he did, he did for himself and for himself alone. The political aspirations, passions and prejudices of his countrymen only interested him to the extent to which he could turn them to his own personal profit. His activities exercised no influence of any kind on the course of contemporary events. Those of his victims whose identities have been established, were all obscure private individuals, and there is no reason to believe that any of those whose identities remain undisclosed were persons of position or influence. On the face of it, therefore, it is strange that it has been deemed politically expedient to deny him the sombre fame which his infamous achievements as a professional murderer indisputably entitle him.

Why has that 'Iron Curtain of Discreet Silence', originally devised to cloak such major political happenings as the mass-deportation of the inhabitants of vast areas in Eastern Europe in accordance of the shameful Yalta and Potsdam Agreements and such momentous crimes of the widest political significance as the Katyn Forest Massacre been used to cloak the doings of a mere private killer?

The answer is that the career of Dr. Marcel Petiot cannot be described without disclosing the surrounding social and political conditions which alone made his crimes possible. It has been realized that however skilfully distorted and toned down, the facts of his career could not be made to harmonise with the official fairy tale which purports to describe the liberation of France during the Second World War. Concerning this fairy tale, dutifully accepted as factual by the British public for a decade, it will be sufficient here to quote Mr. Hampden Jackson's "The Post-War Decade" published in 1955. "There was surprisingly little vindictiveness in France after the Liberation", Mr. Hampden Jackson writes. "Instead of moral degeneration, there was in 1945 a spirit of liberation and renaissance. As Dorothy M. Pickles wrote in *French*

Politics 'there was, for a short time, a sincere spirit of moral and social purpose, of unity and brotherly love, a sense of democratic rebirth which set up Wordsworthian reactions in more than one British observer whose feet were normally planted firmly on the ground'."*

It must be presumed that owing to the curtain of discreet silence surrounding this subject, Mr. Hampden Jackson was not aware that after the Liberation more Frenchmen were done to death by their own countrymen than perished throughout the entire French Revolution: more than four times as many Frenchmen were judicially murdered or lynched in the years 1944-45 as had been put to death by the Germans during the occupation: presumably also, his eyes had not been pained by photographs of droves of Frenchwomen being paraded through the streets stark naked by their chivalrous countrymen before having their heads shaved in public before exultant crowds. It is hard however to explain his complacent assertion that there was surprisingly little vindictiveness in France after the Liberation in view of the fact, which it has been impossible to suppress, that Marshal Pétain after his condemnation at a mock trial in 1945, was detained in captivity on a dreary little island in the Atlantic until his death in 1951 through the implacable malice of his enemies. In 1940 the French Assembly conferred on him dictatorial powers by a majority of 569 to 80: in 1950 the French Assembly overwhelmingly rejected a motion that he should be reprieved, although by that time he was ninety-four years of age and nearly blind.

Paris at the time Dr. Petiot carried on his dreadful profession so long and so successfully was not a city likely to give rise to Wordsworthian reactions in anyone. Human life was of no more account there than it was in Borneo in the days of the head-hunters. Operating against the occupying forces were many gangs of terrorists who directed their attacks not only against isolated German soldiers but against any Frenchman whom the leaders of these gangs might be pleased to consider a collaborator. No one was safe from denunciation, arbitrary arrest, lawless violence and blackmail. In such conditions the disappearance of an individual or the discovery of a human body awakened no surprise. Kidnappings and murders by terrorist gangs and sudden arrests and secret executions by the Gestapo were of frequent occurrence. Dr. Petiot relied on these conditions to carry on his profession. His career of crime would be utterly incomprehensible without reference to these conditions. And so the

* "The Post-War Decade" by J. Hampden Jackson (Gollancz, London, 1955). Page 54.

career of this lone wholesale killer has by tacit consent been discreetly withdrawn from investigation in order that the myth of a "democratic re-birth, of unity and brotherly love" might not be contradicted by facts.

As a result of this tacit ban on investigation, the unique character of Dr. Petiot's achievements in crime has failed to win recognition. The few criminologists who to date have studied his career seem disposed to dismiss him as a mere imitator of Landru. This is in a way a tribute since Landru was without question one of the most dreadful criminals who have ever lived. But Petiot was much more than a mere imitator of 'The Monster of Gambais'. No doubt Petiot was familiar with the career of Landru and may have been influenced by it. But Landru, like his English predecessor, George Joseph Smith, was essentially what the Americans call 'a small timer'. His victims were all lonely women, poor and obscure. The profits which he derived from his ghastly profession were grotesquely out of proportion to the risks which he took. A man of wider intelligence would have abandoned so dangerous and unremunerative an occupation for one honest and better paid. Landru also committed incredible mistakes — in particular the keeping of a diary in which he jotted brief particulars of his crimes. Petiot made no such stupid blunders. If in the end he suffered the same fate as Landru, it was the result of bad luck rather than of faulty judgement. Finally, he did not waste his time appropriating the meagre savings of working-class women: his victims, a most motley collection of men and women, had only one characteristic in common — all of them at the time of their death were in possession of large sums in cash, or valuables and securities readily convertible into cash. From an accountant's standpoint, Petiot's business in the Rue Lesueur was a sound commercial undertaking.

Who then was Dr. Marcel Petiot and what exactly were the achievements in crime which has led one student of his career, M. Paul Gordeaux, to claim that he was, "le plus grand assassin du siècle, et peut-être de l'histoire".*

Marcel Petiot was born in 1897 in Auxerre, a small provincial town, one hundred miles south east of Paris. Socially, he belonged to the lower bureaucratic class, his father being a postal official. Both his parents died before he reached his teens and an aunt acted the role of guardian — somewhat inefficiently perhaps since at the age of sixteen he was in trouble with the police on a charge of stealing from letterboxes by the ingenious device

* See 'Petiot' by Paul Gordeaux, "France-Soir", November 15th, 1952.

of inserting therein a long flexible stick dipped in glue. He was merely bound over and his ambition to become a doctor does not seem to have been in any way prejudiced by this youthful lapse. Modern psychologists assure us that leniency is an infallible cure for the juvenile delinquent. No doubt they would point to the case of Marcel Petiot as a striking example of the exception proving the rule.

The outbreak of the First World War in 1914 found young Petiot studying medicine in Paris. At the age of nineteen he was called up for military service. An individualist, interested only in his own personal problems, Petiot remained completely immune to war propaganda. The orgy of slaughter going on, professedly to make the world safe for democracy, aroused in his heart no enthusiasm. But having no choice in the matter, he joined the army and as a medical student he was sent to serve in the Medical Corps.

The most outstanding of Petiot's many gifts was his capacity to estimate exactly all the possibilities opened up by a novel situation. Within a few months of its commencement, the campaign in France developed into trench warfare, and Petiot soon recognised that on most sectors of the front this consisted of long periods of inactivity broken at infrequent intervals by brief outbursts of bloodshed. The life of the men in the trenches during these periods of inactivity was one of constant danger, hardship and monotony. As a relief from unrelieved nerve strain and boredom any form of artificial stimulus was in urgent demand. At the dressing station to which he was attached, Petiot had access to large stores of drugs. Very soon he was conducting a thriving business as a dope-peddler. For a time the First World War, so far as Petiot personally was concerned, seemed to be serving a useful purpose which otherwise was certainly not apparent. This satisfactory state of affairs was brought to an abrupt end when a disgruntled customer gave him away to the authorities. Petiot was arrested and brought before a court martial.

French military discipline during the First World War was maintained by extreme ferocity. After every reverse, wholesale executions were carried out in order to inspire the survivors with a better fighting spirit. For so grave an offence as stealing government stores, the chances were that his career would be ignominiously cut short by a firing squad. In the case of shell-shocked, nerve-shattered men accused of failing to display a proper martial spirit, courts martial were wont to dismiss curtly and without hesitation the evidence of the psychiatrists called for their defence. But for some reason an exception was made in the case of Petiot. Perhaps because Petiot was a medical student, the psychiatrist called to give evidence on his behalf urged his case with exceptional conviction. It appeared that shortly before his arrest, Petiot had sustained a slight wound in the leg. This, the psychiatrist explained to the Court, would undermine his resistance to temptation and predispose him to steal government stores and peddle morphine to the troops. The Court listened with unwonted respect to the conclusions of modern medical science. So instead of being sent to join next morning the batch of unfortunates gathered to expiate the crime of failing to keep their nerves under proper control "in the presence of the enemy", Petiot was sent off to a hospital for psychopathic treatment, and later was granted an honourable discharge from the army and a small pension for life.

Having returned as a wounded hero to civilian life, Petiot duly completed his medical studies, took his degree as a doctor and set up in practice at the little town of Villeneuve-sur-Yonne, only a few miles from his birth place, Auxerre. Here he remained for some twelve years. He interested himself in local politics and as a Socialist became first a councillor and ultimately mayor of the district.

It is unfortunately necessary to pass lightly over this period of Marcel Petiot's life. After he had been arrested on a charge of wholesale murder, many people in Villeneuve-sur-Yonne and the neighbourhood professed to have long entertained suspicions that he had been responsible for the mysterious deaths of a number of persons with whom he as a doctor had had dealings, which, it might at least be said, occurred very conveniently for him.

From what we know of Petiot's later doings, it is certainly highly probable that his career during this period of his life closely resembled the career one hundred years before of that peer among English wholesale poisoners, Dr. William Palmer. The latter, it will be remembered, also set up in medical practice in a small provincial town and very early in his career it began to be noticed that persons whose deaths might save him from embarrassment or which might bring him pecuniary benefit were liable to die suddenly and mysteriously Exactly the same rumours seem to have been current in Villeneuve-sur-Yonne in the 1920's concerning Dr. Petiot as were current in Rugeley in the 1840's concerning Dr. Palmer.

It is impossible, however, concerning Dr. Petiot's career as a provincial doctor to say more than that several persons connected with him died unexplained deaths. Thus a servant girl with whom he was popularly credited with having had a love affair vanished without trace and a Mme. Debauve, a patient of his, was found murdered in her shop which had been robbed and then set on fire. Another patient who, it was said, had been urging the police to widen the scope of their enquiries concerning Mme. Devauve's death, died suddenly after receiving medical treatment from the doctor. All that is certain is that whatever rumours may have been current, they led to no official action being taken.

Dr. Petiot's career as a provincial doctor and leader in local politics came to an abrupt and ignominious end in 1932 when he was charged with petty larceny of electricity by an extremely ingenious arrangement of wires by which he was able to obtain current without his meter recording it. For this he received a suspended sentence of three months imprisonment. Apart from any ugly rumours which may have gathered round his name, this conviction is sufficient explanation why he should have decided to leave the district. No explanation can be suggested, however, why this conviction had no prejudicial effect on his career as a doctor. Marcel Petiot left Villeneuve-sur-Yonne and set up in practice at 66, Rue Caumartin, a busy street in the heart of Paris, near the Madeleine.

Down to about 1940, Petiot's career as a medical practitioner in Paris followed the same lines as his previous career in Villeneuve-sur-Yonne, except that the scope of his activities was wider and more ambitious. Once again, it is said, he acquired an evil reputation. Later, people remembered various deaths and disappearances among his patients and acquaintances concerning which they professed to have felt at the time the gravest suspicions. With a surgery so centrally situated, Petiot soon became known in the underworld of Paris as a doctor who would readily agree with a patient who insisted that in his or her case a course of morphine or heroin was clearly indicated. It is not difficult to believe that for the second time in his career he became a drug-peddler. Once again no doubt he found it a hazardous, if profitable, occupation. If indeed he had been a criminal at Villeneuve-sur-Yonne, the fact that he escaped detection in any serious crime can be accounted for by the fact that he seems always to have played a lone hand without confederates or accomplices. A drug peddler, on the other hand, lives in constant danger of being betrayed by a dissatisfied customer or by one of the network of touts which he is forced to employ to attract customers. It is suggested Petiot strove to overcome this grave drawback by taking steps to ensure that any customer, relative of a customer or tout who indicated an intention to report his activities to the police died before any such intention could be carried out. Several times his downfall seemed imminent but in each case the danger passed as a result of a timely death or disappearance.

Petiot's professional career in Paris began indeed most inauspiciously. In 1936 he was caught pilfering a technical work from a bookshop—a truly ridiculously trivial offence for a master criminal! For perhaps the one time in his life his defence—that he had pocketed the book in a fit of absentmindedness—may have been true! On the other hand, remembering his conviction as a youth for pilfering and the conviction for larceny of electricity which brought about his downfall at Villeneuve-sur-Yonne, it seems more probable that this master criminal throughout his life was a victim of kleptomania. At any rate the Court which tried him took this charitable view of the matter: Petiot was bound over and advised to undergo voluntarily a course of treatment.

Kleptomania is a weaknesss from which the most unlikely persons may suffer: cases are not rare in which persons of integrity and substantial means have stained a hitherto unblemished reputation for the sake of some article of negligible value. It remains astonishing however that a man so self-controlled, calculating and methodical as Petiot should have been the victim of so irrational an urge.

What is even more astonishing is the fact that Petiot's professional career seems to have been in no way prejudiced by his repeated convictions for pilfering. Whether these convictions indicated that he was a petty criminal or a kleptomaniac, one would expect that the French Medical Council would have taken steps to protect the public from the professional services of a man so clearly suffering either from criminal or irrational tendencies. Nothing whatever seems to have been done however: Petiot was neither suspended nor was his name removed from the medical roll. Incredible as it may appear, it is said no report of any of his convictions was lodged with the governing body of his profession.

In the admirable sketch of this case contained in his book, "Murder in France", Mr. Alister Kershaw speculates on the possible reasons why Petiot should have enjoyed immunity from the penalties usually suffered by professional men as a result of a criminal conviction. While admitting the problem "may be explicable on depressingly commonplace grounds", Mr. Kershaw inclines to the opinion that for twenty years before his execution Petiot was the protege of some powerful organization; he suggests that he may have been a member of the Communist network operating in France under the patronage of the Soviet Government, or that he may have been an agent of one of the German intelligence services.*

After the German occupation of France in 1940 it is quite likely that Petiot made himself useful on occasion to the German Secret Service: it is equally likely that he made himself useful on occasion to the Communist organisation in France. In fact it is probable that he found it desirable to perform services for both by betraying each to the other. Once the war had started he may in addition have been in contact with the British Secret Service and with French patriotic organizations. But if we assume this to be true, we still lack an explanation for an immunity which dates from the time when he was a young general medical practitioner in a small provincial town.

Mr. Kershaw offers no suggestions as to what possible services Petiot could have rendered in return for protection by any such organisation when he was practising at Villeneuve-sur-Yonne. A doctor practising in some important military or naval base or in the neighbourhood of the Maginot Line might conceivably have been a useful agent to the German Secret Service: a distinguished doctor practising in Paris and numbering among his patients persons in important political and official positions, might conceivably have picked up items of information which would have been found useful in the Kremlin. But what military secrets could Petiot have discovered round Villeneuve-sur-Yonne, and what secret information could he have gleaned from the gossip of the small farmers and shop-keepers who formed his clientele in that quiet little town?

The present writer confesses himself quite unable to answer these questions and he must therefore dissent from Mr. Kershaw's views on this puzzling problem. Further, he is unable also to explain Petiot's immunity from the normal consequences of his convictions "on depressingly commonplace grounds". If Petiot had been a man possessing large financial resources or had he been a member of some powerful family with wide connections, either bribery or influence would provide a plausible solution. But although Petiot was never forced to live the hand-to-mouth existence of 'Brides-in-the-Bath' Smith and of the "Monster of Gambais", he was never wealthy: his family belonged to the lower middle class and entirely lacked money or influence.

Down to the outbreak of the Second World War, Petiot's career may be summarised by saying that he was never prosecuted or convicted for any serious offence and that he succeeded in some inexplicable way from suffering the normal consequences of con-

* "Murder in France" by Alister Kershaw (Constable, London, 1955). Pages 162-163.

viction for minor offences. At the outbreak of war in 1939, he was actively conducting a practice as a doctor in the heart of Paris in conjunction with the secret business of a drug trafficker and probably that of an abortionist. Whatever suspicions the police authorities may have recorded in their dossier concerning him, he had never given them an opportunity to take action against him.

Nevertheless, it can hardly be doubted that if a second world war had not broken out, justice would in the end have overtaken him. The pitcher would have gone to the wall once too often. In all walks of life, intelligence and daring rarely achieve success unaided by a minimum share of good fortune. Petiot at several critical moments in his career was the victim of pure bad luck. Although an ingenious, far-sighted planner, he was inclined at times to be careless about details—and, as we have seen, he was subject to irrational impulses. Sooner or later ill fortune or inattention to some minor detail would have led to his undoing. In that case Petiot would have secured a place in the annals of crime only as a criminal who used murder as a means of escaping detection in his other crimes.

The outbreak of World War II in 1939 marked the turning point of Petiot's career. It offered him a unique opportunity to exercise his outstanding gift, the power to recognize all the possibilities of a novel situation and the insight to perceive how these possibilities could best be exploited for his personal profit. Men such as Petiot stagnate in settled conditions: they find scope for their powers only when all those about them are bewildered by unfamiliar circumstances. Instinctively they welcome the strange and unfamiliar.

In 1939, the news of the outbreak of war was received in Paris with no such outburst of joyous jubilation as had welcomed the news of the outbreak of the war in 1914. Many people looked forward to the future with well-justified foreboding: a few even permitted themselves to wonder for what cause they were now being called upon to fight. We may be sure that Petiot remained untroubled by any such doubts or fears. It may appear a bold assertion, but probably no member of the French or British Governments at the time cared less than he "for the integrity of Poland". All that interested him was the certainty that a period of disturbed political, social and economic conditions lay ahead. He faced the future with quiet confidence in his own powers.

For some nine months after the outbreak of war, the situation remained fundamentally unchanged. Dr. Petiot continued tranquilly to carry on his medical practice, together with such other pursuits as drug peddling and abortion as had occupied his time since he had settled in Paris in 1932, and no doubt, he took due advantage of the fact that the attention of the police had become mainly directed to tracking spies and arresting persons guilty of expressing views calculated to cause alarm and despondency. On the 16th May 1940 came the news that the tank spear-heads of Guderian and Rommel had crossed the Meuse and were pushing rapidly towards the Channel coast. On the 14th June, Dr. Petiot may have been one of the numerous spectators who watched the first troops of the advance guard of the German armies marching in triumph down the Champs Elysées.

A little more than a year later, Dr. Petiot purchased a dignified residence in a fashionable residential district of Paris near the Etoile. The inspiration which was destined to put him in a class apart among the world's criminals must therefore have come to him between June 1940 and September 1941 when he became the owner of No. 21 Rue Lesueur since this house was deliberately chosen by him, not as a residence, but as a place in which his inspiration could be put into practice.

We do not know how Dr. Petiot occupied himself during this period. That his activities were not unprofitable may be deduced from the fact that at the end of it he was able to buy an expensive mansion which had formerly been the residence of the famous actress, Cécile Sorel. The occupation of Paris by the Germans created an entirely novel situation every feature of which called for careful study. What to those about him was a cause for alarm, despondency and despair was to Dr. Petiot a subject for careful analysis and reflection.

Robbery dates back to the very dawn of history: no doubt it came into existence concurrently with private property. It was probably not long after the first stone axe head had been laboriously chipped out by some particularly industrious prehistoric man that it occurred to one of his quick-witted but lazy neighbours how much less trouble it would be to steal the finished article than to make one for himself. Long before Robin Hood, the obvious fact was realised that it is more profitable to rob the rich than the poor. Very early also dawned the realization that travellers and particularly those taking long journeys are of all people the most likely to have about them quantities of cash and valuables. The first miscreant to whom this realization fully dawned no doubt set up in business as a bandit and thus became the founder of a form of crime which under various names has flourished ever since in every corner of the world. Down through the ages the fact that travellers are the most profitable people to rob has been applied in practice in many different ways by highwaymen.

footpads, bandits, bushrangers, and even by religious secret societies such as the Thugs of 19th century India. It might well be thought that every conceivable modus operandi had long since been thought out and carried into effect. Nevertheless as a result of his careful study of the situation resulting from the German occupation of Paris in 1940, Dr. Marcel Petiot worked out an entirely novel modus operandi for the despoiling of travellers and which for some years he operated most successfully. It is on account of his activities during the four years when Paris was under German military control that he must be allocated a special niche in the annals of crime.

As we have seen, Dr. Petiot's inspiration came to him, some time during the first year of the German occupation, a period of outward tranquility, very different from the period of frenzied political passions and nationalist animosities which was destined to follow it. Defeat so complete, so sudden and so unexpected, had stunned the French people and had deprived them for the time being of the capacity to feel any emotion excepting only a dull resentment against the politicians who had allowed France to become entangled in another war. In 1940 the French Assembly conferred on Marshal Pétain dictatorial powers by a majority of 569 to 80. Had a referendum been held in that year there can be no doubt that his government would have received an overwhelming vote of confidence from the French people. Towards the invaders little or no hostility was shown. Every Frenchman knew that France had often been victorious in the past and liked to think that on these occasions Frenchmen had always proved themselves chivalrous victors. Now France was experiencing defeat, it was generally felt that the situation should be faced with dignity and even with good humour. Towards the invaders at all events, very few were inclined to risk personal discomfort and danger by parading their feelings for no apparent purpose. It seemed impossible to doubt that the existing situation might continue indefinitely: at least no swift reversal of fortune could be hoped for. France appeared completely isolated politically from the rest of the world. The Soviet Government was not only offering Hitler congratulations on the victories of his armies but was supplying his war industries with raw material. Across the Atlantic, President Roosevelt, to judge by his public declarations, was inspired only by a whole-hearted determination to keep the United States from being involved in the war. Six months after the downfall of France—during the presidential election—he gave his famous 'Mothers-and-Fathers-of-Boston' pledge—"I have said this before but I shall say it again and again and again. Your boys are not going to be sent out into any foreign wars!"

It is easy for us with our knowledge of what was going on behind the scenes to dismiss the attitude of the average Frenchman in 1940-41 as shortsighted and unduly pessimistic. It should be remembered, however, that the average French man-in-the-street in those days had nothing to guide him but public declarations such as Roosevelt's Boston Pledge and Mr. Molotov's congratulatory telegram to Herr Ribbentrop on the German overthrow of France—he had no reason to hope that Hitler was contemplating anything so insane as an invasion of Russia or that Roosevelt was really striving heart and soul (as he explained in a private letter to Viscount Elibank of February 1938*) "to educate American public opinion" to join in the crusade against Hitler—the policy labelled by Clare Luce as "Lying us into War".

For their part the behaviour of the German troops for the first year or so of the occupation of France was exemplary—in all respects the exact opposite of their behaviour from the first moment of the invasion of Russia in the following year. On both occasions, however, they did but display the one really outstanding characteristic of the German race, a susceptibility to become hypnotised into unquestioning obedience by any order, good or bad, given by those in authority over them. The conduct of the German troops when they entered Russia in 1941 can be judged from the fact that in a few months they transformed the fear and hatred felt by the vast majority of the Russian people for Stalin's murderous regime—tens of thousands of innocent people had been executed or had been transported to Siberia during the Great Purge of 1936-39—into enthusiastic and in fact fanatical support. This campaign of terrorism seems to have been a deliberate policy undertaken on express orders from Hitler as part of the Nazi crusade against Communism. But in the preceding year the German troops had been ordered to show every possible consideration and courtesy to the French civilian population. On both occasions Hitler's orders were punctiliously obeyed. The result was that in France after the surrender of the French armies outwardly cordial relations were at first established. The victors carefully refrained from all provocation and few French civilians were ready to risk life or liberty by any expression of patriotic emotion.

Nevertheless however outwardly tranquil the situation might appear there were many people in occupied France unwilling to trust to appearances and anxious to leave the country as quickly as possible. First of all there were the Jews, including many who

* See the article "Franklin Roosevelt: Friend of Britain" by Viscount Elibank in the Contemporary Review of June 1955.

had fled to France after 1933 to escape Nazi persecution in Germany. Although not at the moment molested, no Jew could feel confident that persecution might not be commenced at any moment in the occupied territories. Secondly there were the Communists including many German renegades who had been actively supporting the enemies of their country. True on the surface the relations between the Nazi Government and the Kremlin were most cordial. The occupation of Paris had moved Mr. Molotov to send the Führer his hearty congratulations. Officially therefore for the Communist party in France the German victory was a subject for rejoicing or at least for passive acquiescence. But what Communist could feel any confidence that these brotherly relations would not come to an abrupt end. Obviously the only prudent course was to slip out of France before either Hitler or Stalin came to some "agonized re-appraisal" of the situation.

When an urgent demand exists, it is seldom long before persons are found offering to meet that demand. Very soon after the German occupation began, a novel variety of the travel agency business began to flourish in France. A person desiring for his own good reasons to go abroad, made the necessary contacts, paid the substantial fee demanded and was then taken along one of the secret escape routes leading out of occupied territory. The organizers of these escape routes had no connection with the secret French patriotic associations which also operated escape routes for the benefit of recruits anxious to join the 'Free French' forces mustering in Great Britain or with the British Secret Service which also operated escape routes for its spies and agents. The interests of such private organisers were entirely commercial. For their services they demanded large fees and no doubt earned them since the work of conducting a secret travel agency in war time is both difficult and dangerous.

With his close contacts with the Parisian underworld, we may be sure that Dr. Marcel Petiot soon knew all there was to know about the new travel agency business which started immediately after the arrival of the Germans. No doubt in the seclusion of his surgery in the Rue Caumartin, he carefully considered all the possibilities opened up by this novel development of modern warfare. Probably he finally turned down the idea of going into the business himself by organizing an escape of his own because his personal inclination was always to work alone with as few colleagues and helpers as possible. An underground escape route agency would require a large staff of assistants all of whom would demand a share of the profits and any one of whom would be in a position to betray him. Perhaps he came finally to the conclusion that the profits at best would be hardly sufficient to justify the enormous risks which would have to be undertaken. Capture would have extremely serious consequences. The German Security Police spared no pains to discover underground escape routes and when they discovered one made distressingly little distinction between those established for the entry and departure of British spies and those established for private profit.

While unwilling to enter the travel agency business himself, Petiot must have been reluctant to make no attempt to turn to some account so unprecedented a situation. Unquestionably there were thousands of persons in Paris anxious to travel to foreign lands, many of them people of wealth who would undoubtedly wish to carry with them out of France all their portable property. Was this not a heaven-sent opportunity to apply the ancient criminal maxim that of all people the most profitable people to rob are travellers.

At this point of his reflections, Petiot's great inspiration came to him. To rob! The underground travel agencies had only robbed their clients in the sense they had extracted extortionate fees for their services. But why be content with mere fees? If arrangements were made that these rich travellers came to some fatal mishap on their journey all the wealth which they were carrying with them abroad could be appropriated by those in charge of them. As all arrangements for their journey would have been made in complete secrecy no one would make any inconvenient enquiries in the event of their disappearing without trace. Friends and relations would assume that they had merely slipped out of occupied France by one or other of the underground escape routes to a destination unknown. All well-wishers when a disappearance took place would join in a voluntary conspiracy of silence to prevent the German Security Police obtaining a clue which might lead to the discovery of the escape route by which, it would be assumed, their departure had been effected.

And of course, reflected Petiot, if this plan were adopted, there would be no need to go to the trouble of organizing any escape route at all! The only staff that would be necessary would consist of a few touts to attract likely clients. Both the expenses and the risks would be negligible. As the residuary beneficiary of all the money and jewels which his clients were taking with them abroad, there would be no need to haggle about fees. He would thus be in a position to undercut the market. He would attract clients by offering the same services at much lower prices than his rivals.

Mr. Alister Kershaw thinks it probable that Dr. Petiot began to carry his inspiration into operation during the first year of the German occupation. A number of dismembered bodies were found scattered about Paris and it is certainly possible that these were the bodies of persons who had secretly visited him at his address in the Rue Caumartin with the intention of setting forth from there to foreign parts along the escape route which the doctor had told them he had organized. There is no evidence, however, to support this supposition. None of the bodies in question were identified and no doubt there were many criminals in Paris who took advantage of the abnormal conditions.

On the 22nd June 1941, Hitler ordered his armies to invade the Soviet Union.

This date marked a turning point in European history and also marked a turning point in the career of Marcel Petiot. Down to this date life in occupied Paris had been abnormal but there had been no general breakdown of law and order. In spite of irritating restrictions and ever increasing deprivations the average man-in-the-street went about his business more or less as usual. The civilian police protected life and property: the courts continued to function as usual. Here and there small resistance groups had become active. They were composed mainly of youthful members of the upper classes inspired by patriotic enthusiasm. Their aim was to reverse the decision of the Battle of France and to restore France to her ancient position as one of the Great Powers of Europe. Contact between these groups was maintained by a central directing agency in London from whom they received money, arms and encouragement. They worked in conjunction with the British Secret Service and their activities were directed to acts of carefully planned sabotage. To the Germans they were a nuisance rather than a danger. They had no practical influence on the military situation. Ruthlessly repressed by the German security forces, their main function from the British point of view was that they tended to break down the cordial relations at first existing between the French civilian population and the German army of occupation. The French Communists in deference to the friendly relations existing between Soviet and Nazi Governments held coldly aloof from such bourgeois activities.

Hitler's invasion of the Soviet Union completely transformed the situation. Resistance groups composed of Communists, Fellow Travellers and Leftists quickly formed all over France. In their view, a temporary squabble between capitalist states had developed into the great long-awaited class war between Communism and Fascism. Their inspiration came from the exploits of the Partisan bands operating in Russia in the rear of the advancing German armies. The original resistance groups organized by the British continued to function but were soon completely overshadowed by the new Communist groups. While gladly accepting money, arms and explosives from the British, acts of sabotage against the Germans as directed by the British Secret Service was to the Communist resistance fighters a mere side-line. Their speciality was murder. Any German caught unawares must be disposed of by a knife thrust or by a bullet. In the class war there can be no neutrals. Not only persons actively co-operating with the German Fascists but persons not disposed actively to aid the cause of Communism must be summarily liquidated just as if they had been residents of Mr. Stalin's Soviet Paradise. All over France, acts of liquidation began to take place.

This transformation of the situation in France in the summer of 1941 was a calamity for the French people and from the example it provided to later resistance movements, for the rest of the world. For Dr. Petiot, however, it was a most welcome development. One of the main difficulties to be overcome by a murderer is disposal of the body of his victim. But this difficulty does not exist in a land in which the discovery of the bodies of murdered persons is an everyday occurrence, or in which mysterious disappearances are continually taking place. During the second stage of the German occupation of France a disappearance could be adequately explained in half a dozen different ways. The person in question might for one of a score of reasons have left France secretly by one of the underground escape routes. Or the missing person might have been arrested by the Gestapo as a suspected member of 'La Résistance' and might either be awaiting interrogation in some prison or might already have been found guilty and executed. Again the missing person might have been summarily liquidated as a "collaborator", or what was equally likely he or she might have been murdered by some member of 'La Résistance' in pursuance of some personal grudge, or possibly for some commonplace motive such as robbery. In such circumstances it was impossible for the French police to press an enquiry concerning a missing person very far for fear of awkward facts which might be brought to light: both 'La Résistance' and the Gestapo strongly resented their respective activities being pried into by third parties.

Having given the far reaching consequences of the German invasion of Russia in June 1941, his careful consideration, Dr. Petiot decided that the situation merited a substantial capital outlay on his part. His home and surgery in the Rue Caumartin served well enough for his traffic in drugs and for an occasional abortion or murder but it was too small for business on a scale befitting the new opportunities offered by the changed circumstances. What he needed were large premises of his own, which, he could adapt as he thought fit to make them suitable for carrying out the plan he had in mind. Strict privacy was also essential. The Rue Caumartin is in a densely populated district. What he needed was a large house, centrally situated so as to be easily reached by clients but in a select residential district with as few neighbours as possible.

A dignified mansion, No. 21, in the Rue Lesueur, a quiet street running between the Avenue Foch and the Avenue de la Grande Armée exactly suited all of Dr. Petiot's requirements. Always a quiet backwater for affluence and gentility, the Rue Lesueur was now more secluded than ever since many of the houses were closed— their wealthy occupants having either gone abroad or moved into the country after the outbreak of war for fear of bombing. No. 21 was for sale, no doubt in the circumstances at a very reasonable price. Dr. Petiot purchased this house in September 1941, some four months after the situation had been transformed by Hitler's invasion of Russia. He at once put in hand carefully planned alterations to make this former residence of Mlle. Sorel suitable for the business which he intended to carry on there.

Petiot made no secret of the alterations to the ground floor which he considered necessary in order to adapt it for the business which he had in mind. A lesser man would have tried to have done the necessary work himself. This would not have been an impossible task since the only essential feature of his plans was the provision of a windowless apartment with one strong door. Beneath the premises was a large cellar which only needed the addition of a door strong enough to resist the most frenzied efforts to break it down in order to make it suitable for the carrying out of his purpose. But the doctor scorned any such makeshift arrangements: his undertaking promised very substantial profits and petty economies would be out of place. And as we shall see, he had decided to put the cellar to a subsidiary but yet necessary use. In the strictly one-man business which he proposed to run, it was most desirable that he should himself perform the duties of receptionist, executioner and undertaker. Why should he in addition expend his energies as an amateur bricklayer?

A firm of builders received instructions from the new owner of No. 21 to cut off one end of the large front room on the ground floor by building a partition wall so as to create a small triangular room which, he explained to the builders, he required to house a rather noisy electrical transformer. To prevent the neighbours being disturbed by the noise of this machine, the room containing it

H

must be made as sound-proof as possible. Presumably for this purpose also he directed that the window of this new room should be bricked up, and at the same time a small window, filled with strong plate glass, should be cut in the opposite wall so that the owner of the transformer could inspect its working from the rear adjoining room without the trouble of entering the room containing it. This new room could only be entered through a doorway cut in the partition wall which was to be provided with strong double doors—once again a precaution against noise. Finally, in order to ensure strict privacy, the new owner of No. 21 directed that the boundary wall of the courtyard behind the house should be greatly increased in height so that it should prevent neighbouring residents from observing from their upper windows anything taking place in the courtyard. That he proposed to make some use of this courtyard seemed to be indicated by instructions to dig a pit near the garage, and to fix a block and tackle to a wall alongside this pit.

These instructions may, perhaps, have seemed to the builders a little out of the ordinary, but there was nothing inexplicably sinister about them. Marcel Petiot was a trained man of science, a practising doctor who held himself out as a specialist in a wide variety of electrical treatments. Was there anything remarkable in such a man equipping a new surgery with an electrical transformer either for use in his practice or for the purpose of scientific experiments?

The alterations to No. 21 having been carried out to his satisfaction, it only remained for Petiot to have the boiler in the cellar put in proper working order, to obtain a consignment of quicklime from his brother, Maurice, who conducted a radio repair shop in Auxerre, and to arrange for various touts to conduct a discreet publicity campaign extolling a new escape route recently opened for the service of those desiring to leave occupied France.

To achieve the latter purpose, so essential to his plan, Petiot began by approaching an impecunious patient of his named Raoul Fourrier who, he knew, spent most of his time in the night clubs and cafes of Montmartre. To Fourrier he confided that he was connected with 'La Résistance' and had been put in charge of a newly opened escape route from occupied territory. If, therefore, Fourrier heard of anyone wishing to leave France, he was in a position to arrange it. He would be pleased to pay Fourrier a commission for any would-be travellers introduced by him.

Fourrier was charmed with the suggestion and spoke to a friend of his named Edmund Pintard who generally passed under the name of 'Francinet'. The latter said that he often heard an urgent wish expressed to leave France and readily agreed to act as Fourrier's agent in exchange for a share of the commission payable.

There is no reason to think that either man had any suspicion that the underground escape route Petiot professed to control was entirely imaginery. Their business was merely to introduce prospective clients to him and to draw their commission calculated on the fees paid. Naturally they asked no questions. It was impossible therefore for them to disclose to the authorities what he was really doing. And Petiot ran no risk that they would betray him as a person operating an escape route: believing him to be a member of 'La Résistance', they would know what fate would be meted out to them by 'La Résistance' in the event of their betraying an escape route to the Gestapo.

Dr. Petiot purchased 21 Rue Lesueur in September 1941, and it would not have taken the builders long to complete the alterations which he required. Not one of his clients survived to describe their experiences after they had decided to avail themselves of the services which he offered to them. What these experiences were, therefore, must always remain a matter for conjecture. His trial in March 1946 threw surprisingly little light on what those experiences must have been. We may conveniently pause at this point, therefore, to consider what purpose his structural alterations to his new property might have served. What would a visitor to 21 Rue Lesueur have undoubtedly found had he made an appointment to meet Dr. Petiot there after these alterations had been carried out?

The front door would be opened by Dr. Petiot himself, who would explain that he was alone in the house as a precautionary measure. The visitor would then be ushered into a well-furnished front room, the blinds of which would be drawn to guard against observation by any agents of the Gestapo who might be lurking in the street. Seated in a comfortable armchair, the visitor would then discuss his business with his host seated at his desk. If the visitor on any pretext was asked to enter the next room, naturally his polite host would insist that his visitor went first. If instead of following him, his host had quietly closed the door behind him, the visitor would have found himself shut in a small, bare, triangular apartment, artificially lighted, with the window on the right bricked up, and only a small aperture, filled with plate glass, high up on the wall on the left. In front of him the visitor would see a door which naturally he would try to open. He would soon find, however, that this was only a dummy door fixed to the wall. Having made this disturbing discovery, the visitor would naturally atempt to retrace his steps into the doctor's reception room, only to find that the door had been securely shut. Expostulations and shouts for help would be fruitless since this triangular apartment had, as we have seen, been rendered sound proof.

Up to this point we are on sure ground. The triangular apartment would serve admirably as a trap for an unsuspecting visitor: it is difficult to say what other purpose it could have served. It only remains to add that if a visitor who found himself shut in this triangular, windowless, sound-proof apartment, died there in some way never fully cleared up, there would be no reason why the police should ever learn of the death. Petiot was a trained anatomist to whom the dismemberment of a body would present no difficulties: the house contained a boiler which could be used for the disposal of dissected remains: and for anything left over in the boiler there was a pit in the yard at the rear of the house, sheltered by a high wall from the observation of inquisitive neighbours, and a supply of quicklime in which such remains could be buried.

One feature of this triangular apartment deserves mention if only because it aroused more interest and horrifying speculation than any other feature. On the wall opposite the little plate glass window half a dozen steel hooks had been fixed at varying heights from the floor. No evidence was given at the trial establishing the purpose these hooks were intended to serve: it was not proved whether they had been put there by Petiot or by some earlier occupier of the house. The French Press eagerly adopted the theory that Petiot had provided these hooks so that he could hang from them his dying victims—"par le viseur il prenait un sadique plaisir à contempler leur agonie." The triangular apartment was dubbed 'La Cellule de Torture.'

In complete default of any evidence of sadistic tendencies in Petiot, it is hard to believe that he allowed himself to be distracted from the carrying out of his practical aims swiftly and efficiently by indulging in sadistic gloating over his victims. Until further information comes to light it seems better to dismiss the problem of these hooks on the wall as one of the unsolved mysteries of this extraordinary case.

At his trial which began on the 18th March, 1946, the prosecution named twenty-seven persons whom they alleged had been done to death by Petiot, and produced facts in evidence in support of each of these charges. In most of these twenty-seven cases, however, these facts only proved that Petiot had been in close association with persons who were missing, that he had weighty reasons for wishing that these persons should disappear, and that all these persons had disappeared mysteriously without trace.

In four cases, however, definite evidence linking Petiot with the missing persons was produced by the prosecution in the shape of property and garments proved to have belonged to them which were found by the police in forty-nine suitcases at the house of a bicycle dealer named Neuhausen in Courson-les-Carrieres. It was established beyond question that at the time of his arrest by the Gestapo, Petiot had sent away these suitcases by road from 21 Rue Lesueur. A neighbour came forward to say that she had seen a lorry being loaded with suitcases outside 21 Rue Lesueur, and by tracing the lorry driver the police at last found them in the loft of Neuhausen's house. These suitcases were found to be packed with a varied assortment of clothing and such personal effects as lip-sticks, powder boxes, toothbrushes and handkerchiefs. A few items of this property was subsequently identified as having belonged to persons with whose murder Petiot was charged.

On his part, Dr. Petiot admitted responsibility for the death of no less than sixty-three people. Of these, he claimed, thirty were Germans and the remaining thirty-three were French collaborators. He made no attempt to give the names of all these people but admitted responsibility in eight of the cases included in the twenty-seven charges brought against him by the prosecution.

It would require a lengthy book to set out in detail the facts and circumstances of all the twenty-seven charges brought against him. The facts in all these twenty-seven cases were, however, very similar and in most of them precise details are lacking.

Here, it is proposed to exclude from mention a number of early cases which were unconnected with Petiot's underground travel agency. Thus, among the charges brought against him at his trial was responsibility for the disappearance and presumably for the death of a certain Jan Van Bever, a young man who had denounced him to the Police as a drug trafficker. Very similar was the case of a Madame Kahid who had complained that her daughter, a drug-addict, had obtained her supplies of heroin from him. A third example is that of Mlle. Denise Hotin, a young woman who had secured an abortion with Dr. Petiot's aid and who, he had good reason to fear, was being subjected to pressure to disclose the facts to the police.

In each of these cases, one fact was established beyond question: M. Van Bever, Mme. Kahid, and Mlle. Hotin all disappeared suddenly and completely. In each case, also, it could be shown that Petiot had the best of reasons for welcoming an early and complete disappearance. But in none of these cases was there any direct evidence against him and apart from his later career as a whole-sale killer, it is doubtful if any court would have convicted him on any one of these three charges, had it been dealt with alone, without regard to the mass of evidence indicating that he had adopted murder as a means of livelihood.

It will be sufficient here to deal with only those cases in which either direct evidence incriminating Petiot was produced by the prosecution in the shape of property or clothes belonging to his victims which were later found in Petiot's possession, or in which Petiot admitted having killed the persons in question but claimed that he had killed them for patriotic reasons.

The case of the Kneller family is one in which the evidence against Dr. Petiot was particularly strong, although he did not see fit to give to the Court any explanation concerning it. Kurt Kneller was a German renegade, born in Breslau in 1897, who had fled from Germany in 1933—no doubt for such excellent reasons as an interest in Communism or for some criminal activities. On the outbreak of war in 1939, Kneller enrolled in the French Foreign Legion to fight against his own country. After the surrender of France in the following year, he returned to Paris with his wife, also a German, and their son René, aged seven. At first they were not molested but at the time Kneller first came into contact with Dr. Petiot, he had had one narrow escape from arrest by the Gestapo and was living in hiding with his wife in the flat of a friend, a Mme. Noé, having left René in the charge of the child's godmother, a Mme. Roart. Petiot was most sympathetic and encouraging. They could rely on him to make all arrangements for their immediate escape from France with their possessions. He advised, however, that it would be imprudent for the whole family to travel together: it would be safer, he said, if he and Kurt Kneller went first and then he would return to escort Mme. Kneller and little René out of occupied territory.

As far as his victims and their friends were concerned, the doctor was perfectly open about the part which he was playing in the matter—by his manner he implied that from human sympathy and patriotic zeal he was risking his life to help them and that he did so with complete confidence in their loyalty. Blinded by gratitude, it naturally did not occur to anyone whether *they* could rely with equal confidence on *him*. No one could have been more considerate and indefatigably helpful than Dr. Petiot. He, himself, called at Mme. Noé's flat taking with him two trunks and four suitcases and assisted that lady and Mme. Kneller to pack all the family possessions. He also called at Mme. Roart's house and arranged for the child to join his parents at Mme. Noé's flat. A few days later, he called at Mme. Noé's flat, and Kurt Kneller, having said goodbye to his wife and child, left the flat in the company of his preserver. He was last seen entering a station of the

Paris underground—no doubt on the way to the doctor's premises in the Rue Lesueur.

The next day, Mme. Kneller brought little René to Mme. Noé's flat and the following morning Mme. Noé saw them both leave in the company of Dr. Petiot. Neither of them was ever seen again. Shortly afterwards Petiot called with a large box in which he packed the remaining possessions of the Knellers. He left with this box and did not return. After about two weeks Mme. Roart, the child's godmother, received a card purporting to come from Mme. Kneller stating that Kurt Kneller had been taken ill. A later card merely stated that Kurt Kneller had not recovered. Nothing further was ever heard of the Kneller family. When the police searched the forty-nine suitcases from the cellar of 21 Rue Lesueur, they found certain garments and linen which were identified as having belonged to the Knellers, including the pink pyjamas of poor little René Kneller.

Although Dr. Petiot made no admission concerning the fate of the Kneller family, no reasonable doubt can exist as to what was their fate. Equally well established was his guilt relating to the disappearance of the Woolf family. Not only were some clothes found in the suitcases removed from 21 Rue Lesueur identified as having belonged to the Woolf family, but Dr. Petiot coolly admited responsibility for their fate. Or to put his atittude more correctly, he claimed the credit of having "disposed" of them, a fate which, he said, they richly merited since they were, he had discovered, collaborators and secret agents of the Gestapo.

The case of the Woolf family deserves description in some detail as the facts were clearly established and they will serve to illustrate Dr. Petiot's modus operandi which he no doubt followed in most of his crimes. In particular, this case illustrates how Dr. Petiot established contact with his client-victims and the skilful way in which he obtained their confidence and induced them to avail themselves of his services.

Some time towards the end of 1942 a lady dentist, a Mme. Gingold, practising in Paris, happened to mention to a patient of hers, a Mme. Eryane Kahan, that her doctor had told her that a patient of his had told him that there existed a secret underground organization for smuggling people out of occupied territory. This organization was directed by a Paris doctor whose name, however, he did not disclose. The two ladies agreed that this information was very useful to have in such troubled times.

Shortly afterwards, the lady dentist asked her patient if she could find accommodation in the house where she lived for three acquaintances of hers. So Mme. Kahan made enquiries of her landlord, there proved to be an unoccupied apartment and Mme. Gingold's acquaintances became the tenants. They consisted of a young Dutch Jew named Maurice Woolf, his wife, Liane Woolf, and Maurice Woolf's mother, Rachel Marx. All three had left Germany in 1933 and had taken up their residence in France, bringing with them considerable wealth. In France they had adopted the name of 'Walbert'.

In the course of conversation, Mme. Kahan happened to mention to her new neighbours that she had been told that there existed means of leaving occupied territory for those wishing to do so. The Woolfs declared vehemently that their one desire was to leave France at the earliest possible moment. Mme. Kahan replied that she quite understood how they must feel: in fact, if it could be arranged, she would be delighted to go with them. Mme. Gingold's friend, the doctor, was approached discreetly but all he could do was to put them in touch with the patient who had told him about the existence of this secret organization, said to be directed by a mysterious doctor. In due course, an interview was arranged between Mme. Kahan and this patient, a denizen of the Parisian underworld known as Henri of Marseilles. This man told Mme. Kahan that he could not tell her the name of the doctor who ran the organization as he did not know it himself, but he would make enquiries among his friends, and would telephone her to tell her what he had found out. Later, in accordance with an anonymous telephone message, Mme. Kahan kept an appointment in a cafe in the Rue Tronchet and was there met by two men who gave their names as Pintard and Fourrier. They informed her that they could assist her to make the arrangements which she desired but warned her that the cost would be 75,000 francs for each person. In reply to her anxious enquiry, they agreed a reduction might be made for a number of people travelling together. Finally they asked 200,000 francs for a party consisting of herself and her three friends.

The price asked seems to have staggered Mme. Kahan. She was still energetically striving to obtain some further reduction when a fourth person unobtrusively joined the group who introduced himself as Dr. Eugène. Mme. Kahan declared that she and her friends did not possess 200,000 francs but they would be able to pay 125,000 francs down and the balance when they arrived in the Argentine.

"Dr. Eugène" sternly rebuked his two touts, Pintard and Fourrier. "We are not blackmarket racketeers", he told Mme. Kahan. "We do this for the cause of France. I will gladly help you for 50,000 francs!" An appointment was immediately made for Dr. Eugène—that is to say, for Dr. Marcel Petiot—to visit the Woolfs at their flat on the following day.

In passing, Petiot's shrewd psychology should be noted. Most of his client-victims would willingly have paid all that they possessed to leave France in safety. But even the dangers which surrounded them could not entirely efface the habits of a lifetime. Safety at any price was most welcome but safety at a bargain basement price was even more welcome. Maurice Woolf rejoiced at his good fortune in having found someone prepared to undertake the hazardous task of arranging the escape of himself and his family from occupied France for so small a payment as 50,000 francs—the equivalent of £450. No doubt he dismissed the doctor as a fool who could be left to find out for himself later what was the market price for the services which he was offering. Acting on a sudden impulse, Mme. Kahan declared that she had decided to remain in Paris. But this decision did not discourage the Woolfs. Dr. Petiot told them they could take two suitcases each and urged them to take with them their most valuable possessions, pointing out the impossibility of finding a place of safety for what they left behind. Helpful as ever, Dr. Petiot left in a taxi with the suitcases "to take them to the station". Next day he returned, and Mme. Kahan said goodbye to her friends, probably half regretting the impulse which had caused her not to accompany them. In accordance with the doctor's directions, the two ladies carried, securely hidden on their persons, all their best jewellery.

On that day the Woolf family vanished without trace. Some of their clothes were later found by the police in Marcel Petiot's cellar at 21 Rue Lesueur. Eryane Kahan, thanks to her unreasoning impulse, survived and gave evidence against Petiot at his trial.

No doubt can exist as to the fate which overtook Maurice Woolf his wife and mother, since apart from the clothes identified as belonging to them found in his suitcases, at his trial he frankly admitted having "disposed" of them as collaborators. Although he produced no evidence in support of this allegation, it remains nevertheless quite possible that this allegation was true. Many prudent people in the position of Maurice Woolf tried to secure themselves doubly by joining organizations of both sides. In 1942, it had not become clear which side was going to win. When one side or the other had at last achieved victory, one could always explain away membership of an organization of the defeated side, by saying that one had only joined it in order to betray it.

The disposal of the Woolf family was one of the most profitable of all Dr. Petiot's undertakings. Not only did he collect a considerable sum in money and jewellery but it led directly to another profitable undertaking. Shortly after the Woolfs had departed with Dr. Petiot on the first stage of their journey to the Argentine, another young couple called at Mme. Kahan's flat: their name was Basch and like the Woolfs they were political exiles. They belonged to a wealthy family of Dutch Jews. They explained to Mme. Kahan that they were friends of Maurice Woolf and his wife who, they had been told, were proposing to go abroad. They would like to go with them.

Mme. Kahan replied that the Woolfs had already left and were by this time probably already in South America. She could, however, put them in touch with the patriotic gentleman who had arranged their journey. No doubt he would be prepared to perform the same service for them.

Needless to say, Dr. Petiot's services were entirely at their disposal. He assured them that they could rely on him to arrange that they joined their friends at an early date. In due course they departed in his company and were never seen again. Clothes identified as the property of Gilbert Basch were later found in the forty-nine suitcases from Dr. Petiot's cellar. At his trial, Petiot admitted this "disposal", explaining this by alleging that both Basch and his wife were agents of the Gestapo, an allegation which, for the reason given above, may possibly have been true.

Some six months after the disappearance of Gilbert Basch and his wife, some time in June 1942, Petiot met at a bridge party a Dr. Paul Braunberger, a distinguished doctor of medicine, a man of some sixty-six years of age. After Petiot had left, Dr. Braunberger told the other guests how much he had enjoyed talking with him. The conversation, however, had not been entirely about professional matters. Dr. Braunberger had mentioned how much he would welcome an opportunity to leave occupied territory and Dr. Petiot had replied that he knew of means by which this would be readily achieved. Not long afterwards Dr. Braunberger, in response to a mysterious telephone call, left to keep an appointment from which he never returned. In the days following Mme. Braunberger received several mysterious letters, purporting to come from her husband, directing her to make arrangements to join him in unoccupied France, bringing to a certain meeting place in Paris all her most valuable possessions with her. The mode of address and the style of these letters however aroused Mme. Braunberger's suspicions. She decided not to comply with the directions given her and no doubt as a result, survived. There can be no reason to doubt what was Dr. Braunberger's fate since his hat was found by the police in one of Dr. Petiot's suitcases.

One further case must be mentioned here as it shows that Dr.

Petiot did not limit his activities to rich political exiles who desired to be smuggled out of occupied territory. As in the case of that great Victorian pioneer of the travel agency business, Mr. Thomas Cook, the services of Dr. Marcel Petiot were at the disposal of anyone who desired to avail themselves of them and had sufficient cash to pay for them.

Dr. Marcel Petiot was a lone wolf of crime. He had no confederates entitled to a share in the profits and in a position to betray him. Thus the role of his former patient, Raoul Fourrier, and the latter's friend, Edmund Pintard, alias Francinet, was merely to frequent the bars and night clubs of Montmartre in order to contact any person who had expressed a desire to leave occupied territory. As we have seen, for this service they were paid commission for each client introduced and no doubt they in turn let it be known that they themselves would make it worth the while of anyone who introduced would-be travellers to them. One day Pintard was approached by a professional criminal whose real name was Joseph Reocreaux but who was generally known as "Jo the Boxer". This man said that he was seeking an opportunity to emigrate to South America and understood Pintard could help him. Pintard replied guardedly he knew a "Dr. Eugène" who might be able to help him.

An appointment was arranged between Jo the Boxer and "Dr. Eugène". Jo the Boxer explained that the French civil police were searching for him in connection with a profitable stroke of business which he had carried out in Hautefort, near Toulouse. He, and another professional criminal named Estebesteguy, generally known as "Adrien the Basque", and two other men had just carried out a daring coup. Masquerading as members of the German Security Police, they had gone to the house of a certain M. Emile Joulet, held up the occupants with their revolvers and searched the premises. They had found over 2,300 gold dollars and 530 gold napoleons, besides 7,000 dollars and 500,000 francs in notes. To escape the police of Marshal Pétain's government, they had fled to occupied territory. Now, Jo the Boxer explained, he desired to go abroad, taking with him his two mistresses, Mlle. Annette Petit and Mlle. Claudia Chamoux and a male friend, Francois Albertini, known as "Francois the Strong". The latter ultimately decided to bring his mistress along with him.

As ever, Dr. Petiot was most sympathetic and understanding. He confirmed that he controlled an admirably arranged escape route and providing the terms could be agreed, they could be assured that all five of them would soon be in the Argentine.

The terms were quickly agreed, and the money paid. Dr.

Petiot declared that a party of five was too many for safety and so it was arranged that Jo the Boxer and Mlle. Petit should set forth with him first by the escape route and that he should then return to escort Francois the Strong and the other two women. Everything went accordingly to plan—Dr. Petiot's plan, that is to say. Not one of those five people was ever seen or heard of again.

There is no direct evidence linking Petiot with their disappearance. It might indeed be possible to believe that all five are still alive and well in South America. Dr. Petiot, however, frankly admitted disposing of them on the grounds that they were agents of the Gestapo, and there is no reason to doubt that he spoke truly. And this case is linked with a later case in which, in addition to an admission by Petiot, property of the persons in question were later found in his possession.

In the spring of 1943, shortly before Dr. Petiot was driven out of business by force of circumstances, he received a visit from Adrien Estebesteguy, popularly known as "Adrien the Basque", who had been one· of Jo the Boxer's confederates in the hold-up at Hautefort. Adrien was accompanied by a man whom he introduced as Joseph Piereschi.

"I am given to understand", Estebesteguy explained, "that you arranged a trip to the Argentine for my close friend, Jo the Boxer, and some friends of his. I and my friend Piereschi also urgently desire to leave France at once. You may name your price—money is no object to me. But we want to leave and as soon as possible".

It is unnecessary to· state what was Dr. Petiot's response to so open-handed a proposal. Both men had plenty of money. Estebesteguy who had a long criminal record, still had his share of the booty from the Hautefort hold-up. He had not tried to escape from France at once like his friend, Jo the Boxer, because he was in close association with a man named Lafont who was one of the chiefs of the political police of the Vichy Government. Recently, however, he had imprudently quarrelled with Lafont and so could no longer rely on his protection. Piereschi also had plenty of money since he had just escaped from prison while awaiting trial for a robbery in Marseilles in which nearly 1,000,000 francs had been stolen. A Corsican by birth, popularly known in the Parisian underworld as "Ge", he boasted as long a criminal record as his friend Estebesteguy, starting with a term of penal servitude at the age of eighteen for manslaughter.

All the necessary arrangements were quickly made. Both men desired to take their mistresses with them. Estebesteguy's mistress, Gisele Rossmy, told a friend shortly before the departure that the price charged was 100,000 francs per person. She and Estebesteguy set forth in the company of Dr. Petiot during the last week of March 1943—a couple of days later Dr. Petiot returned to escort Piereschi and his mistress, Paulette Grippay. Paulette Grippay's black satin dress and some shirts belonging to Estebesteguy were later found by the police among Dr. Petiot's effects.

From the facts stated above it can be said that it has been established beyond all doubt that Dr. Petiot was responsible for the deaths of at least eighteen persons, that is to say for the deaths of Kurt Kneller, his wife and child, of Maurice Woolf, his wife and mother, of Gilbert Basch and his wife, of Dr. Paul Braunberger, of Jo the Boxer, Francois Albertini and their three girl friends, and of Estebestguy, Piereschi, Mlle. Rossmy and Mlle. Grippay.

In view of this staggering total of eighteen persons concerning whose fate no shadow of doubt can exist, it seems hardly worth while to undertake an inquiry whether Petiot was also responsible for the death of some, all or any of the other persons named by the prosecution as his victims. Probably he was guilty in the majority of these cases. Probably also, although nothing more than grounds for suspicion exist, he was guilty of such crimes as the murder of Mme. Debauve early in his career as a young doctor at Villeneuve-sur-Yonne. Probably also he was responsible for a number of other murders for which he was never suspected. His own figure of sixty-three victims may well have been an underestimate.

Knowing as a certainty that Dr. Petiot murdered at least eighteen persons, we may now turn to enquire what exactly was the method employed by him. It is a curious fact that the police investigation never cleared up this interesting question. No conclusive evidence on the subject was given at the trial. Mr. Alister Kershaw inclines to the view that it was the doctor's custom at the final meeting with his client-victims in his reception room in the Rue Lesueur to advise them, as a medical man, that they ought to be inoculated against the diseases to which they might be exposed during their travels. On the pretence of inoculating them, Petiot would then inject some deadly drug. Any objections raised to this precautionary measure could be met by pointing out that he could not be expected to take charge of anyone liable to fall ill during the journey: delay caused by illness would put in peril the lives of all taking part.

An alternative suggestion is that the polite doctor at the termination of the interview insisted that his client-victims should drink with him a glass of wine to the success of the journey. The wine given them would of course be poisoned.

There is yet another possible solution. The triangular apartment could have been adapted to serve as a home-made gas chamber. In that case, we must picture the doctor, having politely ushered his client-victim through the doorway leading from his reception room into this triangular apartment, and having securely fastened the door behind him, turning on a tap which allowed some deadly gas to enter the apartment.

To the present writer it seems strange that if this were the method adopted, the fact was not later established by the discovery of at least traces of the equipemnt used to fill the apartment with poison gas. Perhaps, however, Petiot dispensed with equipment and achieved his purpose by tossing into the apartment a gas bomb which broke on impact the instant before he closed the door on his doomed client.

It is of course possible that Petiot varied his technique in accordance with the client with whom he had to deal. Obviously a method which might have been adequate in the case of poor old Dr. Braunberger might not have been suitable in the case of the ex-Legionnaire, Kurt Kneller, who probably came to the interview armed, still less in the case of dangerous criminals like Jo the Boxer or Estebesteguy who no doubt never stirred abroad without an arsenal of revolvers and knives on their persons. Whether inoffensive or formidable, everyone who passed into that triangular apartment passed on via the boiler in the cellar to the quicklime in the inspection pit in the courtyard.

Inevitably the discreet publicity campaign of Messrs. Fourrier and Pintard at length reached the ears of some agent of the Gestapo. The Germans were always keenly on the alert for any rumour which might lead them to the discovery of one of the underground escape routes out of occupied territory used by their foes. The Gestapo decided to investigate the activities of this "Dr. Eugène", whom they soon identified as Dr. Petiot. A certain Alsatian Jew named Yvan, who was a genuine member of 'La Résistance' had fallen into their hands and was awaiting his inevitable fate. The Gestapo offered him a large reward and a free passage to Spain if he would present himself to Dr. Petiot as a person desiring to escape out of occupied territory. Yvan was only too happy to agree. He contacted Dr. Petiot, paid the fee demanded—the Gestapo supplied the money—and in due course presented himself at 21 Rue Lesueur. Presumably he was dealt with in accordance with the doctor's usual technique: at all events he was never seen again by the Gestapo or anyone else.

The Gestapo was puzzled by the mysterious disappearance of their agent but in the end assumed that he had double-crossed them. They decided to adopt direct methods. Dr. Petiot was arrested. The charge against him was that he had aided the departure "of persons having an interest in leaving France". This charge, Petiot indignantly denied: he knew nothing about escape routes or resistance movements. The Gestapo searched his home in the Rue Caumartin but omitted to visit his house in the Rue Lesueur. After some eight months he was released for want of evidence against him.

This is truly most astonishing. We have always been led to believe that the Gestapo was as indifferent to the production of admissable legal evidence against their victims as any war-crimes tribunal. We have been assured that they acted on the principle, later formulated by the London Agreement governing the Nürnberg Trials, that any allegation, whether admissable as evidence or not, could be accepted against a prisoner if it was expedient to deem it as having probative value. There is certainly an unexplained mystery attaching to Petiot's release. The most likely explanation seems to be that as a result of his thriving business in the Rue Lesueur, Petiot was in possession of large funds. No doubt many of the Gestapo chiefs suffered from the general demoralisation and were not inaccessible to bribery.

Petiot's downfall was brought about by a simple stroke of bad luck on his part. On March 11th 1944, some six months after his release by the Gestapo and very shortly after the successful disposal of Estebesteguy and his friends, something went wrong with the boiler in the cellar at 21 Rue Lesuer. The occupier of the adjoining house telephoned the police to complain that a noisome black smoke was issuing from the chimney of the premises next door. On arrival the police found a card pinned on the door of No. 21 inviting callers to communicate with 66 Rue Caumartin. The police telephoned this address: someone, no doubt Dr. Petiot himself, answered the phone and promised to come over at once to help them deal with the smoking chimney. He took so long in doing so, however, and as the oily black smoke continued to pour from the chimney in ever increasing quantities, the police came to the conclusion that the house must be on fire. They therefore summoned the fire brigade and without waiting for the appearance of the owner, forced an entry into the house through a window.

The smoke was clearly coming from the cellar. On entering the police found before them an astonishing and horrible spectacle. The floor of the cellar was littered with human remains, afterwards estimated to have come from at least ten persons. There were numerous leg bones, several human hands, a human skull half reduced to ashes and two nearly complete skeletons. The noisome smoke proceeded from the boiler in which further human remains were being consumed.

Shortly after this gruesome discovery had been made, a short, dark, clean-shaven man arrived at the house on a bicycle. He described himself as the brother of the owner, Dr. Marcel Petiot. He was invited to enter and was conducted to the cellar. Then followed a scene which will remain for ever memorable in the history of crime.

Holding a handkerchief to his nose, Petiot—for of course the caller was Petiot himself—surveyed the ghastly spectacle before him and then turned coolly to the assembled police officers and firemen. "I risk my life here", he remarked. "No, it is not as you may think. You have happened to come across the execution chamber of a group of 'La Résistance'. Here the Boches and their collaborators vanish—particularly the most troublesome ones!"

The explanation to Petiot's hearers seemed reasonable and adequate. It was common knowledge that a number of terrorist gangs had become extremely active of late in Paris. The French police had been receiving frequent complaints from the occupying authorities that German soldiers were continually vanishing without trace. Also numerous French citizens who had collaborated with the occupying forces had mysteriously disappeared. Everyone assumed that all these missing persons had been kidnapped and murdered as part of the great terrorist campaign then raging throughout France, preparatory to the Anglo-American invasion which was expected to take place at any moment. Clearly 21 Rue Lesueur was the headquarters of one of these gangs.

The police officers who had come to investigate a smoking chimney had no wish to become involved in a political matter. If they arrested this patriot they might later find themselves dealt with as collaborators. Anyway as these human remains were apparently those of German soldiers and French collaborators, the least said about the subject the better. In France in 1944 murder had long ceased to be murder. "Slip away quickly, mon vieux", whispered one of the officers. "But don't be seen in this neighbourhood again or we may be compelled to arrest you as a criminal". Petiot thanked them briefly in the name of 'La Résistance', turned on his heel, left the house, mounted his bicycle and disappeared down the street. He was not seen again by the police for seven months.

When however the episode was reported at police headquarters a very different view was taken of it. Reference to the dossier of Dr. Marcel Petiot revealed that he was a man against whom the gravest suspicions had been recorded, a man upon whom the police had long kept an eye as a known drug-trafficker and abortionist. Immediately a frantic search was launched to find the plausible gentleman who had been so foolishly allowed to cycle away from his house by the police on the day on which they had discovered the crimes which he had been committing there. Mme. Petiot, Petiot's brother, Maurice Petiot, and the two touts, Fourrier and Pintarch, were at once arrested. Some suitcases known to have been sent away by Petiot from 21 Rue Lesueur at the time of his arrest by the Gestapo were traced by the police to an attic of a bicycle dealer named Neuhausen living at Courson-les-Carrieres. Both Neuhausen and his wife were promptly arrested. The news that Petiot had been seen was reported from all over France. Nevertheless the doctor remained missing. It was as if the earth had opened and swallowed him up.

On the 6th June 1944 the long expected Anglo-American invasion took place and on the 24th August the Germans evacuated Paris and withdrew eastward. There followed an orgy of jubilation and homicide. The Communists set about the congenial task of liquidating their opponents. Anyone who had made himself prominent as an opponent of Communism was liable to denunciation as a collaborator and to summary arrest and execution, the accusers of the victim acting as judges of their own charges. Not only were thousands of suspected collaborators summarily shot but anyone with personal enemies or who was believed to be worth while robbing was liable to denunciation and execution. Such executions took many different forms. To quote Mr. Sisley Huddleston's *"France: The Tragic Years, 1939-1947"*: —

"The mob, after the manner of mobs in all countries, joined in lynching parties without stopping to enquire what offence had been committed. There were professional criminals who had the chance of their lives to kill and rob with impunity and were responsible for many revolting happenings. Even more shocking were the crimes committed by normally respectable people whose sadistic instincts were aroused and given free reign. There were many cases of personal revenge with no public basis whatever. And there was a great deal of terrorism carried out with purely radical revolutionary aims: the opportunity for the suppression of opponents was too good to be lost".*

The official custodians of law and order, the gendarmes, jailors, magistrates and judges, were hardly less arbitrary and ferocious than the lynching parties. As one example the case may

* "France: The Tragic Years, 1939-1947" by Sisley Huddleston (Devin-Adair, New York, 1955), Page 301.

be cited of Louis Renault, inventor, pioneer of the automobile industry and one of the greatest industrialists of his age. During the critical days of 1918 a great new host of light tanks, designed and built in his factory, turned defeat into victory. At the end of the war he was the only civilian upon whom was awarded the rank of Officer of the Legion of Honour. But in 1944 his outstanding services to France counted for nothing against the long accumulated resentment felt against him in Leftist circles for his many triumphs in industrial disputes. The Front Populaire denounced him as 'the ogre of Billancourt'. He was arrested as a collaborator. After interrogation in his cell, he was removed to hospital a physical and mental wreck. He died of cerebral haemorrhage: an X-ray photograph disclosed a fracture of the first cervical vertebrate, the result of a blow or kick delivered during his interrogation. The authorities curtly refused an enquiry. Although no charge had been made against him, his estate was confiscated.*

The case of Louis Renault is only exceptional because his family had the courage, tenacity and the resources to batter away at the wall of official indifference and evasion. After four years the decree of confiscation was set aside as invalid. In the majority of cases, the relations of persons lynched, judicially executed or murdered during 'interrogation' were terrorised into silence by the fear of suffering the same fate.

According to H. Adrien Tixier, a Socialist who in March 1945 became Minister of the Interior in General de Gaulle's cabinet, between August 1944 and March 1945 there were 105,000 executions. Presumably officially approved lynchings were included by him under the heading 'executions'. No tidings of this blood-bath reached the outside world. Such foreign observers as Mr. Hampden Jackson, quoted above, were able to enjoy "Wordsworthian reactions" thanks to the innocence of their hearts and the curtain of silence drawn around the subject. Deprived of all information concerning what was really happening, they were left free to picture a reign of "unity and brotherly love, a sense of democratic rebirth" which they guilelessly assumed would be the natural result of Liberation.

The time of the new police force established by General de Gaulle's regime was very fully occupied. Their former colleagues who had remained loyal to Marshal Pétain's regime had to be hunted down and arrested: the processions of naked women being paraded through the streets had to be supervised to prevent traffic obstructions: the lynching mobs often required professional assistance in tracking down their victims. Nevertheless, in spite of all

* "Renault" by Saint Loup, Bodley Head, London, 1957.

these distractions the search for Dr. Petiot continued. In the end an act of foolish imprudence on his own part led to his discovery. Several newspapers had declared that the infamous murderer of the Rue Lesueur was a Gestapo agent and at last Petiot was goaded into writing an anonymous letter to the Press indignantly denying the charge and claiming that he was a member of 'La Résistance'. The handwriting of the letter was compared with the handwriting of various leaders of Résistance groups and it was found to tally with that of a Captain Henri Valèry, an energetic officer of the movement stationed at Reuilly.

The police paid a surprise visit to the office of Captain Valèry. They found him immersed in his patriotic duties, including no doubt the preparation of lists of men who were to face a firing squad and of women who were to have their heads shaved in public. Although he had only joined 'La Résistance' six weeks before, he had risen to the rank of Captain, and was awaiting embarkation orders to proceed to Indo-China with the rank of Major, there to take part in the suppression of the revolt which had broken out in that distant province of the French colonial empire. In spite of the beard which he had grown since he had cycled away from the Rue Lesueur nine months before, Petiot was easily identified. On him were found some £300 in francs and a number of identity and membership cards, including one showing that he was a member of the Communist Party. A ration book found on him was later found to have belonged to the unfortunate little René Kneller. Petiot was at once arrested.

The trial of Dr. Marcel Petiot began on the 18th March 1946 before the Assize Court of the Seine. Just as the career of the accused occupies a unique place in the annals of crime, so the trial which ended with his conviction is without a parallel in the history of jurisprudence. Few criminal trials are of greater interest to historians, and particularly to historians interested in the social history of Europe during the 20th century, since not even the story of Belsen shows more clearly the state of utter demoralisation to which a leading European state could sink during the Second World War. To lawyers, on the other hand, this trial is of little interest. The legal conceptions accepted without question by the Court must seem to a lawyer fantastic and repugnant, a gross caricature of hitherto universally accepted legal principles. In all civilised countries, the issue at a murder trial is invariably a simple one, since the definition of murder in all civilised countries is essentially the same. If the accused person be admittedly sane, and if it can be proved that he killed "with malice aforethought" without legal justification, conviction naturally follows.

But in France in 1945 the principle had become tacitly accepted that a French civilian who struck a knife in the back of a German soldier was not guilty of any offence in law, such an act being a patriotic duty worthy of commendation. This principle had soon become extended to cover cases in which French citizens cut the throats of other French citizens who, according to their bona fide belief, had collaborated with the enemies of France. Invariably in such cases the question whether the victim had in fact been guilty of collaboration was held to be a question for the judgment of the self-appointed executioner, and the only issue which could arise for decision by a court of law was whether the judgment of the self-appointed executioner was bona fide. This was often a difficult issue for a court to decide, but in cases when an innocent victim was done to death, due allowance was generally made for the patriotic if misguided zeal of the self-appointed executioner.

The few criminologists who have investigated the case of Dr. Marcel Petiot have treated his guilt as self-evident and have passed over his defence as merely a demonstration of his matchless effrontery. But Petiot's defence was not so treated by the Court. In a nutshell his defence was that he was the leader of a secret terrorist organisation known, so he revealed, as Groupe Fly-Tox. The business of this organisation was to kidnap German soldiers and French citizens who, according to his bona fide belief, were collaborators, murder them and dispose of their bodies at the headquarters of the organisation at 21 Rue Lesueur. In all, his organisation had disposed of some sixty-three persons in this way, of whom some thirty were German soldiers.

It may seem somewhat astonishing to the British reader that the Assize Court of the Seine should have treated such a defence as this as worthy of anxious consideration. The attitude of the Court at the trial of Dr. Petiot to terrorist activities appears astonishing to a British reader because later and painful experience of terrorist activities has caused him to revise the opinion which he himself probably held in 1945 on the subject. In 1945 terrorism carried out by gangs of civilians was a novel phenomenon and the only victims at that date had been German soldiers and persons believed to have been friendly with them. Since that date, however, British soldiers have been the victims of exactly similar murderous activities in Egypt, Palestine and Cyprus. As a result it has become less easy to dismiss the subject by labelling the victims brutal soldiery and their murderers as heroic resistance fighters.

When Dr. Petiot claimed to have directed the activities of a terrorist organisation which he said was known as Groupe Fly-Tox, the members of the Assize Court knew that whether this particular terrorist organisation was a creation of his imagination or not, many terrorist organisations had been operating in Paris and the other chief cities of France and had committed exactly the same outrages which he claimed his organisation had committed. It was these organisations which the Court called to mind when considering Petiot's defence, organisations whose members were being applauded throughout France as national heroes. To the British reader, on the other hand, Petiot's description of the activities of Groupe Fly-Tox calls to mind the activities of such bodies as the Irgun Zvai Leumi and the Stern Gang which committed so many cowardly outrages in Palestine on British soldiers during the period 1946 to 1948.

There was nothing inherently improbable in Petiot's claim to have directed a terrorist organisation in the way he described. Neither was his claim that he believed in good faith that such people as the Woolfs and the Basches had had dealings with the Gestapo, lightly to be dismissed. The Court earnestly entreated Petiot to disclose the names of one person who had helped him to direct Groupe Fly-Tox. All they asked for was corroboration of the existence of this body. Let him only establish that he had been a resistance fighter and then he might be sure that the many errors of judgement which had led to the death of innocent persons would be forgiven him.

But Dr. Petiot would name no one. Or rather he would name no living person: all the persons whom he named as his colleagues in Groupe Fly-Tox proved on investigation to be dead. The leaders of 'La Résistance' professed never to have heard of a terrorist organisation of this name. Petiot claimed that an Argentine diplomat, who he said passed under the name of Dessaix, had helped him to smuggle the victims of Nazi tyranny out of France. But there proved to be no one of this name in the Argentine embassy. Petiot claimed to have invented a secret weapon which he had patriotically given to the Americans. In Washington, however, nothing was known of either him or the secret weapon.

"Petiot", writes M. Paul Gordeaux, "gouailleur, arrogant, vantard, se défend avec autorité, avec adresse, avec humour".* He pointed out that Groupe Fly-Tox naturally kept no written records since it was liable to be raided by the Gestapo at any time. His colleagues in the organisation were distinguished patriots who for reasons of safety passed under assumed names. He declined to disclose their identity without their permission. He himself had been an active member of 'La Résistance' since 1941. He had done

* See concluding article "Petiot" by Paul Gordeaux, in "France-Soir", December 21, 1952.

nothing of which he was ashamed. Far from being charged with crime, he should have been decorated with the Cross of the Liberation as other terrorist chiefs of organisations similar to his had been decorated.

The Court deliberated long and anxiously. It would indeed be a dreadful thing to send to the guillotine a terrorist chief whose dare-devil exploits entitled him to the Cross of the Liberation and a kiss on each cheek by General de Gaulle! The only issue in the case was whether Groupe Fly-Tox had really existed or not. Reluctantly the Court decided that in default of any corroboration this organisation must be treated as a figment of Dr. Peiot's imagination. They decided to convict, comforting themselves with the reflection that if they were wrong, when the news of his conviction was published Petiot's comrades in Groupe Fly-Tox would be sure to come forward to save their chief. Petiot was sentenced to death.

Eighteen months was allowed to pass after Petiot's arrest before he was brought to trial. French justice moves notoriously slowly but it seems likely that in this case the course of law was deliberately delayed in the hope that at the last moment some brother terrorist would come forward to save the accused man. Since no one came forward during this period to testify that any of Petiot's crimes had been committed for 'La Résistance', it was assumed that the judgment of the Assize Court of the Seine was right. On the 24th May 1946 Dr. Marcel Petiot was executed by the guillotine in the Santé Prison.

Dr. Petiot was not only the greatest of French criminals but unquestionably one of the greatest criminals who have ever lived. He possesed iron nerve, great organising ability, complete ruthlessness and an unparalleled capacity to see the possibilities of turning to account a novel situation. The only weakness which can be attributed to him was a propensity to indulge in petty crime. As a result of this strange weakness he several times for no adequate gain unnecessarily attracted the attention of the police to himself. This propensity can be explained by suggesting that he pilfered from letter boxes and stole electric current merely for the pleasure he derived from committing these offences. Alternatively, this propensity can be attributed to kleptomania. If the latter explanation be correct, kleptomania was the one irrational streak in his essentially well-balanced and practical mind.

The discovery of Dr. Petiot's crimes was brought about by a stroke of simple bad luck—an unfortunate combination of a smoking chimney and a querulous neighbour. His capture was brought about by an act of foolish imprudence on his part—the writing of an anonymous letter to the Press denying the allegation that he had been a Gestapo agent. Had he only laid low at Reuilly for only a little while longer, he could have set forth as Major Henri Valéry of the French Army for a life of new experiences and adventures in Indo-China. Had he survived the campaign against the Viet Minh rebels, no one on his return to France as one of the heroes of the defence of Dien Bien Phu would have thought of reviving the by then long forgotten allegations concerning his conduct during the German occupation.

Dr. Petiot's long and successful career of crime must be attributed to his singleness of purpose, his complete indifference to the political passions which distracted his countrymen, and, above all, to his rigid rule to play his own hand unaided by confederates enjoying his confidence and consequently in a position to betray him.

At the same time strange to say, these qualities can be said to have led ultimately to his downfall. His singleness of purpose led him to devote his entire energy to the carrying out of schemes for his personal profit. Apparently, he took no part of any kind in the underground resistance movement until after the discovery of his crimes. He probably dismissed any such activity as dangerous and comparatively unremunerative, for a busy man a waste of time. But some record of such work would have saved his life when the inevitable day of reckoning dawned. Had he devoted a little of his time and energy to carrying through some spectacular resistance exploit, his acquittal by the Assize Court of the Seine would have been certain. With his temperament and rare gifts, we can be sure that he would have carried through successfully and with relish such resistance exploits as the blowing up of the house of some notorious collaborator and his family, or the assassination of some leading German general by some such sensational method as that attempted, fortunately unsuccessfully, by the Cypriot who placed a time bomb beneath the bed of Field Marshal Sir John Harding, the Governor of Cyprus. Petiot would have found such activity highly enjoyable and in the end, when he found himself in the dock, richly rewarded.

Throughout his life Petiot played a lone hand. In the end, when he stood in the dock, there was indeed no one who could betray him. There was in fact no one who knew anything good or bad about him or his doings. When being pressed by the police for information concerning her missing husband, Mme. Petiot remarked, "My husband was not the sort of man of whom one asks questions". Neither she nor the doctor's younger brother, Maurice, who conducted a radio repair business in Auxerre, seem to have had any idea as to what was the real nature of his activities. Mme. Petiot only admitted to the police that he may have used his premises in the Rue Lesueur "to get rid of people reported to him as traitors". Maurice once incautiously confided to a friend that his brother had disposed of at least fifty or sixty collaborators. Both regarded him, quite genuinely, as an heroic resistance fighter.

Dr. Marcel Petiot passed through life without making an intimate friend or a personal enemy. Casual acquaintances liked him: as we have seen, a brother medico, Dr. Braunberger, was much impressed by the medical knowledge which he displayed in a short conversation: when he joined 'La Résistance' a few months before his arrest, he quickly won the regard of his comrades. He certainly knew how to inspire confidence, particularly of women. A few seemed to have felt for him a vague distrust. No one enjoyed his confidence or knew what he really thought or what he was actually doing.

As a consequence, when he stood on trial for his life there was no one who could give corroborating evidence in his favour when corroborating evidence would assuredly have saved him.

CHAPTER V.

THE MARZABOTTO AFFAIR

There is weighty classical authority for the assertion that the inconsistences, follies and hypocrisies of mankind are a constant subject for mirth in the high heavens.

If this be true, the high heavens must have been continually shaken by the resounding laughter of the gods over the political situation which arose in Cyprus in that year of grace 1956. Not that there was anything in the least humorous in the ruthless and treacherous attacks which began in that year on British soldiers stationed in Cyprus as a result of which many were killed and many more injured. In Great Britain, at any rate, this campaign of organised violence aroused nothing but angry indignation, except of course among the British Communists, Fellow-travellers and Leftists. The latter characteristically expressed only solicitude for captured terrorists on whose behalf frantic demands for clemency were always forthcoming. Notwithstanding this noisy clamour by a small minority, public opinion in Great Britain remained firmly convinced that when a terrorist shot a soldier in the back, the only persons entitled to sympathy were the victim and his relations.

Viewed strictly in the abstract, however, the subject had a grimly humorous side. Not only did the Cypriot terrorist organisation, EOKA, use the technique introduced and perfected by the British and their allies during the Second World War for use against the Germans in the occupied countries, but the leaders of EOKA were actually British trained. At the trial of Captain O'Driscoll for man-handling a young Cypriot terrorist, it was disclosed that some ten years before Captain O'Driscoll had trained the EOKA leader, George Grivas, in the secrets of guerilla warfare and underground activity for use against the German occupying forces in Greece. Unfortunately, Grivas proved himself an apt pupil with a retentive memory. What he had been taught by the British in 1944 he remembered in 1955 when he undertook the task of expelling the British from Cyprus.

As the intended gruesome ending did not by a miracle occur, it is hard to deny that there is something humorous in the fact

137

that the time-bomb placed under the bed of the British Governor of Cyprus, Sir John Harding, by a young Cypriot, was of British manufacture, having been supplied to the Greek underground movement in 1944 to be placed, doubtless with similar intent, beneath the bed of a German general. Fortunately after storage for a dozen years this bomb was no longer in working order so that Sir John's slumbers were not disturbed.

But the circumstances which would have most appealed to the peculiar and rather cynical sense of humour which, according to Homer, the gods possess, is that all the time the secret adherents of EOKA were shooting, bombing and stabbing British soldiers there remained in an Italian military prison a certain German major serving a sentence of imprisonment for life for having dealt without proper sympathy and understanding with the adherents of a similar terrorist organisation in 1944!

This major—Walter Reder by name—was accused by the Italians of responsibility for what for want of a more accurate title may be styled the Marzabotto Affair. He was put on trial by an Italian court and, as the reader will not be surprised to hear, convicted. Since then he has remained in prison. A curtain of discreet silence has been drawn around his case so that nothing whatever is known about it by the British or American publics. This blissful ignorance can hardly be justified since in the first place Major Reder was arrested by the Americans: handed over by them to the British, he was in turn handed over by the British to the Italians so that the latter could try their own charges against him.

The British and American publics have indeed been supplied with what purported to be information concerning the Marzabotto Affair. Long since completely forgotten, this information may be briefly summarised as follows.

In September 1944 the German armies in Italy were holding a line about one hundred and thirty miles in length running east and west across Italy from sea to sea. This front was being furiously attacked by numerically superior forces enjoying complete supremacy in the air and undisputed command of the sea on each flank. Towards the end of September, the German troops on the vitally important sector of the front south of Bologna, not content with repulsing repeated attempts to break through, decided for no apparent reason or excuse to attack an open undefended town in their own rear. The small town of Marzabotto was selected for this insane enterprise. Several hundred—some accounts say several thousand—completely inoffensive and defenceless inhabitants of this town, men, women and children, were ruthlessly massacred.

THE MARZABOTTO AFFAIR

One popular version states that this was done by herding them into a church which was then set on fire. Having performed this criminal—and insane—exploit, the perpetrators of this massacre returned to the front, there to repel further desperate attempts by the Americans to break through before the onset of winter. In reliance on this story it has become customary to refer airily to Marzabotto as the Italian Oradour.

Such was the story as it was first presented. Not until long after it had served its purpose as war propaganda did the truth become known. Nothing in any way noteworthy had in fact disturbed the peace of Marzabotto during the Second World War. Like all other towns and villages behind the German front, Marzabotto sustained damage from American bombing. By September 1944 the German front to the south and east of the town had been so far pressed back that Marzabotto came under American shell fire aimed at the German rail and road communications which passed through the town. The following spring the town was evacuated by the Germans without fighting as part of a general withdrawal to the north.

The name Marzabotto, however, continued to be used to label certain fighting which took place on the 29th-30th September 1944 in the mountains lying south of the town. In this fighting the complaint was made that certain Italian Communists carrying on guerilla warfare under the name of the "Stella Rossa" brigade, were encircled and annihilated by German units directed by the above mentioned Major Walter Reder.* His alleged crime or crimes, for which he was condemned to life imprisonment, are now said to have been committed in this mountain fighting which can quite accurately be described as having taken place in the Marzabotto Zone.

At the time this fighting took place in the late summer of 1944, no British, French or American professional soldier had ever been called upon to cope with the problem which then confronted Major Reder, and it is to be feared that for this reason his view of it was long dismissed as unworthy of consideration. To his mind at the time, this self-styled "Red Star Brigade" was nothing but a formidable gang of terrorists, carrying on hostilities contrary to the Geneva Convention one day and posing as inoffensive civilians the next. For long this view was summarily rejected as an indefensible injustice to the memory of a body of "heroic resistance fighters". But now it has become generally admitted that the uniformed soldier attacked by "inoffensive armed civilians" is at least entitled to hold his own opinion on the matter. During the Korean War, American professional soldiers had to deal with

* See Postscript on Page 176.

139

THE MARZABOTTO AFFAIR

several 'Red Star Brigades' operating behind their front: without
hesitation they dealt with Communist guerilla activity in their rear
exactly as Major Reder and his comrades dealt with it during the
campaign in Italy in 1944. In 1955 raids and ambushes by Moroccan
insurgents, and in 1956 raids and ambushes by Algerian insurgents
were dealt with by the French by the same unsympathetic methods:
according to the indignant complaints of the French Communist
and Leftist Press, what may be termed the Oradour technique
was habitually employed against any village near which the
mutilated bodies of ambushed French soldiers were found.* The
The campaigns of the Americans in Korea and of the French in
the mountains and deserts of North Africa are comparable in
difficulty with the German campaign in Italy. Fortunately in Cyprus
the British have only had to contend with isolated outrages without
strategic significance and having politically only a nuisance value.
The survivors of these outrages, however, have reached the same
unsympathetic views of Grivas and his EOKA terrorists as Field
Marshall Kesselring's men reached concerning the terrorists directed
by Mario Musolesi, alias 'Lupo'.

Who was this Mario Musolesi, alias 'Lupo' who was killed
defending his headquarters on Monte Sole, south of Bologna,
on the 29th September 1944? And who was Major Walter Reder,
the German officer who directed these operations which ended
with the death of Mario Musolesi, alias 'Lupo', and the destruction
of the self-styled 'Red Star Brigade' which he commanded? The
story of these operations, which have become known as 'the Marzabotto Affair', is not only interesting in itself but it merits
attention as providing an excellent example of many similar operations
which have taken place since in many widely separated parts of
the world.

Mario Musolesi was born in the district of Bologna, a flourishing industrial city in northern Italy with a quarter of a million
inhabitants. Always strongly left-wing politically, Bologna during
the regime of Mussolini remained a stronghold of the proscribed
Italian Communist Party. The most important fact concerning
his earlier life is that he served in the Italian Army and rose to the
rank of sergeant. What, if any, were his military exploits has
not been recorded: neither is it known when he became a Communist. When Mussolini was overthrown on July 25th 1943 by a

* The report of the committee appointed in 1957 by the French Government to investigate allegations of terrorism by the French forces in
Algeria, long withheld from publication, substantially confirmed these
allegations. See 'Le Monde' of December 13, 1957. In particular it
confirmed that torture had been habitually employed for the interrogation
of suspects.

140

junta of army officers with the connivance of King Victor Emmanual III, Mario Musolesi at once set about establishing in Bologna and the surrounding districts a Communist "SAP" (Squadre di ardimento patriottico), which may be described as the basic unit of a Communist 'combat' organisation, being composed of a few individuals, male and female, who band themselves together to carry out such simple forms of underground activity as the distribution of seditious literature, the collection of subscriptions from sympathisers, and the organisation of secret political gatherings. The main purpose of a "SAP" unit, however, is to serve as the nucleus for the formation of a "GAP" (Gruppe di azione patriottica), a unit which undertakes definite terrorist activities. It was not long before Musolesi's energy and zeal had evolved out of the original "SAP" group established by him a "GAP" unit which operated so skilfully and ruthlessly that it soon became as dangerous for a German soldier to go about Bologna unarmed and alone as it has now become for a British soldier in Nicosia. In addition to the murder of isolated German soldiers caught unawares, Musolesi's "GAP" unit specialised in throwing bombs into passing military vehicles, in acts of sabotage on the railway and in the assassination of leading members of the anti-Communist parties.

It should be stressed that the Communist underground movement in Northern Italy, of which Musolesi soon became one of the most powerful chiefs, began immediately after the downfall of Mussolini's regime in the summer of 1943. Marshal Badoglio's notorious wireless broadcasts from Brindisi urging all Italians as a patriotic duty to murder every German within reach, only began after that military gentleman had fled from Rome and the Anglo-American invasion of Southern Italy had begun. To do them justice, Mario Musolesi and his brother Communists were probably quite uninfluenced by the bloodthirsty exhortations of Badoglio, whom they probably despised, not without justification, as a time-serving be-medalled flunky in the service of that least majestic of monarchs, King Victor Emmanuel III. When the Germans occupied France in 1940, the French Communists had held coldly aloof from what they regarded as a mere capitalist squabble: in 1940 the Third Reich and the Soviet Union had been on the most cordial terms. But in 1943 this capitalist squabble had become in the Communist eyes the great class war which Karl Marx and Lenin had predicted. No Italian Communist therefore had occasion to hesitate for an instant as to the course which he should adopt when the regime of Mussolini collapsed. In 1943 the Third Reich was at war with the Soviet Union: Big Brother Stalin had actually signed a treaty of alliance with the Western Powers, had met their leaders, Roosevelt and Churchill in conference, had shaken their capitalist hands, had made them all sorts of promises in return for material assistance, and had even expressed the opinion that it would be in the interests of Communism if the Western Powers emerged from the war as the apparent victors. With such authoritative guidance, humble Communists like Mario Musolesi had no need for advice or encouragement from Marshal Badoglio whose military gifts were approximately on a level with his political integrity.

In passing it may be observed that Marshal Badoglio's incitements to murder over the wireless from Brindisi in 1944 seem to have faded from memory remarkably quickly and completely. Otherwise it is hard to understand the indignation recently so forcibly expressed in France at the incitements to murder directed to the Algerian insurgents by the Cairo radio. Equally hard to understand is the indignation expressed in the House of Commons concerning the similar incitements to murder directed to the Cypriot terrorists by the Athens radio. Even the British Leftists who denounced attempts to silence the Athens radio by jamming as a violation of the sacred right of free speech, admitted that the language of these broadcasts justified complaint. In all innocence, Field Marshal Sir John Harding told a press conference that never before in the history of the world had responsible men publicly and persistently urged others to commit murder and glorified the most abominable outrages. "No political purpose", the Archbishop of Canterbury solemnly assured the House of Lords, "can excuse deliberate crime!" These weighty words of spiritual guidance should be kept in mind when considering the oratory of Marshal Badoglio and the doings of Mario Musolesi, alias Lupo, and his Red Star Brigade.

Although probably little influenced by Marshal Badoglio's exhortations to commit "deliberate crime", the Italian Communists were not too proud to accept material help provided by those for whom he acted as a docile mouthpiece. The British and American invaders not only supplied him with the wireless equipment for his broadcasts but offered to supply anyone willing to carry his words into effect with the means of doing so. Weapons, ammunition and money were dropped by British and American planes at all the known centres of resistance. Very soon Mario Musolesi found himself able to extend the scope of his operations. No longer had he to be content with arranging for a bomb to be tossed into a passing lorry: convoys of lorries were ambushed in operations in which hundreds of well-armed men took part. In place of an occasional shot fired into the back of some unsuspecting soldier, followed by a wild scamper for safety, his men began organised attacks on small German units which they caught at a disadvantage and in particular on the barracks and headquarters of the Italian police and Fascist Militia. Fierce and often protracted skirmishes began to take place. After these skirmishes the terrorists, instead of scattering and becoming again inoffensive civilians, retreated to prepared strongholds in the mountains.

The following description of an attack on a police barracks will serve as an example of the activities by the Red Star Brigade before it had developed its full strength. In 1945 the Italian Union of Partisans published a booklet entitled "Epopea Partigiana" in which various forms of partisan activity are described and glorified by various contributors. One of the contributors was Bruna Musolesi, a sister of Mario Musolesi, who was an active member of the 'Brigade' with a rank which may be translated "Female Liaison Officer" or perhaps better "Female Courier". Bruna Musolesi writes:

"In May 1944 the police barracks at Marzabotto were attacked. Our 'ragazzi' (lads) disguised themselves in captured uniforms of the Fascist Militia and escorted to the barracks three English soldiers who happened to be with them at the time. They explained to the sentry that the three Englishmen were escaping prisoners of war whom they had captured and wished to hand over. The Police Sergeant in charge opened the gate and was immediately shot dead. A fierce fight ensued in which three of the Militia were killed and three wounded".

"As a result of this gallant exploit", Miss Bruna concludes complacently, "panic spread among the police barracks of the neighbourhood".

At first the activities in Northern Italy of such Communist leaders as Mario Musolesi were treated by the German High Command rather as a nuisance than as a menace. After his rescue from Campo Imperatore by S.S. Major Skorzeny, Mussolini established a new Fascist regime in Northern Italy under the name of the Italian Social Republic. It is customary to refer to the Italian Social Republic as a mere puppet state created by Hitler. In fact it possessed an active, independent life of its own, entirely lacking in that part of Italy which under duress professed allegiance to King Victor Emmanuel. The latter was indeed a puppet state, inspired by no principle or inspiration of any kind. The military clique which had brought about Mussolini's downfall relied for support on a group of ex-Fascists which it distrusted and feared and on the Communist Party in Southern Italy which it distrusted and feared still more. Its sole policy was abject acquiescence to any demand the Allies might be pleased to make. To the support of the Italian Social Republic, on the other hand, there gathered many able and experienced men who had served under Mussolini for twenty years and who knew that their fortunes and probably their lives were at stake. It is not open to dispute that could all foreign influence have been expelled from Italy, the Social Republic led by Mussolini would quickly have extended its jurisdiction throughout Italy.

But of course Mussolini could no more rid himself of German military support than King Victor Emmanuel could persuade the Allies to withdraw their troops from Italian soil. The existence of Marshal Badoglio's regime and the existence of the Italian Social Republic depended solely on the outcome of the Second World War. The respective military strength of the rival regimes in Italy did not influence this outcome in the slightest. Under pressure from President Roosevelt, the unhappy Badoglio announced that his government considered themselves at war with Italy's ally, Germany, and with great difficulty he managed to raise a few units for service in the war on the Allied side. After a short trial, however, Field Marshal Alexander declared that he would prefer not to have their assistance. In the Social Republic, Mussolini's Minister of Defence, the able Marshal Graziani, raised a Fascist army of some 150,000 men which, when given the opportunity by the Germans, fought well. But the recollection of the repeated occasions in North Africa and in Russia when they had been let down by their Italian allies, culminating in Badoglio's treachery, had filled the German High Command with a determination, however urgent the need for men, never to entrust any important sector of the Front to Italian troops. As a result, the bulk of the armed forces of the Social Republic found their activities limited to maintaining law and order in those parts of Italy subject to its jurisdiction.

At first therefore, the activities of such Communist organisations as that of Mario Musolesi were dealt with most effectively by Mussolini's police and militia. The latter needed no encouragement from the Germans to hunt down and execute Communists. Feeling throughout Northern Italy was very bitter as a result of the Communist reign of terror against former Fascist adherents being carried on in those parts of Southern Italy occupied by the Anglo-American invaders. For the first few months after the invasion started, the Germans were able to ignore Communist activity behind their front and to concentrate on the task of repelling the Anglo-American invasion.

Gradually however, the situation changed. In every theatre

of the war the tide of battle was turning against the Axis Powers. The Russian hordes began to advance slowly but irresistably upon Europe: an Anglo American army landed in Normandy. In Italy, the complete Allied supremacy in the air made it impossible for the Germans to do more than conduct a fighting retreat. As one defensive line after another was finally broken, the area of the Social Republic became smaller, and it became increasingly clear which side was going to be ultimately victorious. Behind the German front, more and more of Mussolini's supporters threw in their lot with the Communist Partisans while there was time before the day of vengeance dawned for those who held out to the last.

While the theatre of war in Italy was moving gradually northward from the Gulf of Taranto to the foothills of the Apennines in Tuscany, Mario Musolesi's tiny "SAP" organisation carrying on seditious propaganda in Bologna developed into a formidable "GAP" organisation carrying out acts of terrorism, which in turn developed into a semi-military unit styled the Red Star Brigade. No longer were Musolesi's followers armed with revolvers and knives and such rifles as they managed to capture from the Fascist Militia. Like manna from heaven bountiful supplies of war material descended from the skies in which the Allied air forces reigned supreme. The arms so supplied included not only rifles but heavy machine guns and trench mortars.

Throughout the Social Republic numerous other Communist 'combat' organisations flourished. Some of them were large and some were small but none achieved so important an influence on the course of events as the Red Star Brigade. This may have been due to the personal qualities and military training of its leader, Mario Musolesi, who at length promoted himself to the rank of 'major'. Or it may have been due to the chance that its area of operations happened to be situated behind the most vital sector of the front to which Field Marshal Kesselring's armies at last withdrew for a final stand. This front, known as the Gothic Line in memory of the exploits of the Teutonic hero, King Totila, in the sixth century, extended across Italy a distance of about 120 miles from Leghorn on the Mediterranean to Pesaro on the Adriatic, a few miles from Rimini. The centre of this front stretched along the Apennines. Behind it to the North were the principal German lines of supply, the railway and main road running behind the front from Milan to Rimini. At the important railway junction at Bologna the main line branched southward across the Apennines to Florence and Rome. At the beginning of September 1944, the German centre was falling backwards north of Florence to the Gothic Line along the Apennines behind them. All supplies for these hard-pressed troops had to be brought from Bologna by two routes. One was the above mentioned railway from Bologna to Florence which from Bologna ascended the northern slopes of the Apennines by the valley of a mountain stream named the Setta. The other was the railway running from Bologna to the westward of and roughly parallel to the main line up the valley of another mountain stream named the Reno, and from there over the Apennines to Pistoria and so to Florence. The Reno and the Setta join at San Marconi a few miles south of Bologna to form one river flowing into the Po.

Between these mountain streams, the Reno and the Setta, is a ridge of hills and mountains rising to nearly 3,000 feet, broken by deep gullies and covered for the most part with dense scrub. Except for a few small and widely scattered hamlets this triangular strip of barren mountain country was uninhabited. 'Major' Lupo the former Sergeant Musolesi, established his headquarters near Monte Sole, a mountain lying roughly half way between Marzabotto, a small town to the West on the Reno river and Vado on the Setta to the east.

From a strategic point of view the position was admirably chosen. All supplies for the German troops holding the central sector of the Gothic Line along the edge of the Apennines to the South had to pass within a few miles of 'Major' Lupo's headquarters, either up the Reno Valley on one side or up the Setta Valley on the other.

General Max Simon, the German commander on this sector, soon found that he was concerned with more serious matters than an occasional act of sabotage on the railway, a lorry or two blown up by a land-mine, or a patrol ambushed and massacred. Wide sections of the two railway lines were repeatedly torn up and work parties sent to repair them shot down: only strongly guarded convoys could proceed slowly to the front along the systematically damaged and mined roads: ambushes carried out by hundreds of heavily armed civilians often developed into serious fighting necessitating the immediate despatch of reinforcements from the hard-pressed battle front. Attempts to pursue the Partisans retreating to their mountain strongholds only resulted in further fighting and losses.

In the booklet quoted above entitled "Epopea Partigiana", 'Major' Lupo's sister, Bruna Musolesi describes fighting on a very considerable scale at the end of May 1944 between a German punitive expedition and the Red Star Brigade. The good lady writes as follows:

THE MARZABOTTO AFFAIR

"On the 28th May 1944 strong German forces amounting to a division launched an attack in the entire area from Sassa Marconi where the Reno and Sassa streams join, to Marzabotto and Vado. The battle lasted fifteen hours. The Germans had 554 killed and 630 wounded. The survivors escaping from our bands were pursued by us as far as the railway bridge at Vado. The dead were collected three days later but many were left lying where they fell".

The reader may well hesitate to accept this story as factual. Obviously the Communist contributors to "Epopea Partigiana" were not amateur historians bent on providing posterity with facts and figures but propagandists only concerned with glorifying the achievements of Communist Partisan fighters. No doubt the claim that a German division was defeated by the Red Star Brigade is absurd and the figures given are nothing but imaginative estimates. On the other hand "Epopea Partigiana" was intended mainly for reading by members of the Communist Party in Northern Italy, many of whom would have some independent knowledge of the facts. We may accept it therefore as probable that 'Major' Lupo's men engaged in successful fighting on the above mentioned date. Probably the Germans did in fact send strong detachments into the mountainous country between the Reno and the Setta to round up the Partisans operating from there and found their opponents more numerous and far better armed than had been expected. In such difficult country the casualties from snipers may well have been severe. Possibly some of the detachments were overwhelmed and massacred. It would of course be vain to seek any reference to such unsuccessful fighting in the German official communiqués.

During the summer of 1944 the situation on the German front astride the two main routes from Florence to Bologna became increasingly critical. While the British 8th Army under General Leese fought its way slowly along the Adriatic coast, the American 5th Army fought its way step by step up the southern slopes of the Apennines in the direction of Bologna. As early as the 2nd July the Allied High Command felt so confident of an early breakthrough that orders were issued for a general advance to the Po when the collapse of the German front which it was believed might take place at any moment should occur. On the 24th September the Americans captured the Futa Pass to the eastward of the main Florence to Bologna railway. From here their way stretched downhill into the Po Valley. At this point only a few miles separated them from the district between the Reno and the Setta dominated by Lupo and his Partisans.

Nothing throws a greater strain on the morale of troops resisting strong frontal attacks than the knowledge that their line of retreat is dominated by enemy forces, even if, as in this case, these enemy forces consist only of armed civilians. The situation clearly demanded some drastic remedy. It was risky to withdraw troops from the hard-pressed front but General Max Simon decided that the risk must be taken. Half measures would be useless. First class troops must be sent to the rear with orders to dispose of the danger finally and as quickly as possible.

General Simon's choice fell upon Reconnaissance Panzer Unit No. 16 of the 16th Panzer Division then engaged a few miles to the South in desperate fighting with the advancing 5th American Army. This division was signalled out for special and generous praise by Field Marshal Lord Alexander in his report on the operations in Italy between the 3rd September 1943 and the 12th December 1944. (See the Supplement to the London Gazette published the 4th June 1950, No. 38937.) In particular, speaking of the fighting at Cecina between the 29th June and the 1st July, the British commander-in-chief observes. "The 16th S.S. Panzer Division had been brought in here to strengthen the German defence and fought with skill and fanaticism". Later, referring to the struggle for Rosignano during the first week of July, Lord Alexander records, "The town was defended by the 16th S.S. Panzer Grenadiers against the 34th United States Division with the same stubbornness as they had shown at Cecina".

The gravity of the situation can be judged from the fact that in order to deal with it crack troops such as these should have been withdrawn from the front in the midst of an enemy offensive.

The commander of Reconnaissance Panzer Unit No. 16 was a certain Major Walter Reder who with Mario Musolesi, alias Lupo, was destined to play the two principal roles in the so-called Marzabotto Affair. We must pause here therefore to state briefly who he was and what had been his career down to the date when he was ordered to leave the front with his unit in order to dispose of the Red Star Brigade.

At the outbreak of the Second World War, Walter Reder was a professional soldier with a commission in the German Army. He was then only twenty-four years of age. Having served in the campaign in France, he volunteered for service in Russia in a unit of storm troops. He fought in the front line throughout the Russian campaigns of 1941 and 1942 and was several times wounded. In the recapture of Kharkov in March 1943 he was so severely wounded that his left forearm had to be amputated. He was awarded a number of high decorations for courage and leadership under fire and finally received the much prized Knight's Cross of the Iron Cross. After recovery from his wound, he was made commander of Reconnaissance Panzer Unit No. 16 and saw service in Jugo-Slavia. Promoted to major, he and his unit were sent to the Italian front in May 1944. For his services on this front against the American 5th Army he was several times mentioned in despatches.

The task assigned to Major Reder at the end of September 1944 was a difficult one. The Partisans commanded by the Communist leader 'Major' Lupo held strongly entrenched positions in the mountains between the Reno and the Setta, with their headquarters near Monte Sole, a peak 2,171 feet in height, and strong outlying positions to the south west round Monte Salvaro of 2,854 feet. From the Futa Pass the Americans had steadily thrust forward so that their front line had become only some five miles from the Partisan headquarters. Time was of the essence, as the lawyers say, since if the Americans achieved a breakthrough, the position of the German troops retreating down the Setta and Reno valleys on Bologna would be desperate. At any moment also the Americans might decide to reinforce the Partisans by dropping paratroops. If this happened, Major Reder's difficulties would be increased tenfold.

Major Reder decided to carry out his mission by delivering a converging attack from all sides. While detachments pushed northward against the Partisan positions round Monte Salvaro, the main German attack was directed from the east from across the Setta Valley against the entrenchments of the Partisans near Monte Sole. Owing to an injury to his knee, Major Reder was unable to lead his troops himself: throughout the action he remained on a hillside overlooking the Setta stream, directing by wireless the main attack in a westerly direction.

It should be noted that the small town of Marzabotto was quite outside the area of operations, being merely the starting point of the detachments advancing against the Partisans from the north. The town was some six miles in a straight line from the hillside where Major Reder remained throughout the fighting. The troops under his direct command never reached Marzabotto: having captured 'Major' Lupo's headquarters near Monte Sole, they were halted and then withdrawn to the Setta Valley.

A possible explanation of the complaints made later that the inhabitants of Marzabotto suffered violence at the hands of the German troops during these operations, is that the detachments which set out to attack from this town, began by making a search for secret bases of the Partisans in the town itself. If such a search

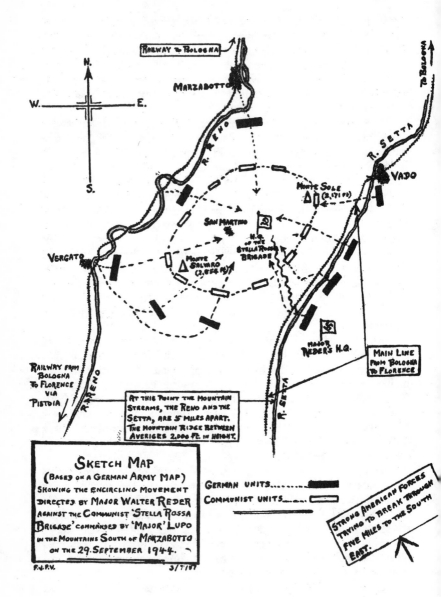

N.

W.————————E.

S.

RAILWAY TO BOLOGNA

MARZABOTTO

TO BOLOGNA

R. RENO

R. SETTA

VADO

MONTE SOLE
Δ (2,171 FT)

SAN MARTINO

H.Q.
OF THE
STELLA ROSSA
BRIGADE

VERGATO

MONTE
SALVARO
Δ (2,854 FT)

MAJOR
REDER'S H.Q.

MAIN LINE
FROM BOLOGNA
TO FLORENCE

RAILWAY FROM
BOLOGNA
TO FLORENCE
VIA
PISTOIA

R. RENO

AT THIS POINT THE MOUNTAIN
STREAMS, THE RENO AND THE
SETTA, ARE 5 MILES APART.
THE MOUNTAIN RIDGE BETWEEN
AVERAGES 2,000 FT. IN HEIGHT.

R. SETTA

SKETCH MAP
(BASED ON A GERMAN ARMY MAP)
SHOWING THE ENCIRCLING MOVEMENT
DIRECTED BY MAJOR WALTER REDER
AGAINST THE COMMUNIST 'STELLA ROSSA'
BRIGADE' COMMANDED BY 'MAJOR' LUPO
IN THE MOUNTAINS SOUTH OF MARZABOTTO
ON THE 29. SEPTEMBER 1944.

P. v. P.V.   3/7/47

GERMAN UNITS.........
COMMUNIST UNITS.......

STRONG AMERICAN FORCES
TRYING TO BREAK THROUGH
FIVE MILES TO THE SOUTH
EAST.

150

had resulted in some lair of the Partisans being discovered, fighting would no doubt have taken place, Partisans would have been killed and property damaged.

This explanation will be found on reflection highly improbable. We have the evidence of Lupo's sister, Bruna, that in the barracks of Marzabotto was a force of Fascist Militia. As an important point on the railway from Bologna to Pistoria, it is certain that the town had also a permanent German garrison. It is most unlikely therefore that troops sent to Marzabotto as a starting point for an expedition into the mountains to the south would start by searching the houses in the town itself.

Had 'Major' Lupo when he saw that he was to be attacked in force, reverted to his former tactics and ordered his men to scatter, hide their arms and become again inoffensive civilians, probably in such difficult country the majority of them would have been able to slip away and to live to fight—or rather to murder—another day. The German forces must have been too few completely to surround the extensive area held by the Partisans. There must at first have been wide gaps between the converging columns through which individuals could have escaped. Had these prudent tactics been adopted, Major Reder would have found himself in the position of a boxer whose punches are wasted in the empty air. His men would have occupied some peaks, seized some arms and ammunition and arrested a few inoffensive civilians. But no doubt 'Major' Lupo was unwilling to abandon the large stores of war material which he had collected round Monte Sole. Perhaps to the very last he expected the Americans, only a few miles away across a single mountain ridge, to break through to his rescue.

At daybreak on September 29th four companies of Panzer Unit No. 16 moved forward to the attack on the positions of the Partisans on each side of Monte Sole. They were received with heavy rifle and machine gun fire. When this resistance was broken, the Partisans fell back on their headquarters which were also attacked by the detachments advancing from the north and east. In the area of the fighting were a number of small hamlets and groups of houses, the largest of which was San Martino with about 200 inhabitants. The Partisans took refuge in these places which they defended desperately. There is no reason to doubt that the inhabitants joined in the fighting; whether willingly or unwillingly is immaterial since in Communist partisan warfare a civilian who refuses assistance is deemed a self-confessed traitor to be dealt with accordingly. In any event their fate would have been the same since resistance in these hamlets—only two, San Martino and Cadotto, are mentioned by name in the reports—was only overcome by the employment of handgrenades, bazookas, flame-throwers and shell fire. A last desperate stand was made on Monte Sole. By evening the Red Star Brigade had been wiped out. 'Major' Lupo was among the killed. By midday on the following day, the 30th September, the mopping up operations had been completed. By that evening Major Reder and his Panzer Unit No. 16 was back in the front line taking part in a successful counter-attack to eliminate a penetration which the Americans had succeeded in making during the course of the day.

That the scale of the fighting with the Red Star Brigade was relatively small is shown by the fact that the German casualties in this operation amounted to only 24 dead, including one officer, 40 wounded and six missing. Probably the majority of the Partisans, estimated to have numbered nearly 2,000, were killed, but many undoubtedly managed to slip away including 'Major' Lupo's sister, Bruna Musolesi, who survived to describe her recollections of the encounter in her previously quoted contribution to the Communist booklet, "Epopea Partigiana". Her account adds nothing of importance, however, to the above outline of the facts except that she discloses that her brother was warned by a priest named Don Fornasini, who acted as a spy for the Partisans, that an attack was to be expected. Her admission proves that Major Reder did not owe his success to surprise, and it is also of interest as showing the active part played by priests in guerilla activity—in Italy in 1944 as in Cyprus in 1956. Bruna Musolesi estimates the number of German troops taking part in these operations as four divisions—an absurd exaggeration of course—and declares that the attack was supported "by artillery, tanks, mortars, flame-throwers and weapons of every kind". She adds, "There was not a corner in the whole zone which was not struck by projectiles. I cannot explain how I and my sister escaped. I can only remember thinking that the day would never end. Night at last closed over the fire of the conflagrations. Lupo was missing. We did not know what had become of him."

In view of what was to be alleged later, what is most noteworthy concerning Bruna Musolesi's story is her omission to make a complaint of any kind against the conduct of the German troops. She makes no attempt to represent her brother Lupo as an inoffensive civilian with an amiable if eccentric weakness for calling himself a 'major', who with two thousand other inoffensive civilians went on an excursion into the mountains and there, while innocently admiring the magnificent scenery was attacked and done to death by brutal German soldiery. On the contrary, she claims, no doubt with justice, that her brother and his comrades put up a determined resistance in prepared positions to an expected attack by regular troops supported by flame-throwers, tanks and shell fire.

Such are the facts of the Marzabotto Affair down to the destruction of the Red Star Brigade on the 29th September 1944. Down to this point the story may be described as highly creditable to all concerned. The men of Panzer Unit No. 16 under the command of Major Reder carried through a difficult operation in an extremely workmanlike manner fully justifying the high opinion formed of their soldierly qualities by Field Marshal Lord Alexander. For their part, 'Major' Lupo's men displayed a steadfast courage rarely displayed by partisan fighters. Although warned that an attack was pending, the majority at any rate preferred to defend their mountain stronghold rather than to slip away to safety in the guise of inoffensive civilians in accordance with the invariable practice in partisan warfare. Concerning Lupo himself, we may assume that he deliberately elected to die with his men since the fact that his two sisters managed to slip away proves that escape was not impossible. If as a terrorist chief he was responsible for many cowardly outrages, at least it can be said for him that he atoned by his death for his crimes. His sister's claim that he should be ranked as a Communist hero, unlike so many similar claims, seems supported by facts.

No doubt this minor operation behind the German front in Italy would have been quickly and completely forgotten but for the chance that a few days later a member of Major Reder's Panzer unit, named Julien Legoli, deserted to the Americans. No doubt to ingratiate himself with his captors, this man told them a story that before launching his men to the attack on the Partisans, Major Reder had given them a 'pep' talk in which he ordered that no quarter was to be given to civilians offering resistance. In view of this statement Legoli was handed over by the Americans to the dreaded Deuxiéme Bureau at the 'Free French' headquarters in Rome where he embellished his statement to the effect that Reder had ordered that in the event of fire being opened on the advancing troops by the partisans all civilians in the neighbourhood were to be summarily shot as a reprisal.

Legoli's statement was passed on by the Deuxiéme Bureau to the Italian authorities appointed by Marshal Badoglio to prepare a list of 'war-criminals' upon whom vengeance was to be demanded when 'unconditional surrender' had been achieved. Major Reder's name was solemnly added to this list. All his later experiences originated from this statement of the double traitor and deserter Julien Legoli. The only charge of any substance which Reder had to face at his trial was based on this alleged 'pep' talk given by him on the hillside overlooking the Setta Valley just before the attack on the Red Star Brigade. The prosecution contended that what he said amounted to an order to shoot all civilians, regardless of age or sex, in the area of operations as a reprisal if resistance was offered. In accordance with the usual practice in 'war-crimes' trials a number of quite distinct and frivolous charges were added to the indictment in order to give a sinister background to the main charge. These additional charges need not concern us here. In a nutshell, whenever a reprisal had been carried out against the partisans in an area in which or near which Major Reder's unit might have been, he was charged with having personally directed it. The bulk of these charges were at his trial first dismissed as not proven: on appeal he was pronounced not guilty.

It may well be thought that as the only direct evidence against Major Reder consisted of the testimony of Julien Legoli, the issue upon which Major Reder's trial turned was whether this testimony was to be believed or the denial of the defendant that he gave this alleged 'pep' talk. On oath Major Reder swore that he gave no 'pep' talk to his men. He only admitted calling his company commanders together before the attack to give them his directions in the course of which he said, "Die Operation ist ohne Rücksicht auf beiderlei Verluste zu führen"—"The operation is to be carried through without regard to losses on either side".

Here clearly is a clear-cut issue of fact. The reader will no doubt assume that the Court having heard both Legoli and Major Reder in the witness box, decided to accept the evidence of the former. Having accepted Legoli's evidence as the truth, the Court naturally convicted Major Reder. The reader will assume that Legoli was the 'star' witness for the prosecution and that his cross-examination by Major Reder's counsel was the highlight of the trial.

The reader will therefore be astonished to learn that Julien Legoli was never called as a witness at Major Reder's trial although what he had said was the only direct evidence against the accused: as at the trial of General Max Simon, Major Reder's immediate superior, by a British military court at Padua four years before on similar charges, only a written statement by Legoli was put in evidence by the prosecution. Contrary to the rules of evidence and in defiance of elementary principles of justice, this written statement was in both so-called trials accepted in place of the sworn testimony of this vital witness in the witness box. By this shabby manoeuvre Reder's counsel was prevented from testing the truth of Legoli's story by cross-examination.

In fairness to the British military court at Padua which

tried General Simon and to the Italian military court at Bologna which tried Major Reder, it should be said that in dispensing with the presence of Legoli in the witness box they were but following a practice firmly established in 'war-crimes' trials. Article 19 of the so-called Charter annexed to the London Agreement dated the 8th August 1945 expressly authorised the International Military Tribunal of Nürnberg to disregard the rules of evidence and to accept inadmissible evidence if it would help to bolster a conviction. After the lapse of a decade, this article appears so incredible that it is only fair to quote it here in full. Article 19 reads as follows: —

"The Tribunal shall not be bound by technical rules of evidence. It shall adopt and apply to the greatest possible extent expeditious and non-technical procedure, and shall admit any evidence which it deems to have probative value".

In accepting a written statement by the double traitor Legoli in the place of sworn evidence in the witness box, the Italian military court which tried Major Reder was only "adopting and applying to the greatest possible extent" the direction given by Article 19 for the trial of prisoners of war, a direction also "adopted and applied to the greatest possible extent" by the Nürnberg Tribunal of which those distinguished English judges, Lord Justice Lawrence and Mr. Justice Birkett, were members. By what principles of law or common sense a burglar, a fraudulent promotor or a motorist who drives without due care and attention should be entitled to claim the protection of the rules of evidence as a matter of course and the unfortunate soldier who has had the misfortune to be taken prisoner should not be entitled to claim this protection, is a question which has never been answered. Even that stalwart apologist for 'war-trials', Professor Goodhart, has never ventured to suggest an answer. The fact remains that this strange principle was expressly laid down for the trial of the 'major war-criminals' at Nürnberg and was naturally followed afterwards by less august tribunals. Thus as late as 1949 the British military court which tried Field Marshal von Manstein at Hamburg, carried Article 19 to its logical conclusion by dispensing with witnesses altogether. In that case, some written statements by some German prisoners in American hands were accepted by the court as having "probative value", although these prisoners were alive and available to give evidence in the witness box.

In the case of Julien Legoli, it is open to question whether he was available to give evidence. All we know for certain is that the French authorities produced a statement which they said had been made by him and that the British and Italian military courts accepted this statement at its face value. We do not know whether either the British or the Italian military authorities asked that arrangements should be made by the French authorities for Legoli's personal attendance in court. We can only assume that no such request was made or that if it was made it was rejected.

The fact stated above that this deserter from Major Reder's unit Julien Legoli, was a French subject, born in Alsace, must have struck the reader as very astonishing. How could it have come about that a French subject should be found serving in a German S.S. Panzer unit? No doubt Legoli himself explained the matter by saying that he had been forced to join by the brutal Nazis. But this explanation cannot possibly be accepted: certainly the French authorities would not have entertained it for an instant. It was of course a fact that many Alsatians were forced by threats to work in Hitler's labour battalions and a few may have been induced to join one of the combatant services. But the 16th S.S. Panzer Division of which Legoli became a member was a crack corps composed of carefully picked men. Not only as in the paratroop divisions was the standard of physical fitness demanded very high, but in addition in the S.S. formations assurance had to be given that the would-be recruit was politically 'sound'—in other words, that he was genuinely an ardent National Socialist. Julien Legoli would only have been accepted after rigorous medical and political tests of fitness.

In the eyes of the 'Free French' authorities, therefore, Legoli would be regarded as the blackest of collaborators. We know the fate of even the most inoffensive collaborator: after the Liberation no less than 105,000 collaborators were executed, with or without trials, in the space of eight months, of whom the majority were accused of nothing more serious than making a show of friendliness to the German troops occupying France. How then would a man be regarded who had not only voluntarily joined Hitler's armed forces at the time of the downfall of France in 1940 but had gained admission by proving that before the outbreak of war he had been a secret adherent of Hitler!

Perhaps the worst offence committed by Julien Legoli in the eyes of his countrymen was that he had helped to dispose of one of the most cherished of French political myths, the myth that the entire population of Alsace was filled with ardent and unswerving French patriotism. Ever since Alsace had been recovered by France in 1919 the fact had been strenuously denied that there existed in Alsace a numerous minority which desired to remain German. Even more unwelcome was the fact that after the establishment of a National Socialist regime in Germany in 1933 there were many in France and particularly in Alsace who were attracted by Hitler's political theories as an alternative to the French democratic political system for which they blamed France's decline.

When Legoli volunteered in 1940 to serve in the German armed forces he knew what his fate would assuredly be in the event of Germany's defeat. By September 1944 Germany's ultimate defeat had become a certainty. His desertion was clearly only a desperate effort to save his life which he had undeniably forfeited. His denunciation of his commanding officer, Major Reder, was obviously a forlorn attempt to ingratiate himself with his countrymen. Did this forlorn attempt succeed? It may well be doubted. Of course Legoli would have been only too happy to say anything his captors wanted him to say. Had he proved obstinate over some detail, the Deuxiéme Bureau had their own methods for overcoming obstinacy. Why then should the French authorities make any bargain with him? Having signed the document placed before him, the probability is that he was forthwith taken out and shot as a traitor. What purpose could be served by sparing his life? What impression would such a man make in the witness box? Under cross-examination he would have to admit that he had been a Nazi, and that he had been a traitor to France: his story that he had been forced to join the S.S. would be disbelieved by his own countrymen. How then could the prosecution venture to ask a court to accept him as a witness of the truth? Probably Legoli had long been in his grave at the time of Major Reder's trial.

The course of events down to the opening of Major Reder's trial in Bologna in October 1951 can fortunately here be passed lightly over since they reflect little credit upon any of the parties concerned.

Major Reder himself won fresh laurels during October in the fierce fighting in the Apennines in which was repulsed the last desperate attempt of the Anglo-American armies to break through into the Po Valley before the onset of winter. In February 1945 he was transferred to Hungary through which the Russian hordes were pressing irresistibly. In March he sustained severe injuries to both knees. Soon after the general capitulation of the Axis Powers, he was arrested as member of the S.S. and interned. Owing to his disabilities—his left forearm had been amputated in Russia and he was still incapacitated by his knee injuries—he was shortly released. He was living under 'open arrest' in Salzburg when he was arrested by the Americans on account of a charge lodged against him by the Italians that he was a war-criminal responsible for the Marzabotto Massacre.

For two years—from September 1945 to September 1947—he was detained in an American prison camp at Glasenbach in which were detained some 7,500 men and 500 women, including former cabinet ministers, generals, privates, farmers and industrial workers. Against the great majority no specific charge had been made: they were merely detained on suspicion of having been Nazi sympathisers until someone could get around to deal with their cases. The camp was terribly overcrowded and the death rate among the prisoners as a result of the shortage of food, the cold of winter and the lack of all but the most primitive sanitary arrangements very high. After two years the Americans found time to examine the charges against Major Reder. To the Americans they seemed to be entirely lacking in substance but the ruling had been laid down that any member of the S.S. was prima facie a war-criminal. If the British wanted him, they were welcome to him. So in September 1947 Major Reder was handed over to the British military authorities in Austria.

The British military authorities investigated the Italian charges against Major Reder with praiseworthy care. At first his interrogation was carried out by a Major J. E. McKee. Later his interrogation was completed by a Major W. G. Aylen. Neither of these gentlemen spoke German so that the services of an interpreter, a Dr. Hans Susserroth, was necessary. At Major Reder's trial in Bologna, this man Susserroth gave evidence that he himself had interrogated the accused who had denied taking any part in any operations against the Italian Partisans.

In affidavits sworn for Major Reder's appeal to the Supreme Italian Military Court in Rome, both Major McKee and Major Aylen swore that Susserroth had given false evidence. He had been employed, they both testified, only as an interpreter, never as an interrogator. Further they both testified that Major Reder had freely admitted having directed the operations against the Red Star Brigade south of Bologna in which its commander 'Major' Lupo was killed. In fact Major Reder had claimed that his detachment had borne the brunt of the fighting on that occasion.

Major McKee concluded his affidavit by stating, "Throughout his interrogation by me, Major Reder behaved with dignity. He repeatedly affirmed his innocence. He denied ordering excesses against the Italian civilian population or having received orders from his superiors to carry out excesses. On one occasion Major Reder could without difficulty or danger have escaped from British custody. He explained that he had refrained from escaping as he was quite prepared to face a trial on the charges made against him".

At the time this interrogation was proceeding, the British authorities had just carried through to a successful conclusion the prosecution for war-crimes of Major Reder's commander-in-chief, Field Marshal Kesselring. A British military court, sitting in Venice, had in April 1947 condemned this famous soldier to death. There is fortunately no occasion to deal here with the facts of this so-called trial round which the 'Iron Curtain of Discreet Silence' has been draped with special and understandable care. Even after more than ten years have elapsed, no account of this trial has been published in English. Referring to the conviction of Field Marshal von Manstein by a British military court in Hamburg in 1949 Captain Liddell Hart, the famous military critic, wrote to the "Times", "His condemnation appears a glaring example of gross ignorance or gross hypocrisy". The present writer can only respectfully concur but must repeat the opinion which he has previously expressed in another book that in comparison with the trial of Field Marshal Kesselring, the trial of Field Marshal von Manstein was in every respect a model war-trial.

Having disposed of Field Marshal Kesselring, the British authorities turned their attention to Major Reder's immediate superior, General Max Simon. In January 1948 he was brought to trial before a British military court at Padua and sentenced to death. Parenthetically it may be mentioned that the death sentences passed on Field Marshal Kesselring and General Simon were both shortly commuted to sentences of imprisonment for life, and in due course both men were rather shamefacedly released.

Having disposed of General Simon in January 1948, it would seem that only two courses lay before the British authorities in regard to Major Reder. If they were satisfied that a prima facie case had been made out against him, they could send him for trial before a British military court as they had done with his two superior officers. If they were not satisfied that there was a prima facie case against him, then nothing remained to be done but to release him forthwith.

Neither of these courses were adopted. On the 13th May 1948 Major Reder was handed over by the British to the Italians.

The present writer regrets that he can find no clue suggesting an explanation for this extraordinary procedure. In itself, this is not perhaps remarkable. The working of the British military-legal or legal-military mind during the post-war years is generally quite beyond mere human comprehension. Possibly closer investigation of the political situation in May 1948 would disclose that there was some special reason at that time for making a gesture which would conciliate Italian public opinion. Some cynical politician in London may have decided that an obscure S.S. officer in captivity in Austria would serve as a convenient subject for such a gesture. A simple but adequate explanation is that the British military authorities in charge of Major Reder's case had got themselves into a muddle and decided that the easiest way out of it was to follow the precedent set by Pontius Pilate long ago. Clearly the Italians were convinced that Reder was guilty. If therefore the case was handed over to them so that they could act as judges of their own charges, the matter would be disposed of quickly.

The trial of Major Reder which began in Bologna in October 1951 was not such a complete farce as might reasonably have been expected. True, the prosecution allowed themselves three and a half years to prepare the charges and permitted the defence only two months to prepare to meet these charges. But this preliminary injustice is the invariable practice in nearly all trials for "war-crimes". Bologna where the trial took place was not only one of the greatest strongholds of Communism in Italy but was the headquarters of the Union of Italian Partisans. Throughout the trial mobs demonstrated outside the court house: witnesses for the prosecution who failed under cross-examination were maltreated and the lives of witnesses for the defence were threatened. Defending counsel had to appeal for police protection. The issue of the case was openly proclaimed to be political. The court had to decide whether it supported this Fascist officer or the late lamented 'Major' Lupo. The latter had indeed been posthumously decorated with the Gold Medal for Valour on account of his exploits as a Communist Partisan fighter, but the result of the trial would show what the Italian officer class, to which the members of the Court belonged, really thought of their fellow-countryman. If Reder were acquitted, every gallant Partisan fighter throughout Italy would regard the verdict as a personal insult.

It can hardly have been an intended impertinence to the Court but the person appointed to conduct the prosecution was neither a lawyer nor a soldier but a youthful Communist student named Stellacci who as a reward for his alleged exploits as a resistance fighter had been given a commission in the Italian Army with the rank of captain. A theatrical and excitable little creature with a toothbrush moustache which gave him a striking resemblance to Charlie Chaplin when he was acting for the Keystone Comedies, Stellacci knew nothing of law or of military matters. Unable to comprehend the issues raised at the trial, he wasted the time of the Court with long tirades against the defendant and with eulogies of the departed heroes who had laid down their lives to make the world safe for the dictatorship of the proletariat. Seemingly his antics in court counted as military service since during the course of the trial he was promoted to the rank of Major. Reder listened

Major Walter Reder in the uniform of a captain in the
3rd Panzer Grenadiers, taken on service in Russia. Later
he was accused of civilian massacres in the Italian town of
Marzabotto.

Major Reder being confronted with a female witness. Not one witness was called who claimed to have seen him present or taking part at any of the crimes alleged.

unmoved when he heard himself described as "beast", "murderer", "scamp" and "criminal" but was roused at length to protest when Stellacci proclaimed his disbelief that so contemptible a malefactor could have been decorated for valour. Proof having been given that Major Reder had received the Knight's Cross of the Iron Cross, Stellacci declared the accused stood self-convicted since everyone knew this decoration was exclusively given for murdering Soviet babies.

The issues raised at the trial will be dealt with briefly later. Having listened to all the evidence produced and having endured a passionate harangue from Stellacci describing the era of universal happiness which would dawn when at last Communism dominated the world, the Court adjourned to consider their verdict.

Had the Court considered Major Reder guilty, they would undoubtedly have sentenced him to death. The fact that they did not sentence him to death proves that they considered him innocent. On the other hand, a verdict of acquittal was clearly impossible in view of the political situation. The existence of the Italian Government depended on a precarious majority possessed by a coalition of the leading anti-Communist parties. Reder's acquittal would raise such a storm of outraged political feeling that the downfall of the Government might result which in turn might well be the first step towards the establishment of that dictatorship of the proletariat in Italy which Stellacci had described to them in such glowing terms. The blood of the members of the Court ran cold at the very thought. Clearly Caiaphas had known what he was talking about when he advised that occasions can arise when it is well that one man should die for the people.

The verdict was very carefully framed. Of the eight charges, five were mere make-weight charges added to provide a background for the main complaint. These five charges were dismissed for want of evidence. On the remaining three charges Reder was found guilty. The first of these related to the shooting of certain terrorists and hostages at Bardine. Reder denied that either he or his unit were in the neighbourhood at the time of these executions and no evidence was produced by the prosecution to contradict him. The second charge upon which the Court returned a verdict of guilty related to a punitive expedition carried out north of Massa-Carrara on the 19th August 1944 against certain Communist bands who styled themselves the "Lunense" Brigade. This operation was similar to but on a smaller scale than the operation above described against the Red Star Brigade some six weeks later. No direct evidence was given that Major Reder was responsible for the loss of life and the damage to property done during this operation. The

K

third charge upon which Major Reder was found guilty related to the attack on Lupo's Red Star Brigade. This was admittedly the main charge against him. In support of this charge the prosecution claimed to possess direct evidence against the accused in the shape of the testimony of the Alsatian deserter, Julien Legoli, but, as we have seen, the prosecution refrained from calling this evidence.

In view of these findings, the Court sentenced Major Reder to imprisonment for life *"for causing loss of life to the Italian civilian population and for causing damage to Italian civilian property"*.

This verdict may be described as a skilfully devised compromise which on the one hand preserved Major Reder's life and on the other saved the Italian Government from a dangerous political crisis. It must unfortunately be recorded that the Court for some inexplicable reason added to the sentence of imprisonment for life the additional penalty that Reder should be deprived of his military rank.

Of course this Italian military court had no more authority to degrade an officer of the army of a foreign Power than, say, the British Board of Trade would have to direct that a Portuguese colonel should be promoted to the rank of general or that a Chilian admiral should be degraded to the rank of lieutenant! One can only suppose that the minds of the Court had become befuddled by Stellacci's turgid eloquence or that this additional penalty was added at the last moment to placate the furious Communist mob demonstrating outside the court house. This patent absurdity was rectified in due course by the Supreme Italian Military Court to which Major Reder appealed in March 1954. This court quashed the sentence of degradation as ultra vires, and also substituted a verdict of 'Not guilty' in place of 'not proven' in respect of what we may call the background charges. In regard to the other charges, including the charge relating to alleged offences committed in the Marzabotto Zone, the appeal court confirmed the verdict of guilty together with the sentence of life imprisonment.

The decision of the Supreme Italian Military Court was given on the 16th March 1954. We must now go back to the 26th June 1953 to a very remarkable reply of this date sent by the Italian Minister of the Interior, Signor Scelba, to a letter dated the previous 16th January written to him by the Austrian State Secretary, Graf, appealing for Major Reder's release as an act of clemency.

Signor Scelba replied courteously apologising for his delay in replying which he explained by saying that he had had first to consult with the Minister of Justice and the Minister of Defence.

THE MARZABOTTO AFFAIR

Rejecting emphatically this appeal for clemency, Scelba wrote: —
"A revision of the trial by an appeal to the Court of Cassation
against the death sentence passed on Major Reder by the
Military Court at Bologna on the 31st October 1951 is not
possible.

Reder was condemned as a participant in the gravest war-
crime: the destruction of the entire town of Marzabotto,
whose inhabitants, about 1,700 persons, men, women and
children, were killed without exception, together with the
Pastor, in the church whither they had fled. The church was
set on fire with the houses and destroyed. This exceptionally
grave happening still lives in the memory, and the village
to which the Gold Medal has been awarded, is regarded as a
sanctuary. In view of these facts it would be impossible to
recommend the Chief of State to pardon Reder."

This letter is a truly astonishing production. Signor Scelba
was a leading Italian politician, and no doubt a well-informed
and experienced man of affairs. No doubt he had at his elbow
books of reference of every kind. He had only to call upon his
staff in the Ministry of the Interior to have a detailed statement of
the facts laid before him. He declares that before replying to the
Austrian State Secretary Graf, he consulted with his colleagues,
the Ministers of Justice and Defence. Presumably they were as
ignorant of the facts as himself. But it still remains astonishing that
when at length he dictated his reply, his secretary, presumably a
well-informed person, did not correct him along the following
lines: —

"Pardon my presumption, your Excellency, but may I humbly
point out that you are talking through your hat. In a couple of
paragraphs of only some hundred and thirty words you have made
no less than five grave misstatements of fact. Major Reder was not
condemned to death in Bologna or anywhere else: he was sentenced to life imprisonment. No one has ever charged him as a
participant in the destruction of the entire town of Marzabotto.
This town was in fact never destroyed entirely or in part: it
was only considerably damaged by American bombs and shells.
No evidence was given at Major Reder's trial that its 1,700 inhabitants, men, women and children, were massacred in the church
or anywhere else. Permit me to doubt whether the church at
Marzabotto is large enough to accommodate 1,700 persons. No
mention was made at the trial of the untimely decease of the Pastor
of Marzabotto: there is no reason to think, so far as I know,
that this clerical gentleman is not still alive and well: at any rate
Major Reder has never been charged with having caused his death.

163

THE MARZABOTTO AFFAIR

Before you summarily dismiss me for insolence, may I suggest that I get you the file relating to Major Reder's case. You will there find exactly what charges were made against him and of what offences he was found guilty. At the risk of your ordering me to be thrown downstairs, may I suggest that in the amiable innocence of your heart you have muddled together the facts of Major Reder's trial and a propaganda myth invented by our Ministry of Information which is based, rather slavishly it must be confessed, on the French story of Oradour. In that story, you may remember, the inhabitants of a village, according to some accounts numbering 2,000 but according to other accounts less than 200, were locked in a remarkably capacious church and there burnt to death as a reprisal for outrages by French Partisans. The story of Oradour may have some basis of fact. But the story of Marzabotto is a pure propaganda myth. Our propaganda department has simply adopted the French story and broadcasted it with only the name Marzabotto substituted for Oradour".

This is what Signor Scelba's secretary could have said with perfect truth. Perhaps it would be asking too much of a secretary to expect him to speak with such frankness to his principal. Still in view of the remarkable collection of errors which Signor Scelba had managed to crowd into one short letter, his secretary might at least have hinted the letter would be no worse for checking. Apparently he said nothing however. Perhaps he was as ignorant of the facts as Signor Scelba. All that is certain is that Signor Scelba's letter, uncorrected, was duly despatched to the Austrian State Secretary, Graf. No doubt its contents astonished that gentleman greatly.

In fairness to His Excellency Signor Scelba, it should be stated that his view of Major Reder's case was that held by nearly everyone who remembered the case at all. Blame only attaches to him for giving an uncompromising refusal to a plea for clemency without bothering to find out the facts. By the public of the United States and by the public of Great Britain Major Reder had long been completely forgotten with the exception of a few people who dimly remembered him as a German officer who had been convicted of the appalling crime of shutting a number of civilians in a church and then setting it on fire. Hardly anyone remembered the name of Marzabotto as the place where this alleged atrocity was supposed to have taken place. In fact this crime, if associated in the public mind with any particular place, is generally linked with the French village of Oradour sur Glane. Although Major Reder was over three hundred miles away at the time of the Oradour atrocity, as a result of all this confusion its shadow has fallen across him.

The main difficulty in the way of arriving at the truth concerning the Marzabotto Affair arises from the fact that this name has become applied to two distinct happenings or alleged happenings.

First of all there are the alleged happenings said to have taken place in the little town of Marzabotto referred to in Signor Scelba's letter quoted above. If any such happenings had in fact occurred, they would unquestionably have been at least mentioned in Major Reder's trial. No mention or reference of any kind to any such happenings was made at Major Reder's trial and the obvious explanation for this omission is that the alleged Marzabotto massacre is nothing but a Communist propaganda fairy tale.

So exactly do the alleged happenings at Marzabotto resemble the alleged happenings at Oradour that there seems no escaping the conclusion that the Italian propagandists, either from lack of inventive powers or just from simple laziness, borrowed the French story and put it forward as their own. Probably they selected Marzabotto as the scene of this propaganda myth because the name of this little town had become familiar owing to the fact that the exploits of 'Major' Lupo and his Red Star Brigade were performed in the Marzabotto Zone.

Against this simple and obvious explanation it may be objected that it leaves out of account the conviction still widespread in Italy that bloodshed on an outstanding scale took place in 1944 in the town of Marzabotto. Visitors to Marzabotto are now shown an impressive stone mausoleum erected in 1948 in which are inscribed the names, said to number 1,830, of the victims of this alleged massacre, which visitors are assured included five priests and eighty women burnt to death in the church.*

It is certainly hard to believe that all these names are fictitious. On the other hand it is hard to understand why if a massacre of civilians on however small a scale took place in the town of Marzabotto, no evidence concerning this massacre was produced at Major Reder's trial. Such evidence would have been most relevant to the charges brought against him since he was admittedly in charge of the operations being carried out at the time and the perpetrators would therefore presumably have been troops under his command.†

To the present writer the most probable explanation appears to be that the mausoleum at Marzabotto was erected by the Communist-controlled local authorities for a two-fold purpose; to glorify the exploits of the Communist Partisans of the district and to perpetuate the Communist propaganda myth, which had already

* See the article 'Lebendig Begraben' in the Austrian newspaper "Echo der Heimat" of the 12th May, 1957.
† See Postscript on Page 176.

become widespread, that the German 'Fascists' had carried out a great massacre of innocent civilians in the town. The names inscribed in the mausoleum are not fictitious but are the names of all the inhabitants of Marzabotto and the surrounding districts who lost their lives during the Second World War. If this is what was done, the total of 1,830 persons does not seem an incredibly high figure, bearing in mind the fact that the protracted Allied bombing and shelling of the town must have led to many casualties, while as the most populous place in the district, probably a large proportion of the members of the Red Star Brigade were residents of Marzabotto, and no doubt many of these lost their lives when the brigade was surrounded in its nearby mountain stronghold and destroyed by Major Reder's men.

Turning from speculation to the facts established at Major Reder's trial at Bologna in October 1951, it now only remains to enquire what exactly were the facts which the Court considered merited punishment by a sentence of imprisonment for life. At the same time we can consider whether the findings of the Court can be justified either by law or by common sense.

The findings of fact by the Court upon which it based its sentence are too vague to be of much assistance. It will be remembered that Major Reder was sentenced to life imprisonment for having been responsible "for causing loss of life to the Italian civilian population and for causing damage to Italian civilian property".

It is not open to question that Major Reder was responsible for the death of 'Major' Lupo and his band of Communist guerillas. As we have seen he frankly admitted responsibility when questioned by the British Major McKee, and later he made the same admission at his trial at Bologna. Lupo's Red Star Brigade numbered about 2,000 men. No doubt a number managed to slip away but probably the majority perished. The scene of the fighting was mainly barren and pathless country but here and there were tiny hamlets inhabited by shepherds and goatherds. The Partisans barricaded themselves in these places which they defended desperatly until overcome by shell fire and flame-throwers. Loss of life inevitably resulted with damage to civilian property.

To what extent was Major Reder personally responsible for this loss of life and damage to property? We may leave out of account the doings of the columns advancing from the north and west, but the attack from the east was directed by wireless by Reder himself. Admittedly this attack was directed against the village of San Martino near which was the Partisan headquarters where Lupo himself fell. No doubt San Martino and the neighbouring hamlet of Cadotto were destroyed and many of their inhabitants killed.

The prosecution apparently made no complant concerning the death of Lupo and those members of his gang who resisted to the last. Relying on the statement given by the deserter Julien Legoli, the prosecution alleged that on Major Reder's express orders no quarter was given to the Partisans and that in San Martino and in the neighbouring hamlets the inhabitants as well as the Partisans were killed by Reder's men.

The first of these allegations was not seriously pressed by the prosecution. In fighting between regular troops and armed civilians quarter is rarely given by the troops to the civilians whom they capture for the very simple reason that regular soldiers captured by civilian combatants are never given quarter. The so-called 'Red Star Brigade' commanded by 'Major' Lupo was only the original terrorist organisation formed by him greatly enlarged and provided from the air with Allied weapons so that it was able to undertake military operations. Its methods of warfare remained the same. As British troops have learnt from experience in Palestine, Egypt, Malaya and Cyprus, terrorist gangs rarely take prisoners. The aim of a terrorist gang is to inspire terror by killing the soldiers of what they regard as a hostile state by any means whenever possible. When in the course of operations a soldier is captured, he is immediately murdered as a matter of course. The only variation of this practice occurs when captured soldiers are kept prisoner to be murdered later as a formal act of reprisal for the execution of captured terrorists. Examples of British soldiers so murdered in reprisal can be readily quoted. The activities of the Stern Gang in Palestine in 1947 included several such outrages: so did the activities of the EOKA terrorists in Cyprus in 1956. In general, however, the practice of terrorists is never to grant quarter. There is no reason therefore why terrorists should be entitled to claim quarter when captured by regular troops.

Sir Winston Churchill once quoted with approval the definition of a prisoner of war as "a person who once wanted to kill you and now asks you not to kill him". The right to claim quarter is a development of what is known as civilised warfare. It is a strictly reciprocal right. The uniformed troops of a civilised state spare the lives of enemy soldiers who surrender and grant them honourable treatment on condition that the enemy troops treat soldiers who surrender to them in the same way. The uniform of a soldier entitles him when captured to claim the rights of a prisoner of war from his uniformed opponents.

But of course Lupo and his gang paid no more attention

to the requirements of the Conventions of Geneva and the Hague than did later the Jewish Stern Gang or the Cypriot EOKA. They themselves wore no uniforms so as to be able, when the occasion demanded it, to throw away their arms and slip away in the guise of inoffensive civilians. A few indeed wore captured uniforms stripped from the bodies of the German soldiers or of the Italian Militiamen whom they had murdered. The reader will remember the story of Bruna Musolesi quoted above of how the police barracks at Marzabotto was attacked and the officer in charge murdered by terrorists dressed in captured uniforms of the Militia.

It may be remarked that the practice of stripping the bodies of murdered opponents is a common one in partisan warfare. The simple purpose of a terrorist campaign is to inspire terror. With this aim in view it is also a common practice of terrorists to mutilate the bodies of fallen foes. That this vile practice is effective in achieving the desired result is indicated by its widespread adoption. It was employed by the Spanish guerillas during the Napoleonic Wars, it was employed in Italy and many of the occupied countries, particularly in Greece and Jugo-Slavia, during the Second World War, and at the time of writing it is being employed by the Algerian insurgents in their terrorist campaign against the French. It suffers, however, from one serious drawback: it tends to make the surviving comrades of murdered and mutilated men extremely unsympathetic with any terrorists who later fall into their hands.

If we accept the statement of the deserter, Julien Legoli, it appears that before the attack on the partisan positions round Monte Sole, Major Reder told his troops that if they were fired on —as of course it was certain they would be—all civilians found in the neighbourhood of such shooting should be summarily shot. Can it be said that this order, if given, doomed to an undeserved death any harmless goatherd, quite unconnected with the Red Star Brigade, who might be found looking after his flock near the position defended by the Partisans?

The answer is that no goatherd or other person unconnected with the Red Star Brigade would by any chance have been found minding his own affairs in the neighbourhood of the brigade's headquarters. Communist Partisans never acknowledge the right of any member of the civilian population to remain neutral. The unescapable duty of every member of society is to do everything in his or her power to help bring about the early establishment of the dictatorship of the proletariat, the ultimate goal, according to Karl Marx, of human development. The Communist maxim is that those who are not with us are against us. Refusal to perform this plain duty would have been treated by Lupo and his fellow terrorists as an admission of being a sympathiser with Fascism. The hypothetical harmless goatherd postulated in the above question would not have been found looking after his flocks near the Partisan's headquarters after he had informed Lupo that he knew nothing and cared less about Communism and Fascism and that he intended to maintain a policy of strict neutrality. The popular catchword 'peaceful co-existence' had not been invented in Lupo's day. The hypothetical harmless goatherd would have been promptly taken out and shot. Had any of the inhabitants of San Martino shown any disposition to remain neutral Lupo would have ordered their immediate liquidation as self-confessed Fascist sympathisers and a standing danger to his organisation.

We may take for granted therefore that all the able-bodied inhabitants of this thinly populated mountain district joined with the Partisans in resisting the German attack. It is impossible to say how many did so because they were adherents of Communism and how many from fear of the Partisans. Their doom was certain from the start of the German attack: if they assisted the defence, they would be shot by the Germans, and if they refused to assist the defence they would be liquidated by the Partisans as Fascist sympathisers.

The charge was made at the trial that a number of women and young persons were killed during the German attack. There is no reason to doubt the truth of this charge. The Red Star Brigade contained many active female members who on occasion joined enthusiastically in the fighting. As the British have recently learned in Cyprus, women and young persons perform many essential tasks in underground guerilla warfare. Women are particularly useful for spying, maintaining communications and for decoying soldiers to selected spots where they can be safely done to death. Young persons are employed chiefly in spying and carrying messages. In Cyprus they have been also used as screens for their adult colleagues. In Nicosia, for example, British troops have been repeatedly attacked with stones by organised mobs of schoolchildren, both girls and boys, behind which 'heroic resistance fighters' can lurk in safety waiting for a favourable opportunity to add a bomb to the shower of missiles.

In Major Reder's defence it was argued that the Partisans had no right to claim the protection of the rules of civilised warfare since they paid no attention to these rules themselves. As they gave no quarter to their opponents, they themselves had no right to quarter. Even the operation in question on the 29th September 1944 provided an example of this. One German scouting party

belonging to the column advancing from the south allowed itself
to be surrounded by a strong force of Partisans dressed in captured
German uniforms. The whole party was massacred to a man. What
reason was there that any discrimination should be given to the
female members of the Red Star Brigade who were as fanatical and
if possible even more treacherous than their male comrades? And
why should discrimination be made in favour of the more youthful
members of the gang, some of whom indeed seem to have been little
more than schoolboys? Under the English Common Law anyone
over the age of twelve is deemed capable of forming a felonious
intent. A similar assumption is accepted in all legal systems. It
is hard to conceive a clearer indication of a felonious intent than
the joining of an organisation formed for the express purpose of
carrying out wholesale murder!

Admittedly the fate of the women and children who lived in
San Martino and the neighbouring hamlets was both terrible and
undeserved. The houses in which they lived were barricaded by
the Partisans whose resistance was only overcome by bombs and
flame-throwers. Their fate was however only the fate normally
suffered in warfare by civilians so unfortunate as to reside in a
place where a battle takes place. Grim as their fate was, it was
no worse than the fate of the inhabitants of villages lying in the
path of the American troops advancing into Germany in 1945.
The American High Command announced that in the event of
American troops being fired on by snipers from any German
village, the village in question would be treated as a defended place
and subjected to obliteration bombing by the American Air Force.
This threat was ruthlessly and often quite unnecessarily carried into
effect.

The objection may be raised that no true comparison can be
made between the position of the German troops holding the Gothic
Line in 1944 who had to cope with Lupo and his Communist
Partisans and the position of the British troops garrisoning Cyprus
in 1956 who had to cope with George Grivas and his EOKA
Partisans. It must be admitted that an essential difference indeed
exists between the two cases which renders comparison difficult.
To make the position of Field Marshal Sir John Harding in Cyprus
in 1956 really comparable with the position of Field Marshal
Kesselring in Italy in 1944 we must try to imagine Sir John's
position if in addition to having to cope with George Grivas and
his EOKA terrorists, he had to defend Cyprus from invasion by a
Greek army superior in numbers to his own and enjoying complete
supremacy in the air and undisputed command of the sea. We must
further imagine this Greek army fighting its way to within a few

miles of his headquarters and the activities of the EOKA terrorists increased tenfold by abundant supplies of arms and ammunition dropped them from the air. Finally, we must imagine the news from home being so bad that it might be announced at any time that Great Britain had been forced to unconditional surrender, in which event Sir John Harding himself and all his men would face the certain prospect of having to stand "trial" before Cypriot courts in which Cypriots would fill the roles of accusers, judges, and in due course no doubt, executioners.

If we succeed in imagining such a transformation of the present situation in Cyprus, we should be able to make allowances for the nerve strain endured by Field Marshal Kesselring and his men as the shadows began to close down on them during those autumn days of 1944.

It not infrequently happens in a criminal trial that after the presiding judge has condemned in scathing terms the conduct of the accused, one is left wishing that in addition to condemning the accused for what he did, the judge would go on to say what in his opinion the accused in the circumstances should have done.

Apparently the Bologna court accepted the version given by the deserter Julien Legoli of the alleged 'pep' talk which he said that Major Reder had given his troops before launching them to the attack on the positions of the Red Star Brigade early in the morning of the 29th September 1944. Presumably the court strongly condemned what they decided he had said on that occasion since this alleged 'pep' talk was the sole direct evidence upon which the sentence of imprisonment for life could be justified. The Court gave no indication as to what they considered should have been his attitude. Assuming that a 'pep' talk was necessary and possible before this attack, which Major Reder denied, presumably the Court considered he should have addressed his men along the following lines:

"My men, you are now going to advance up yonder hillside. You will be fired on with rifles and machine guns from the top and some of you will be killed and wounded. When you reach the top you will find some hundreds of civilians standing about admiring the view. Although you will find a number of weapons lying about, there will be no direct evidence that any particular one of these civilians had been making use of any particular weapon. You must act strictly on the assumption that all these civilians are innocent persons until they have been brought to trial and convicted. I take the heavy responsibility on myself of directing you to arrest these civilians on suspicion. Although most of them will be the scum of the slums of Bologna you must treat them as

171

if they were the Knights of the Round Table. March them to the rear. I think that you will be justified in the circumstances in searching them for concealed knives and revolvers. I advise you to do so carefully as they will undoubtedly murder you if they have the chance. When you have proceeded further in the direction of the headquarters of the Red Star Brigade near Monte Sole, you will come to the little village of San Martino. No doubt you will be fired on from the windows. Some of you will be killed and wounded. But on no account must you return this fire because women and children may be sheltering in the houses. You must ask the persons firing at you from the windows to surrender, but if they refuse, which of course they will, there is nothing you can do about it. You cannot of course use force as this would endanger the lives of innocent non-combatants. I know that for the last two years hundreds of German women and children have been killed every night by the indiscrimante bombing of German towns and villages but you must dismiss this fact from your minds. On no account must innocent human life be put in peril by warfare".

This clearly is what Major Reder should have told his troops prior to the attack—in the considered opinion of the Italian military court which tried him at Bologna over seven years after the events in question. It is exceedingly strange to find a military court—and above all an Italian military court—laying down such principles for the conduct of warfare. Has any war before or since been conducted in accordance with such principles? Can any trace be found indicating that Italians armies have been influenced in their operations by such principles? Probably some members of the court which tried Major Reder were old enough to have taken part in the Turko-Italian War of 1911. In that war the inhabitants of Tripoli started rioting in the rear of the Italian invaders advancing from the town into the interior. The Italian commander-in-chief, General Caneva, immediately ordèred repressive measures as a result of which over 4,000 men, women and children were killed and many native villages burnt as a reprisal. In the forty years which had passed since then, the precedent laid down by General Caneva had been faithfully followed by Italian commanders. For example, in May 1936 a revolt broke out among the civilian population of Abyssinia, then recently conquered by Marshal Badoglio with the aid of mustard gas. The revolt was ruthlessly repressed, over 8,000 inhabitants of Addis Ababa were shot or hanged in the space of twenty-four hours. During the Second World War bitter complaints concerning the brutal conduct of Italian troops were officially made by the Greek and Russian Governments. Many Italian officers—including Marshal Badoglio himself—were named as war-criminals. The Russians were in the fortunate position of being able to try a number of their own charges against Italian officers taken prisoner by them during the campaign in Southern Russia. The reader will not be surprised to learn that the Soviet authorities found their own charges duly established: many of the accused were executed and the remainder sentenced to life imprisonment. The present writer at any rate would not presume to suggest that in dealing with alleged war-crimes, the Soviet authorities were any more liable to err than was the International Military Tribunal.

In view of the precedent set in Tripoli by General Caneva in 1911 and followed faithfully by Italian commanders ever since, it is truly astonishing that the Italian military court at Bologna should have demanded of Major Reder a standard of super-human restraint never exhibited by any military leader of any nation at any time in history.

In justice to the Italian military court it is only fair to suggest that at the time they gave their verdict they were probably concerned mainly with the task of saving Major Reder's life. This they achieved at considerable personal risk to themselves. The Italian Communist Party was the largest in Western Europe and the strongest single party in Italy. A relatively small change in public opinion would have brought about the downfall of the anti-Communist coalition and led to the formation of a Communist Government. In that event the members of the Court would certainly have faced the charge of having conspired to save the life of a Fascist officer and to defame the glorious memory of that great Communist hero, the late lamented 'Major' Lupo. A court composed of Communist adherents would of course have adjudicated on this charge.

In the circumstances in which the trial was held, the Court probably attached little importance to the actual sentence passed. That it should sound severe was all that mattered when an angry Communist mob was demonstrating outside the court house demanding Reder's blood. No doubt the Court assumed that in a very short while the trial would be forgotten when Reder would be surreptitiously set at liberty.

In the following chapter the somewhat similar case of General Ramcke will be described. The unhappy experiences of General Ramcke can partly be attributed to his unfortunate capacity to antagonise in turn all the various persons in whose hands his fate lay. No such explanation is possible in the case of Major Reder who seems to have been liked by all those who came in personal contact with him. His misfortunes may be attributed, not to the malice of his enemies, but to the fact that he was clearly born under an unlucky star.

In the first place, it was pure bad fortune that the renegade Alsation Legoli should have decided to desert a few days after the operations against the Red Star Brigade. Had he not done so, these operations would have attracted no general attention and would soon have been forgotten.

Secondly, it was most unfortunate that the Italian propagandists should have adopted the French story of Oradour to form the basis of a propaganda myth of their own and should, quite fortuitously have decided to label this myth Marzabotto, the little town on the outskirts of the area in which the Red Star Brigade was destroyed by Major Reder's detachment. As a result his name became associated in the public mind not only with an imaginary happening at Marzabotto but also with the real happenings at Oradour. In the popular mind he is remembered as the man who set fire to a church with a number of persons shut up in it.

Thirdly, it was unfortunate for Major Reder that he was attached to a S.S. Division. Throughout the war this division was under the direct command of generals of the German regular army. Although he never took an active part in politics, the fact that he was an officer in a S.S. unit created the strongest prejudice against him.

Fourthly, if when he was interned at Glasenbach, the American authorities had delayed going into the facts of his case a little longer, he would never have been surrendered by them to the British or to anyone else. The outbreak of the 'Cold War' between the U.S.A. and the Soviet Union, followed by the invasion of South Korea by the Communists, completely transformed the situation. In American eyes Major Reder would have ceased to be a wicked Nazi soldier who had been charged with murdering inoffensive Italian citizens and would have become a German officer who had earned the gratitude of all right-thinking people by ridding the world of a gang of Communist thugs.

Fifthly, it was an inexplicable stroke of bad fortune that the British, after putting on trial and convicting his immediate superior officer, General Max Simon, did not proceed with their intention of dealing likewise with Major Reder themselves. If only the evidence against him had been a little stronger, probably the British would have done so. In that case Major Reder would have followed General Simon to the British military prison at Werl and would in due course have been released with him. Because the evidence against him was so flimsy, the British authorities could not decide to put him on trial themselves. On the other hand, they could not bring themselves to release him. Apparently for no other reason than to save themselves the bother of coming to a decision, the British authorities handed him over to the Italians to judge their own charges against him.

Finally, Major Reder was outstandingly unfortunate in regard to the place of his birth. Born at Freiwaldau in Bohemia in 1915 a subject of the Austro-Hungarian Empire, in a district now belonging to the Soviet satellite state, Czecho-Slovakia, he counted for some obscure technical reason as a citizen of Austria. As an Austrian citizen, the German Government had no right to intervene on his behalf. Had he been a German subject, the friendly relations established between Germany and Italy, backed by the influence which Dr. Adenauer came to enjoy at Washington, would have quickly led to his release by the Italian Government. But as an Austrian subject, the Americans, who had arrested him in the first place, maintained the matter was no concern of theirs from the moment when they had handed him over to the British: the British maintained that they had washed their hands of responsibility for his fate when they surrendered him to the Italians. Everyone agreed that the problem was one to be decided by the Italian and Austrian governments.

The Italian Government only desired to be allowed to forget the whole subject. But the association of Reder's name with the still widely believed Marzabotto myth made a succession of Italian cabinets reluctant to go out of their way to bring down on themselves a storm of protests from the strong Communist opposition for permitting Reder's release. Appeals for clemency were shelved: a more propitious moment for Reder's release would come shortly. On its part, the Austrian Government took but a languid interest in the fate of a man who was only technically an Austrian: the fact that during Hitler's regime Major Reder had distinguished himself by loyal service in the German Army did not commend him in the eyes of many Austrians.

At the time of writing Major Reder still remains in an Italian military prison, having now been in captivity for over eleven years. All but a few of the so-called 'war-criminals', many of them convicted, rightly or wrongly, of the gravest crimes, have long since been released, including a score of Italian war-criminals convicted of far graver offences than Reder's by the Soviet courts. Assuming that his trial by his Italian accusers was a fair trial and accepting the verdict as justified by the facts, put at its highest Reder was only convicted of repressing Communist partisan activity with undue severity in accordance with the orders of his superiors. Both his commander-in-chief, Field Marshal Kesselring, and his immediate superior, General Max Simon, upon whom the main responsibility for this severity clearly rests, were set at liberty long ago. Reder however remains in prison.

Major Reder remains in prison only because no one is concerned to secure his release.

Postscript to Page 139 and Page 165.

In a letter to the author Major Reder points out that he was in command only of his own unit, the Panzer Reconnaissance Unit 16, which delivered the main attack from the East across the Setta Valley against the front Monte Sole-St. Martino. The encircling operation against the Stella Rossa Brigade as a whole was under the direction of the Divisional Commander of the 16th Panzer Grenadier Division. General Max Simon.

This fact was admitted by the Court at Bologna which tried Major Reder. He was convicted only for acts alleged to have been committed by men of his own unit.

General Bernhard Herman Ramcke surrenders to the Americans at Brest. General Troy H. Middleton, Commander of the American Forces, described the defensive operation at Brest as the finest he had ever seen.

(Wide World)

At his trial General Ramcke was sentenced to five years imprisonment even though all testimony pointed only to legitimate destruction of civilian property for purposes of defense. It was the Communist and Leftist press in France which labeled him "The Hangman of Brest" without evidence.

CHAPTER VI.

THE FATE OF A HERO

On the 19th March 1951 a specially appointed military court assembled with due solemnity in the dark and musty little court room in the grim Prison Cherche-Midi in Paris. First of all the President of the Court, Monsieur Ménéquaux, resplendent in crimson robes, took his seat. Then six French Generals in full uniform, their breasts adorned with medals and decorations took their place alongside him. Finally the three prisoners of war whose trial was to begin that day were marched into the dock where they underwent a preliminary ordeal of being photographed by flashlight from every conceivable angle by the swarm of eager journalists attending the proceedings.

When at last order was restored and the journalists had returned to their seats, the Court had an opportunity for the first time to see the men whose alleged misdeeds the entire French Press had for weeks been vainly striving to describe in adequate terms of horror and vituperation. The military members of the Court gazed with curiosity at the eldest of the three prisoners, a man of equal rank to their own whose exploits as a general of paratroops had won him an undisputed place among the bravest front-line soldiers of the Second World War. This, however, did nothing to temper the severity with which they regarded him. Neither were they in the least influenced by the fact that he was a brother professional soldier, nor by the fact that most of them had spent the Second World War as prisoners of war during which they had been accorded without question the treatment to which as prisoners of war they were entitled by international law in accordance with the Hague and Geneva Conventions.

Illogically, perhaps, the latter fact indeed seems generally to have operated exactly in the opposite direction. In 1945 a new dispensation in regard to the treatment of prisoners of war had been introduced. True, the Hague and Geneva Conventions had not been formally repudiated, but it had been decided that a prisoner of war only enjoyed the rights given him by these treaties so long as he remained a prisoner of war and that his captors

177

possessed the right at any time to declare that he was no longer a prisoner of war. This alteration of status was achieved very simply either by symbolically releasing the prisoner from custody or by transforming him into a civilian by formally declaring he was discharged from the Army. Generally discharge was accompanied by depriving the prisoner of his uniform or by stripping from his uniform all insignia showing his rank. These simple formalities having been performed, his captors could then treat him as a person in custody awaiting trial on criminal charges or in any other way they saw fit.

After 1945 this new dispensation was enthusiastically adopted throughout Europe by military tribunals sitting in judgment on prisoners of war. Especially enthusiastic were courts composed of soldiers who had themselves been prisoners of war and who had enjoyed the privileges of the old dispensation. To demonstrate their wholehearted acceptance of the new dispensation, former prisoners of war under the old dispensation invariably dealt with prisoners of war brought before them with unflinching severity.

Everyone that day in the dingy little court of justice in the Prison Cherche-Midi knew that far-reaching political issues of the first importance were involved in the trial which was about to take place. For some years all pretence of friendship between the United States and Soviet Russia had been abandoned. Open hostility was no longer disguised and the possibility that the Red Army might proceed to occupy Western Europe was freely discussed. With this prospect in mind, the American Government was becoming more and more insistent that Western Germany should be recognised as a sovereign state and that a new German Army should be created to help to defend Europe from invasion.

Naturally this proposal had filled with rage and dismay the hearts of every Communist, Fellow-Traveller, Pale Pink and Leftist throughout the world. Rage and dismay were particularly vehement in France where approximately one third of the electorate had elected Communist candidates to the National Assembly. In France there was thus a ·solid mass of opinion opposed to any step which would put the least obstacle in the way of an invasion by the Red Army. Supporting this opposition were all those who while not anxious to see France over-run by the Red Army, much preferred to run the risk of this calamity rather than to accept Germany as an ally in the defence of Western Europe. The prospect of conquest by armed Communist hordes from Eurasia was so novel as to seem unreal in comparison with the ancient feud with Germany dating from the days of Louis XIV. To a wide section of the population, history had stopped in 1919 when Sedan had been so signally avenged. Politically this section may be described as suffering from retarded mental development. As usual the Leftists joined in the frantic clamour, less possibly from love for Communist Russia than from hatred for 'reactionary' Germany. The opinion was vehemently expressed that the presence of the smallest German military unit in Europe would constitute a menace to the peace of the world. The employment of German military prowess must be strictly limited to regions where it could be usefully but safely employed. In French Indo-China, for example, it had been found necessary to conduct the war against the Vietminh "rebels" by means of the Foreign Legion, 80% of whom were Germans, owing to the refusal of the French public to permit the youth of France to be sent out to die in defence of the French Empire A German soldier in the jungles of Tonquin was one thing but a German soldier on the Rhine was quite another matter.

Such being the state of public opinion in France at the time, the trial of the three German prisoners of war which began in Paris on the 19th March 1951 was eagerly seized upon by the opponents of German re-armament as a heaven-sent opportunity to revive memories of the German occupation which had ended nearly seven years before. The entire Communist and Leftist Press exhausted the resources of the French language in an effort to describe adequately the enormities which were attributed to the three prisoners. The indictments contained charges of murder, arson and plundering—crimes by themselves sufficiently grave, one would think—but the Press considered these quite inadequate and attributed to the prisoners the commission of every atrocity which the mind of man had to that date been able to conceive. In this Press campaign against the prisoners even such publications as "Le Monde" and "Figaro" abandoned their usual restraint and joined in the chorus of denunciation and vituperation. Needless to say the entire Press accepted the principle laid down at Nürnberg by the Russian Judge, General Nikitchenko, that a prisoner accused by his captors of the commission of a war-crime must be presumed guilty from the moment his captors decided to label him as a war-criminal, the subsequent trial being merely a sort of formal confirmation of the attachment of this label.

This campaign in the French Press was no mere random expression of a long-standing animosity against Germany. It served a two-fold political purpose. If latent hatred of the French people against Germany could be revived to fever-pitch, no French Government would dare to propose the ratification of any agreement by which Germany regained national sovereignty and with it the right to re-arm. With public opinion solidly behind them, the

French Cabinet could then tell the Americans not to presume to meddle in a European question which was considered in France to be an essentially French concern. Secondly, if these three German prisoners of war were convicted and hanged, German public opinion would be so aroused against France that Dr. Adenauer would no longer be able to offer German support to the United States as the price of the restoration of Germany as a sovereign state. If these men were done to death, six years after the conclusion of hostilities, what answer could Dr. Adenauer give to the question which so many of his countrymen were already asking—"Why should Germans be expected to risk their lives fighting to protect Paris and London from the fate which, with the assistance of the French and British, had overtaken Berlin?"

From the foregoing the reader may have jumped to the conclusion that these three defendants in the dock of the court house in the prison Cherche-Midi were German soldiers captured in battle by victorious French troops when attempting to invade the sacred soil of France in accordance with immemorial Teutonic custom?

Such a conclusion is on the face of it reasonable, but it is entirely without foundation. These defendants were German soldiers who indeed had taken part in 1940 in the invasion of France. But they had not surrendered to the French. On the contrary, the French had on that occasion surrendered to them—the entire French Army in fact. They found themselves brought to trial by a French military court in 1951 because they had surrendered to the Americans in 1944.

How on earth, it may well be asked, did this come about? The Second World War ended in 1945. According to international law, their captors, the Americans, were bound to release them as soon as reasonably possible after the termination of hostilities. Assuming that they were released in 1946—as by international law they should have been—did they later have the temerity to enter France some time prior to 1951, where they committed the murders, acts of arson and of plundering for which they were duly brought before the tribunal sitting in the prison Cherche-Midi presided over by the learned Monsieur Ménéquaux?

Once again this is a reasonable assumption but one entirely baseless. In spite of the requirements of the Conventions of the Hague and Geneva the Americans did not release these three prisoners of war as soon as reasonably possible after the termination of hostilities. In fact they never released them. They did not indeed hand them over to the French. The Americans handed these three prisoners over to the British. By the British they were handed over to the French, who after several years delay, brought the charges against them on which in 1951 the learned Monsieur Ménéquaux and his military colleagues assembled to adjudicate.

Before, therefore, describing this memorable trial it is necessary to explain the legal principles upon which it was based. At the conclusion of the Second World War the victors decided to bestow upon themselves the right to put on trial any enemy prisoner in their hands whom they might decide to charge with having committed a 'war-crime'. No definition of a 'war-crime' has ever been authoritatively put forward, but it is generally agreed that to constitute a war-crime two essential characteristics must exist. The person charged with the act in question must be a subject of a vanquished state. Proof that the person charged is guilty of being on the losing side is a preliminary requisite to every war-crime trial: unless this can be established a war-crimes tribunal has no jurisdiction to deal with the charge. Secondly, the act in question must be an act which the victors have declared to be a war-crime. The date when the act was committed is immaterial because the declaration by the victors that the act in question is a crime has retrospective effect.

The legal principle upon which war-trials are based is that an accuser is the best person to act as judge of his own charges. Some may find this principle hard to accept. Lack of space prevents an enquiry as to the objections which can be urged against the acceptance of this principle. It is sufficient here to state that when first propounded in 1945 it was readily accepted by some of the highest legal authorities. As late as May 19th, 1949, no less an authority than Lord Justice Wright in a speech to the House of Lords complained bitterly that "it seemed very unfair and irrelevant to criticise war-crimes tribunals as conqueror's law. The only question was, did the man have a fair trial? To condemn a judgment merely because the court had been appointed by or consisted of belligerents was quite unsustainable".

This may seem an ingenious and novel defence but it is in fact of hoary antiquity. It is only the stock explanation put forward in extenuation of every lynching, namely, that the lynching party only carried into effect the conclusion which a hypothetical court of justice would have come to had it been given an opportunity to adjudicate. Of course, if it be assumed that a fair trial by an impartial court and the doings of a party of lynchers would lead to precisely the same ultimate result, the complaints of the victim would be "unsustainable". But why should such a sweeping and unverifiable assumption be made?

Relying on the authority of Lord Justice Wright, the reader

must make an effort to regard the tribunal composed of the learned Monsieur Ménéquaux and his six military colleagues as an entirely impartial body, quite unprejudiced by any personal experiences its members may have had during the German occupation of France, and uninfluenced by the frantic clamour which had been going on for months in almost the entire French Press for the blood of "the Hangman of Brest" and his two assistants in crime. To fail in this effort would, according to Lord Justice Wright, be unfair to Monsieur Ménéquaux and his military colleagues.

It must be stressed that the above principle is that an accuser is the best person to act as judge of his own charges and not merely that an accuser is a fit and proper person. The victors in 1945 agreed together that whenever possible a charge brought by a certain state should be decided by a court appointed by that state. Thus if a German soldier was captured by the French and the Czechs accused him of having previously committed a 'war-crime', a French court was considered unfit to adjudicate. In such a case the prisoner would be handed over by the French to the Czechs so that the latter could "try" their own charges against him.

As a result of the application of this principle in accordance with the above mentioned agreement, a wholesale interchange of prisoners of war took place between the victorious states in the years following the termination of the Second World War. An irrebuttable assumption existed that every country which had fought against Hitler and his allies must not only be inspired by the same lofty ideals but must also possess the same conceptions of justice. Although, of course, everyone knew that to hand over a prisoner of war to such peoples as the Czechs, the Poles or the Serbs, was equivalent to condemning him to death, probably by torture, yet the pretence was rigidly maintained that the unhappy prisoner was only being sent for trial. What was his ultimate fate was no-one's concern: the only duty of those in charge of such a prisoner was to take stringent precautions to prevent him committing suicide.

Although the three prisoners in the dock at the Prison Cherche-Midi had surrendered to the Americans who had handed them over to the British, neither the Americans nor the British admitted any responsibility for their fate once they had been handed over to the French. It would have been quite in order for the French, had they been so minded, to have passed them on to say the Czechs or Abyssinians. Fortunately for the prisoners however, the French decided to proceed with their own complaints, and after a delay of some four years these complaints were set forth in a lengthy indictment in accordance with French law, and a court was convened to adjudicate thereon. However much the trial which began on the 19th March, 1951, may appear in retrospect as irregular, not to say eccentric, from the foregoing explanation it will be seen that it was entirely in accordance with the views accepted by the highest legal authorities at the time. Indisputably the three defendants were guilty of being on the losing side and were therefore prima facie war-criminals: if we agree that the accuser is the best judge of his own charges, then we must admit that as the charges were French, a French court was the proper court to try these three prisoners.

It now only remains to describe the circumstances in which the alleged crimes of the defendants were committed, to set forth the charges brought against them, to trace the course of the trial and to comment on the verdict reached. First of all, who was the Hangman of Brest and what were the crimes which he was alleged to have committed?

The Hangman of Brest was the appellation bestowed by the French Press—together with a rich variety of similar appellations —on General H. B. Ramcke, a general of paratroops, whose last military assignment had been to take command of the German forces cut off in Western Brittany by the successful American invasion of Normandy in June, 1944, and to defend himself in the fortress of Brest until he was finally overwhelmed.

General Ramcke provides a good example of that new type of general which had evolved during the Second World War to meet conditions which had fundamentally changed during the twenty years of peace which followed the First World War. Or perhaps it would be more correct to say this type was merely a revival of an ancient type. In the days when battles were won by charges of cavalry the main duty of a general was to direct and lead in person cavalry charges. As late as the 17th century leaders like Gustavus Adolphus and Cromwell engaged in personal combat with sword and pistol among their squadrons. Conditions slowly changed, and by the time of the First World War senior officers, generally men in late middle age, sat securely in shell-proof headquarters out of range of artillery fire, directing by telephone their troops "going over the top". The invention of the tank restored to a great extent the conditions of the 17th century: a tank spearhead cannot be adequately directed by telephone. A commander of tanks, like a commander of cavalry, must lead his unit in person. Still less can the operations of paratroops be directed by telephone. A general of paratroops must be prepared to drop with his men over enemy territory in order to take command of them on arrival. For such work youthful nerves and athletic limbs are essential.

Having taken part in the short and victorious campaign in France in 1940, General Ramcke had taken a leading part in the conquest of Crete, the most spectacular, and from losses incurred, the most ruinous exploit by paratroops during the Second World War. Later he had distinguished himself as a front-line commander in the campaigns of North Africa, Russia and Italy. In the winter of 1943-44 he returned to Germany to supervise the reorganisation of the 2nd Parachute Division which had been decimated in the recent heavy fighting in South Russia, preparatory to being sent to reinforce the German armies in France, then awaiting the long-expected Anglo-American invasion. On the 12th June General Ramcke left the military training base at Wahn near Cologne to take over his new command in Brittany. So complete had the Anglo-American command of the air become that he was expressly forbidden to travel by plane in view of the danger of his plane being shot down on the way by some wandering enemy fighter. Travelling by train had become slow and uncertain owing to the destruction or damage of many railway bridges by air attack. So General Ramcke left Wahn by car and reached Nancy that evening— June 12th. The date is important since on the following 20th September he became a prisoner of war of the Americans. However numerous his misdeeds, therefore, all were committed within this short space of three months, during the first part of which he was feverishly occupied preparing for the arrival of his paratroops from Wahn and during the latter half directing a hopeless resistance in Brest against overwhelming odds.

From Nancy General Ramcke continued his journey, via Orleans and Tours, to Auray on the borders of Brittany, some 80 miles from Brest. The last stage of the journey was begun on the afternoon of the 15th. In the same car with the General were two of his senior officers, Staff-Major Schmidt seated beside him and the adjutant, Major Paul, seated beside the driver. Following was another car with an escort armed with a machine gun. Some eight miles south of Pontivy a Breton peasant was seen to run across the road in front. A few moments later there was a burst of sub-machine gun fire from behind a stone wall bordering the road. Five bullets struck the General's car, one grazed his coat and another passed through his hat. Staff-Major Schmidt next to him was less fortunate. He was killed instantly by a bullet through the heart. The cars had been travelling at 50 miles per hour and by the time the escort had halted and alighted, the assailants had fled. Only a glimpse was caught of a number of civilians disappearing into a neighbouring wood.

THE FATE OF A HERO

The killing of Staff-Major Schmidt has no direct bearing on the trial of General Ramcke which took place nearly seven years later. This killing—to use a colourless word—was not indeed mentioned at the hearing although we may be sure that had General Ramcke and his comrades succeeded in overtaking their assailants, a charge of murdering some innocent French civilians would assuredly have been added to the charges brought against him. At the time these lines are being written the Press has been reporting the details of a similar surprise attack by armed civilians near Nicosia in Cyprus upon a British army car which resulted in the death of the British army driver and of the leader of the terrorist gang, Charalambos Mouskos, who was shot dead by the surviving occupant of the car, Major Coombe. We may say with confidence that if the military tribunal in the Cherche-Midi had been called upon to adjudicate on a charge against General Ramcke of having caused loss of life to Staff-Major Schmidt's murderers, it would have come to precisely the same conclusion as a court composed of the comrades of the late lamented Charalambos Mouskos would reach if Major Coombe was ever so unfortunate as to find himself being tried by them.

Although this particular Partisan exploit did not figure in the charge sheet at General Ramcke's trial, it contained numerous charges alleging that he was indirectly responsible for the loss of civilian lives in many similar Partisan exploits. All these charges may be lumped together and summarised in one general allegation that during the innumerable attacks by armed French civilians on the German forces during the campaign in Normandy and Brittany from June to September, 1944, certain French civilians had lost their lives and that General Ramcke as a commanding officer in that theatre of war was therefore responsible for this loss of life.

Fortunately for an understanding of the trial of General Ramcke, it is unnecessary to go deeply into the rights and wrongs of attacks by armed civilians upon soldiers. In 1944 the practically unanimous opinion was held in all the countries at war with Germany that civilians in the occupied countries who shot down soldiers unawares, de-railed trains, sabotaged factories and committed other acts of violence were splendid heroes. Dissent from this view came only from those few who still mourned persons dear to them who had been done to death by Sinn Fein gunmen during the troubles in Ireland in 1919-1921. In those years indeed exactly the opposite view had been general in Great Britain. It was then felt that great allowances ought to be made for soldiers who found themselves among a bitterly hostile population containing a fanatical minority pledged to kill them by hook or by crook at the first opportunity. But in 1944 the Troubles of 1919-1921 had long been forgotten. The struggle in which General Ramcke found himself engaged appeared simply as one between starry-eyed patriots on the one hand and brutal soldiery on the other.

We are told that the mills of God grind slowly. As a general rule no doubt this is true but occasionally they grind with breath-taking rapidity. In the ten years following the 'resistance move-ment' in France during the Second World War, British troops have had to contend with 'resistance movements' in countries as widely separated as Palestine, Kenya, Egypt, the Malay States and Cyprus. The French themselves have had to deal with attacks by armed civilians in Indo-China, and later in Tunisia, Algeria and Morocco. The Americans have had not only the same experience in Korea but concurrently have had to resist an invasion by formidable regular armies—an experience no British army has ever had. It is noteworthy that in the Korean War the American High Com-mand completely disregarded the principles laid down at Nürnberg by the so-called International Military Tribunal and adopted by other war-crimes tribunals. When American troops engaged in resisting the invasion by the Chinese armies were attacked in the rear by Communist guerilla bands, the same methods were adopted as those adopted by the French during the Peninsular War. Civilians found with arms were summarily shot: areas in which outrages occurred were cleared of inhabitants who were put in concentration camps for questioning, generally under torture, by Syngman Rhee's political police: roving bands of partisans were rounded up and exterminated.

It is not suggested here that these methods were in the circumstances unjustifiable. It may well be argued that the first duty of a commander is to take all possible steps to protect the lives of his men. The only point which it is here desired to make is that the situation which faced General Ramcke and his colleagues in Northern France in 1944 was not unique in history. It had often been faced—in less acute forms certainly—by commanders in the past, for example by Napoleon's generals in Spain during the Peninsular War. It has since been faced by the American generals during the Korean War.

Whatever view the reader may take concerning the interven-tion of civilians in warfare, so far as the trial of General Ramcke is concerned the position can be simply summarised. Among the tasks which he found confronting him when he took over his command in Brittany in June, 1944, was a 'resistance movement' of the civilian population, organised, financed and armed on an unprecendented scale. The Anglo-American landing on the 7th

June was the signal for a frenzied outburst of guerilla activity throughout France. The life of no German was safe. It is not hard to believe that in such a situation the nerves of the German armed forces often gave way just as during the Troubles in Ireland the nerves of the "armed forces of the Crown", in far less trying circumstances, admittedly on occasion gave way.

There exists no longer any inclination to idealise the French 'resistance' movement. The driving force behind this movement was Communist. Its real character was disclosed after the 'Liberation' when after the work of killing Germans was over, more French citizens were done to death by their fellow countrymen of 'La Résistance' than perished throughout the entire French Revolution! The generally accepted estimate is 100,000 victims. For over a year an orgy of murder, robbery and rape raged. The excuse usually given in extenuation of this orgy of cowardly violence is that the victims had collaborated or were suspected of having collaborated, with the German occupying forces. In fact, although personal grudges or simply a desire to steal the property of the victims often provided the motive, in the great majority of cases the motive was simply that the victims were anti-Communists.

There is no occasion to dwell further here on this subject. Reprisals by the Germans for the assassinations and atrocities of the Partisans undoubtedly took place, but General Ramcke was not charged with having personally directed or even with having inspired such reprisals. It was merely alleged that as a commanding officer the ultimate responsibility for reprisals rested on him. This contention was not however pressed by the prosecution and it would appear that this group of charges was only added as an afterthought in order to disguise the threadbare character of the principal charges.

On the 31st July the Americans achieved their decisive breakthrough at Avranches. The German forces in Brittany were ordered to move reinforcements eastwards in order to fill the gap in the front. But it was too late. The American tank spearheads had already poured through the gap, branching out to the East and to the West. The German troops moving eastward from Brittany, including many units from General Ramcke's command, were attacked and overwhelmed. The main German forces defeated in Normandy began to withdraw in disorder eastwards. The problem then arose as to what should be done about the German forces away to the West, in Brittany and along the shores of the Bay of Biscay. Should they be ordered to abandon their coastal fortifications and to do their best to fight their way across France in order to link up with the main German armies for the defence of the western frontiers of Germany?

So far as the German troops in Brittany were concerned, the German High Command decided that owing to the lack of mechanised transport and the destruction of so many bridges by air attack, a successful retreat across the path of the American tank spearhead would be impossible. These troops must be regarded as cut off without hope of relief. The only service which they could now render their country was to hold out in the Breton Peninsula as long as possible and so deprive the victorious Americans of the use of the port of Brest which in the First World War had been the chief port of disembarkation for the American army sent to fight on the Western Front against the Kaiser's armies.

On the 12th August General Ramcke was appointed to take command of all the German forces cut off in the north western corner of France.

This date is of outstanding importance in the story of General Ramcke's trial. On the 20th September he became a prisoner of the Americans. His place in military history mainly rests on what he accomplished during these thirty-nine days. We may safely disregard the charges based on the contention that he was responsible for whatever individual members of his command may have done without his knowledge or approval during the preceding two months. To any lawyer, including even learned Monsieur Ménéquaux, such a contention appears absurd. His place in criminal annals—if he has any place—rests therefore on what he did during these thirty-nine days. Like the learned Monsieur Ménéquaux and his six warrior colleagues in the Cherche Midi Court House we must study with care his doings during this short period. He was accused, it will be remembered, of acts causing loss of civilian life, of destruction of civilian property and of plundering. We must consider carefully whether his situation during these thirty-nine days afforded him an opportunity to commit such crimes.

Brittany is a peninsula about 150 miles in length from east to west: from the Channel coast on the north to the Bay of Biscay to the south is approximately 75 miles. At the north west corner lies Brest, the chief base and arsenal of the French Navy. In 1694 fortifications designed by the great Vauban proved their worth when a combined naval and military attack by the English and Dutch under Lord Berkeley was repulsed with great loss. No pains or expense were subsequently spared to render Brest impregnable, and in 1914 it ranked as one of the strongest fortresses in Europe. In 1940 it was surrendered to the Germans without a shot being fired. As a vital sector of the Atlantic Wall, the Germans erected many new fortifications at or near Brest. All these new fortifications, however, were designed to repel an attack from the sea. As at Singapore, little or nothing was done to meet an attack from the landward side. As a result General Ramcke found himself in possession of numerous long-range naval guns, all pointing seawards and so surrounded by massive concrete emplacements that they could take no part in an attack coming from the land side. Efforts to turn them round to face the advancing American troops were only partially successful.

Following the breakthrough at Avranches, one mechanised American column turned westward and pushed along the road to Brittany. Four years before, after a similar breakthrough, Field Marshal Rommel with a single mechanised division had raced across Normandy and within twelve hours of reaching Cherbourg, had overawed into surrender this strongly fortified naval base with a garrison of 30,000 men, none of whom had as yet fired a shot in the war. The Americans expected to repeat this exploit at Brest, but to General Patton's wrath, precious time was wasted in overcoming a pocket of resistance at Dinan. Having covered the two hundred miles between Avranches and Brest, the American tank spearhead attempted to carry the fortress by a coup de main. They occupied the airfield of Guipavas and captured the village of Gouesnou, only five miles north of Brest. General Ramcke counter-attacked strongly and the American advance was halted with heavy loss. It was clear that the possibility had passed of taking the fortress with a rush: reinforcements and heavy artillery would be needed for a siege.

It is hard to understand why the American High Command decided to undertake this siege. Shut up in Brest, Ramcke and his men would have been as completely out of the war as if they had been in Patagonia. A screen of French Partisans, stiffened by a few American or British troops should have been sufficient to prevent their escape. Further, if Ramcke's men had succeeded in breaking out of Brest, their complete lack of mechanical transport would have placed them at the mercy of the swiftly moving American mechanised divisions. They would quickly have been rounded up and forced to surrender. On the other hand, if left undisturbed in Brest, when Germany finally capitulated, they would of course have surrendered. In that event, Brest would have been recovered by the French without even a pane of glass in a single window being broken.

Flushed by victory, however, General Eisenhower and his advisers were in no mood to permit the obstinacy of one pocket of resistance to deny them the use of the magnificent natural

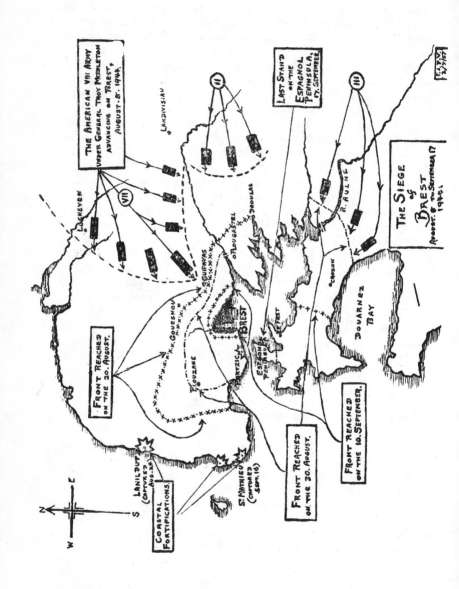

THE AMERICAN VIII ARMY UNDER GENERAL TROY MIDDLETON ADVANCING ON BREST, AUGUST 5, 1944.

LANDIVISIAU

LAST STAND ON THE ESPAGNOL PENINSULA, 17. SEPTEMBER

LANDERNEAU

VII

R. AULNE

THE SIEGE of BREST AUGUST 6 TO SEPTEMBER 17 1944.

PLOUGASTEL

DAOULAS

BREST FOREST

FRONT REACHED ON THE 20. AUGUST.

GOUESNOU

GUIPAVAS

BREST

CROZON

BREST

DOUARNEZ BAY

POUZANE

KERTZIOU

ESPAGNOL PENINSULA

FRONT REACHED ON THE 30. AUGUST.

FRONT REACHED ON THE 10. SEPTEMBER.

LANILDUT (CAPTURED AUG. 26)

ST. MATHIEU (CAPTURED SEP. 10)

COASTAL FORTIFICATIONS.

190

harbour of Brest with its recently constructed docks covering 100 acres and port installations of the latest type. It was decided to crush out resistance forthwith by a major exertion of strength. No less than three infantry divisions with strong artillery and air support were diverted from the pursuit of the main German forces retreating across France. By a letter of instruction dated the 10th September the army besieging Brest was given "first priority" for supplies. It seemed impossible that Brest could resist an attack on this scale for many days. In the summer of the previous year, the Italian island fortress of Panthellaria had surrendered after only a few hours of mass bombing. There appeared to be no limit to the power of concentrated bombardment from the skies.

But the American High Command had overlooked a more recent and far more instructive lesson also from the Italian theatre of war. The long drawn-out battle for Monte Cassino which had raged from February to May of that year had demonstrated that ruins resulting from concentrated bombing provide ideal cover for small units of crack troops armed with tommy-guns who were prepared to resist regardless of their own lives.

The same lesson was to be repeated six months later at Brest. Between August 7th and August 20th the outlying defences of Brest were gradually overwhelmed by a major exercise of artillery and air strength. In all throughout the siege, lasting from August 7th to the 20th September, there were no less than thirty-nine major air attacks by heavy bombers on Brest, while throughout this period fast fighter bombers cruised continuously over the town, practically undisturbed by anti-aircraft fire, industriously destroying selected targets. In one raid on September 12th six hundred bombers took part. By the beginning of September indeed the garrison held only the town itself and the old harbour fortifications. These were soon reduced to ruins by a ceaseless rain of shells and bombs. The fighting among the ruins continued however for another three weeks!

Fantastic though it may appear, the principal charge brought against General Ramcke was that his defence of Brest had caused loss of civilian life and the destruction of French civilian property.

In regard to the charge that civilian life in Brest had been lost as a result of General Ramcke's defence of the town, it is hard to imagine how any life could have survived in that inferno of bursting bombs and shells, falling buildings, streams of burning phosphorous and blazing wreckage. At the beginning of the siege the population of Brest consisted of some 40,000, about half its original population. Few of these would probably have survived the siege had not General Ramcke on the 13th August, some days before the main attack was launched, proposed an armistice for the evacuation of the entire civilian population. General Roy H. Middleton, the American general in command of the besieging army, accepted this proposal, and the evacuation duly took place. Only a few Partisan bands elected to remain in the town in prepared hiding places in order to be able to harass the defenders by attacks from the rear. It is not hard to believe that most of these Partisans perished during the bombardment.

In regard to the charge that he was responsible for the destruction of French civilian property, it is an admitted fact that while the garrison was holding up the attacks of the American army, the systematic destruction went on of the German coastal fortifications, the docks and port installations. No charge could however be brought in regard to this destruction since it was strictly in accordance with the recognised rules of war, the purpose of this destruction being to render Brest useless to the Allies for the disembarkation of troops and stores for the coming invasion of Germany. In regard to the ethics of this destruction, it will be remembered that at the time Ramcke's trial took place, for five years a systematic destruction of factories and docks had been going on throughout Germany, not for any military purpose but to reduce Germany's potential as a trade rival. This policy of destruction had in fact only been abandoned through a change in the political situation. Once it had become necessary to enlist Germany as an ally against Soviet Russia, the policy of destruction was reversed and money had to be lavishly advanced to repair the damage.

Very prudently, therefore, the prosecution limited the charge that General Ramcke was guilty of causing damage to civilian property to allegations that he had blown up certain buildings outside the old walls because they obstructed his field of fire and also certain buildings in the town which had served as strongholds for the Partisans. It was found, however, quite impossible to prove these allegations since the whole town had been practically obliterated by ceaseless shelling and bombing. At the end of the siege, writes General Ramcke in his memoirs,* "Brest looked like a crater on the moon".

In fact Brest did not consist after the siege of a number of badly damaged and shattered buildings. When the last pocket of resistance had been overcome, in many parts of the town it was impossible to distinguish between the remains of one building and the remains of another. The town consisted of masses of brickwork and masonry which had been repeatedly churned over by

* See "Fallschirmjäger" by General H. B. Ramcke, Lorch-Verlag, Frankfurt am Main, 1951.

bombs and shells. Everything combustible had been consumed by the phosphorous bombs and by the liquid fire throwers with which the American infantry covered their advance. No one could do more than guess where the Rue Siam, the main shopping street of Brest, had run: the memorial in the Place du Post to those who had fallen in 'The War-to-End-War' had simply vanished: the Place Liberté could only be identified approximately with the aid of a map. The Cathedral of St. Martin was badly damaged by bombs: the great post office was simply a great heap of ruins. The only structure which remained moderately intact was Vauban's wall although this had been the scene of most desperate fighting, the besiegers at length capturing it with the aid of scaling ladders in the manner of medieval warfare.

On the 13th September, after the siege had lasted over a month, General Troy H. Middleton sent an appeal to surrender to General Ramcke, "as one professional soldier to another". Further resistance, he pointed out, could only delay the inevitable outcome. "Your soldiers have fought well. Approximately 10,000 are prisoners. You know your own losses. Much of your necessary war material must be exhausted and your troops are enclosed in a narrow space. You have completely fulfilled your duty to your country. I hope that you, an experienced and responsible officer who has served honourably and who has already carried out his duty to his country, will give favourable consideration to this proposal".

But the work remained to be done to render the port facilities of Brest entirely useless for the remainder of the war. General Ramcke declined General Middleton's request for surrender.

For yet another week the fighting continued. Step by step the besiegers fought their way through the ruins of the town and of the outlying suburb of St. Pierre. At last there only remained the peninsula of Espagnol with its old fortifications on the south side of the harbour. Subjected to concentrated artillery fire and intensive bombing for two days, and with only rifles and revolvers left, General Ramcke and the last survivors of the garrison of Brest surrendered at 7.0 p.m. on the 20th September.

Thus was reached the inevitable end. But the defenders had achieved their purpose. For the remainder of the war, Brest had been rendered useless as a disembarkation port.

By his captors General Ramcke was treated with every courtesy. He was taken at once by car to the American head-quarters at Lesneven, and the next day was formally received by General Middleton who heartily congratulated him on the resistance which he and his men had offered and expressed his thanks for the care which had been given to the American prisoners and wounded who had fallen into German hands during the siege. Had only a painter with the gifts of Velasquez been present at the American headquarters that day, he would have found a subject for a picture worthy to be set alongside "The Surrender of Breda". The manner in which the surrender of Brest was carried out offers indeed a striking and welcome contrast to the manner in which a number of similar surrenders were destined to be carried out during the ensuing nine months.

From Lesneven General Ramcke was driven to an American prisoner of war camp for officers near Cherbourg. Later he was transferred to a prison camp in England and from there by an air liner across the Atlantic to Washington. The last stage of the journey, "by comfortable Pullman", was to the great prisoner of war camp, Fort Clinton, near Jackson, Missippi.

Down to this point no suggestion had been made by anyone that General Ramcke was other than an honourable soldier who by the fortunes of war had become a prisoner. As he himself admits, he had no ground for complaint of any kind until after the unconditional surrender of Germany had taken place. Immediately, however, unconditional surrender had removed the possibility of reprisals, a violent Press campaign commenced in the United States against the good treatment until then enjoyed by German prisoners of war. As a result of this campaign rations were reduced and many privileges withdrawn.

General Ramcke made himself conspicuous by the energy and warmth with which he joined in the protests made by the helpless prisoners against this petty persecution. In this, he probably did his comrades little good: he undoubtedly brought great troubles upon himself. In fact it is not too much to say that from the action he took at this time can be traced all his subsequent sufferings ending with the trial six years later in the Cherche-Midi Prison at which his life was at stake.

In his memoirs, entitled "Fallschirmjäger" (Lorch-Verlag, Frankfurt am Main, 1951) General Ramcke gives quite unconsciously an extremely vivid character sketch of himself. A general of paratroops must of necessity possess great courage and determination. The part which he had played in the conquest of Crete in 1941 shows that he possessed these qualities. But two incidents which he naively describes in his book show that he possessed to an equally remarkable degree another quality, namely, an outstanding lack of tact.

Thus he tells us that when he returned to France in June 1944 to take over his command in Brittany, he took the opportunity

194

to renew his acquaintance with certain French families with whom he had been friendly when he had had a command in the army of occupation in those parts four years before. In 1940 the vast majority of the French population had submitted to the German occupation philosophically: the possibility of a change of fortune seemed remote and the only sensible course seemed to be to make the best of a bad job. For their part, the German soldiers had received orders to behave with consideration to the French civilian population. As a result, for the first year or so of the occupation, cordial relations generally existed between the occupying forces and the local inhabitants. But by 1944 this tranquil state of affairs had passed away. Outrages and assassinations organised and financed from abroad and savage reprisals by the German security police had shattered for ever the original friendly relations. To be seen speaking to a German was dangerous: to show any signs of friendliness was to incur the suspicion of being a collaborator, a crime punishable by assassination. The last thing which a French family desired in 1944 was to be reminded of a friendship with a German soldier four years before. Such friendships had indeed been common enough but those who had formed them knew it was a matter of life and death that their neighbours should forget their indiscretion.

Yet in June 1944, a couple of weeks after the Anglo-American landing in Normandy had given the signal for a terrific outburst of Partisan activity, General Ramcke tells us that he visited the Mayor of Auray who in 1940 had committed the unpardonable indiscretion of praising the discipline of General Ramcke's paratroops. The terrified Mayor begged to be excused—which response seems to have surprised General Ramcke. Similarly the relatives of some French prisoners of war for whose early release he had used his personal influence with the authorities in Berlin. He found their manner towards him reserved, he tells us, "and in the presence of other French people extremely anxious". If indeed they escaped being murdered after the "Liberation", they probably spent the next couple of years explaining away the General's lack of tact.

Another example from General Ramcke's memoirs illustrating his curious inability to grasp the realities of a situation, will be found in his description of his journey by an Atlantic air liner from Great Britain to the United States. During the flight he received the same treatment as the other passengers on the plane—American officers returning home on leave for one reason or another. He tells us that during the flight he had a most interesting discussion on international affairs with some of his companions to whom he predicted that immediately Germany was overcome a greater conflict was inevitable between the United States and the Soviet Union.

Fortunately for himself, General Ramcke's political predictions were not taken seriously. His hearers all knew as an indisputable fact that complete identity of interests existed between the peace-loving and benevolent President Roosevelt and the equally peace-loving and benevolent Joe Stalin. Probably the views which he expressed seemed too absurd to arouse the resentment of his hearers. Otherwise he would in all likelihood have found himself on arrival in America labelled an unrepentant Nazi and been treated accordingly.

Throughout his experience of prison camps and prisons lasting six years, General Ramcke never seems to have grasped the new conception of what was the only fit and proper attitude to his captors of a prisoner of war belonging to the defeated side. Quite genuinely the victors in the Second World War were oppressed by a consciousness of their own righteousness and by the fundamental wickedness of the vanquished. In such circumstances the only relationship which could exist between a prisoner of war belonging to the vanquished side and a member of the victorious side was on the one hand humility and deference, and on the other, magnanimity.

Temperamentally, General Ramcke was utterly unfit to play the role which one group after another of his captors considered it right and proper that he should play. A man who had leapt with a parachute over the Cretan mountains could neither be browbeaten nor intimidated. He knew precisely the rights given him as a prisoner of war by international law: when these rights were infringed, he expressed his indignation without restraint. He was in fact what any prison governor would label "a difficult prisoner". At Fort Clinton, finding his protests to the authorities without effect, he managed to crawl beneath the barbed wire fence surrounding the camp, obtained a lift in a passing car to the nearest town, posted a number of letters setting forth his complaints to various leading senators and politicians, and returned to the camp before his absence had been noticed. The letters were signed and addressed from the camp: in due course the prison authorities were required by their superiors in Washington to explain what they had been doing. Naturally General Ramcke was placed under arrest for breaking out of the camp and no doubt the prison authorities found themselves in difficulties with their superiors. Ramcke claims that as a result of his action the grievances of his comrades received redress. But he only achieved this at the price of making himself conspicuous as a troublesome prisoner. It is quite likely that all his subsequent sufferings can be traced back to the spite of some petty bureaucrat at Fort Clinton whose authority had been flouted and whose knuckles had been rapped by those above him.

At that time the victorious Powers were industriously exchanging lists of prisoners of war wanted by one or other of them for questioning in regard to alleged war-crimes. So far as the American military authorities were concerned, General Ramcke was a distinguished prisoner of war entitled to special honour on account of the part which he had played in an American military exploit. So, in all probability, he might have remained until the wave of war hysteria had subsided had he only refrained from focusing attention on himself. But a personal grudge once earned could easily be satisfied by arranging that his name should be included in one of these lists of persons wanted for questioning. From what followed, there can be little doubt that this is what happened. In due course a reply was received from the British military authorities that although they themselves had at the moment no complaint against General Ramcke yet they would be pleased to take charge of him in order to interrogate him concerning the part which he had played in the conquest of Crete.

No intimation was given to General Ramcke of the fate which was in store for him. He was merely informed that it had been decided to send him back to Europe. With a truly remarkable incomprehension of the realities of the situation, he understood from this that he was to be returned to Germany to be released. Hostilities had been over for nearly a year and according to international law a prisoner of war must be released as soon as reasonably possible after the conclusion of hostilities. Apparently he believed in all sincerity that his captors and their allies still troubled their heads concerning their obligations under the Hague and Geneva Conventions.

General Ramcke was sent by train to New York where he was embarked with 1,400 other German prisoners of war on a liner bound for Europe. To his surprise, the ship docked at Liverpool where his comrades were landed. He learned long afterwards that they were merely a consignment of slave labour being exported from the United States to work in Great Britain.

Unshakably optimistic as ever, General Ramcke assumed that he and one other prisoner named Kochy were being sent on in advance to Germany for an early release. When the ship docked a few days later, he was astonished to find himself not at Bremerhafen as he had expected but at Antwerp. A further surprise was in store for him. To describe what followed in his own words:

"Hardly had the ship made fast at the quay at Antwerp when we were informed by an American officer that we were to be handed over to the British. A British officer of Police, a sergeant and six policemen took us in charge. Their manners were brutal. With rough cuffs and thumps they fastened Kochy and I together with handcuffs and chains and thrust us with kicks ("mit Fusstritten") into a waiting lorry. We were then driven through Antwerp, under the Scheldt by the celebrated Scheldt Tunnel, via Bruges, to P.O.W. Camp No. 2226 near Ostend".*

This account by the victim was published in 1951. It has never been denied. In default of denial it must be accepted as true. Unbelievable as it may appear if judged according to pre-1945 standards, according to contemporary standards there is nothing about it to justify surprise or comment. In 1945 it was decided that all prisoners of war should be divided into three categories. First of all were those against whom some charge of personal misconduct could be directed who thereby became officially labelled "war-criminals" until such time as some court composed of their accusers formally confirmed their guilt. (Certainly after this confirmation they soon ceased to belong to any earthly category!). Secondly, there were those prisoners belonging to certain units such as the U. Boat Service, the S.S. formations and, for some extraordinary reason, the paratroops. Members of such units were deemed prima facie criminals whose records required careful investigation with a view to transferring them to the first category. In the meantime as prima facie criminals, they were detained in rigorous custody. Finally there was the third category of prisoners composed of men who had been neither charged with any particular offence nor were deemed prima facie criminals from the units to which they belonged. Only to this third category of prisoners were the rules laid down by international law admitted to apply, and then only, of course, at the discretion of their captors.

Without warning or explanation and indeed before he knew of the introduction of this novel system of classifying prisoners of war, General Ramcke found himself placed in the second of the above mentioned categories. Neither his knowledge of the history of his profession nor his own recent experience helped him to understand the situation in which he found himself. Only eighteen months before when he had surrendered to the Americans, they had treated him strictly in accordance with the traditions of warfare between civilised nations. Why should the British—to whom he had not surrendered—now treat him as a convicted

* "Fallschirmjäger" by General H. B. Ramcke, Lorch-Verlag, Frankfurt am Main, 1951, Page 101.

criminal? When General Percival surrendered to the Japanese at Singapore in 1942 and when General Townsend surrendered to the Turks at Kut-el-Amara in 1916, no one had deemed it fit and proper to use handcuffs and chains. Why should the British lapse below the examples so recently set them by Japanese and Turks?

At the time it took place, no doubt the incident could be readily explained by attributing it to the aberrations of some half-witted British junior officer in command of a particularly uncouth selection of military policemen. Unfortunately, this experience on the quay at Antwerp proved to be only a foretaste of what was to follow. It is unnecessary to set out in detail here General Ramcke's experiences between that day in March 1946 when he was handed over at Antwerp by the Americans to the British to that day in March 1951 when he was marched into the dock in the Cherche-Midi Prison on trial for his life. It is sufficient to say that throughout this period of five years he was treated as a convicted criminal, was frequently put in chains and several times was subjected to periods of solitary confinement.

The British indeed never brought any charge against him. Having kept him in rigorous custody for nine months, including a sojourn in the notorious 'London District Cage', Kensington Gardens, the British handed him over to the French on the 4th December 1946.

It still remains a matter for speculation why the British decided not to bring any charge against him and why the French decided to ask that he should be handed over to them. All that we know for certain is that the British obtained the surrender of General Ramcke from the Americans for reasons which have never been disclosed and that having kept him in the strict custody usually accorded to convicted criminals, they preferred no charge against him but handed him over to the French on the 4th December 1946. We do not know what reasons the French gave for asking for his surrender to them. All we know is that he was handed over at the Gare du Nord, Paris, to the French police, whence he was taken, handcuffed and chained, through the streets of Paris to the prison celebrated in the annals of French justice as the first place of incarceration of Captain Dreyfus, the Prison Cherche-Midi. After a week here, in indescribable insanitary conditions, he was taken to the prison of Rennes in Brittany. Shortly after his arrival he was informed that a charge of murder against him was under consideration in connection with the blowing up of the Sadi-Carnot on the 9th September during the siege of Brest.

It is noteworthy, however, that no such charge was in fact ever brought. Presumably it was found impossible to account for this explosion which caused the death of a number of German soldiers as well as of a few French civilians. Partisan sabotage or a random bomb or shell offer possible explanations: the cause of this explosion will probably always remain a mystery. No further mention of this subject was ever made.

It was not until the 25th April 1950 that General Ramcke was presented with a copy of the first edition of the indictment which had at last been provisionally settled. The reader will remember that he was put in chains as a criminal on the quay at Antwerp in March 1946. During the ensuing eleven months this indictment was several times revised, corrected and amended so that a substantially different document was read by the Clerk of the Court on the 19th March 1951 to learned Monsieur Ménéquaux and his six warrior colleagues.

General Ramcke in his memoirs complains bitterly of this delay. It may well appear a travesty of justice to detain a prisoner of war in strict confinement in appallingly insanitary conditions under rigorous discipline enforced by such penalties as terms of solitary confinement in chains, without disclosing to him what offence he was suspected of having committed. To this delay, however, General Ramcke was unquestionably indebted for his life. Had he been brought for trial immediately after the French took charge of him, he would in all probability have been automatically condemned and executed. It was fortunate for him that the administration of Justice in France moves so slowly. He was so to speak at the end of the queue: a great number of other cases were awaiting disposal before his. From his cell, he tells us, he often heard the firing squads carrying out the final stage of the process of disposal.

On the other hand, General Ramcke was very unfortunate in regard to the time when it was ultimately decided to bring him to trial since this decision happened to coincide with a sudden outburst of political tension in France. By 1950 war hysteria had so far subsided that many prisoners of war awaiting trial had been unobtrusively released by order of the French Government without public opinion in France being aroused to any significant extent. It is possible that but for the reputation which he continued to maintain of being "a difficult prisoner", General Ramcke would have been among them. Perhaps it may be said that his own temperament was his undoing. Half-starved, living in a bare, overcrowded, insanitary cell, and subjected daily to personal indignities, he was not the man to keep silent concerning his treatment or to refrain from drawing attention to the rights given him by international law. We may be sure that those in charge of him were often pained and displeased to find how far short he constantly fell below that standard of submissive contrition which had come to be regarded as the fitting demeanour of a prisoner of war guilty of having been on the losing side in a great war. As at Fort Clinton, Mississippi, as in the 'London Cage', Kensington, so in the various French prisons in which he was confined he doubtless made enemies. As a result he was still a prisoner awaiting trial when public opinion in France was stirred to the depths by the proposals being vigorously urged by the American Government that the sovereignty of Germany should be restored and a new German army shoulud be created for the purpose of helping to defend Western Europe from an invasion by the Red Army. Very naturally, Communists and Communist sympathisers throughout the world were aghast at a proposal to put difficulties in the way of a Communist crusade to extend by force the blessings of Communism to the shores of the Atlantic. The obvious way to combat this proposal was to inflame Franco-German relations. The readiest method of achieving this purpose was to put to death yet another German general after a trial at which the victim's alleged crimes could be broadcast with the maximum publicity. Except for General Ramcke, all the well-known German leaders in French hands had already been tried: they were either dead or were serving long sentences of imprisonment. But as the defending commander in the most desperately contested siege of modern times, General Ramcke was a public figure familiar to both the French and the German peoples. His execution for murder, sabotage and plundering could be relied on to have the gravest political repercussions.

Having regard to the political requirements of the moment, General Ramcke was the obvious choice as the focal point for an anti-German campaign. The Communist and Leftist Press immediately labelled him "The Hangman of Brest" and launched strident appeals for an early extermination of the human monster. The French Government reluctantly bowed to the storm: the indictment which had been prepared was hastily rescued from some dusty pigeon-hole, once again amended and the machinery of the law set in motion. Within another six months or so General Ramcke found himself in the dock of the court house of the Cherche-Midi Prison.

The person most deserving sympathy during the trial was not, however, General Ramcke or either of his two subordinate commanders, Captain Kamitschek and Lieutenant Marsteller, who were defendants with him in the dock, but the presiding judge, Monsieur Ménéquaux. To the six French generals who had been appointed to sit with him and who more or less carried out the functions of a jury, the case presented no worry or difficulty. Like the Gallant Six Hundred who charged at Balaclava, theirs was not to reason why. They knew their duty and they took their places determined to carry it out with unflinching courage. Whatever the evidence, these three Boches should receive their deserts.

But to a trained lawyer like Monsieur Ménéquaux the indictment must have seemed an extraordinary document. The first part was obvious nonsense. It alleged that General Ramcke was responsible for a score or so of acts, which for convenience we may label 'Black-and-Tan outrages', alleged to have been committed by German soldiers in Brittany during the period starting from his arrival there in the middle of June down to the commencement of the siege of Brest. Down to the 12th August when he was given command of all the forces cut off in Brest, General Ramcke was himself only a subordinate commander: his command, the 2nd Paratroop Division, formed part of the troops in Brittany under the orders of the General commanding in that theatre of war. It was not alleged by the prosecution that General Ramcke had taken any personal part in these outrages or reprisals: the allegation was that the perpetrators were men under his command, that is to say were members of the 2nd Paratroop Division. Except in one case the prosecution failed to produce any evidence showing to what unit the perpetrators belonged. This one exception related to the execution of three partisans concerning whose case Captain Kamitschek and Lieutenant Marsteller had been concerned. This was the reason, no doubt, that it had been decided to put these two officers on trial at the same time as General Ramcke since admittedly both had been under his command.

The facts of this particular charge were very simple. On the 24th June the bodies of three German ambulance men, naked and horribly mutilated, were found on the road leading from Sizun to Chateaulin. A peasant of Sizun named Cavoloc gave evidence for the prosecution that after this gruesome discovery his son and two other young men were arrested by a detachment under the command of the two defendants, Kamitschek and Marsteller. He admitted that all three men were members of 'La Résistance' and were found in possession of weapons, but he insisted that these weapons had not recently been discharged. He himself had been arrested as an accomplice but had been released next day. His son and the two other men had been handed over by Kamitschek to the German Security Police by whom they were later shot at Chateaulin.

Assuming that these three Partisans were innocent of the

murder and mutilation of the unfortunate ambulance men, and ignoring the fact, admitted by the prosecution, that their lives had in any case been forfeited since they had been found carrying arms on a battlefield, the only connection General Ramcke had had with the matter was that the soldiers who had arrrested them were men of the 2nd Paratroop Division and were thus under his command.

In answer to Monsieur Ménéquaux, General Ramcke maintained bluntly that the three Partisans were rightly shot: he himself knew nothing of the matter at the time but on the evidence given by the prosecution it was clear that his subordinates had acted strictly in accordance with the rules of war. Monsieur Ménéquaux passed on, probably with an inward sigh of relief, to the charges in the second part of the indictment which related to alleged misdoings committed during the siege of Brest.

It will be remembered that this part of the indictment charged General Ramcke with murder, destruction of civilian property, and plundering during the siege. Unfortunately for the prosecution, Brest was evacuated by its entire civilian population before the siege commenced and later was almost completely destroyed by shells and bombs. It was in consequence utterly impossible to prove the death of any civilian or the destruction of any particular building was attributable to the garrison.

In support of the charge of murder, evidence was given by a Partisan leader named Le Roy. This witness said that four of his men had been purposely left behind in Brest at the time of the evacuation of the civilian population in order that they might "observe" the doings of the garrison. He said that he had been told that the secret Partisan 'hide-out' in which these men had secreted themselves had been discovered and attacked by the Germans. He felt sure that all four had been shot by the Germans—at any rate no trace of them had been found. Who could doubt that they were dead? He could not swear of his own knowledge that these men had not been killed by shells or bombs. He himself had been outside Brest during the siege "on other business".

The charge of having destroyed civilian property during the siege was not seriously pressed. The allegation was made that ·the Germans had obstructed the work of the fire brigade in its attempts to put out fires caused by the bombardment: but no explanation was offered why the garrison should wish to carry on the fight among the burning buildings. It was further alleged that the Germans had purposely destroyed certain buildings used as 'hide-outs' by the Partisans and other buildings which had obstructed their field of fire. As, however, practically the entire town had been destroyed by the bombardment of the besiegers, it was quite impossible subsequently to establish how any particular buildings had been destroyed.

No charge was of course preferred in connection with the systematic destruction of the fortifications, the docks and the port installations. It was tacitly admitted that this was legitimate destruction carried out in accordance with the laws of war.

Perhaps the most absurd of all the charges upon which the unfortunate Monsieur Ménéquaux found himself called upon to advise his military colleagues, was the charge of plundering. The garrison of Brest, closely shut in on all sides by overwhelming forces without hope of escape, was alleged to have spent the short time of freedom remaining to them in plunderirng the town! A less auspicious occasion for plundering is hard to conceive. Surely a regiment composed entirely of burglars, housebreakers, jewel thieves and highwaymen could be safely let loose in Regent Street or Hatton Garden if they knew beyond all question that it was merely a matter of days, or at the most weeks, before they would be prisoners when of course anything which they had stolen would be taken from them. In such circumstances, appropriating the Crown Jewels would be hardly worth the trouble. The prosecution indeed showed little imagination in bringing such a charge.

Poor Monsieur Ménéquaux had an exhausting task trying to extract from all this nonsense a few facts which he could declare had established one definite charge. He is entitled to every sympathy for his thankless efforts, as well as credit for the dignity which he displayed in trying circumstances and for his courtesy to the prisoners. General Ramcke, on the other hand, deserves no commiseration since he so obviously enjoyed every minute of the trial. During the long five years which had passed since he was handcuffed on the quay at Antwerp, he had been compelled to bottle up his indignation or, at best, to direct it at indifferent prison governors, policemen and warders. Naturally he grasped the opportunity given him by the trial to express in the most public manner possible what he had been burning to say for so long. With undisguised delight he tore in shreds the case for the prosecution.

Not of course that this had the least influence on the final result. All war-trials are at bottom political: their purpose is not to punish crime but to fulfil some political purpose. The trial of General Ramcke was purely political: it was launched to serve a burning political purpose of the moment. Had it remained unsupported, General Ramcke's refutation of the charges made against him would have been airily waved aside.

But General Ramcke's refutation of the charges made against

him was not left unsupported. It received support of a kind which could not be airily waved aside. The defence had succeeded in obtaining the evidence on commission of General Roy H. Middleton, the American conqueror of Brest.

General Middleton began by disposing of the charge of plundering by testifying that no articles of plunder had been reported to him as having been found on the captured members of the garrison when they were searched after the surrender.

General Middleton was then asked: "What impression did you form of the methods of conducting war of the German soldiers in Brest and particularly of the 2nd Paratroop Division?" General Middleton replied, "During my entire professional service in two world wars I have never come across better fighting soldiers than the German troops in Brest. This applies particularly to the men of the 2nd Paratroop Division. They impressed me as well disciplined well trained and remarkably obedient to orders".

In reply to the question, "Have you any knowledge of brutal acts or criminal behaviour on the part of the garrison of Brest?" General Middleton replied: "No acts of brutality or of unlawful methods of warfare were reported to me by my troops. Those of our men who became prisoners of the German troops in Brest were as well treated as one can expect in war. I consider that the measures taken by General Ramcke for the prisoners in his hands were better than I have ever before observed in warfare".

Finally General Middleton was asked: "Have you any observations to make concerning General Ramcke?" To this question, he replied: "Of the many German commanders I have met in war and of the round dozen German generals who fell into the hands of my troops, I rank General Ramcke as the most outstanding soldier. I consider that he conducted the defence of Brest in accordance with the•best soldierly traditions".

The evidence of General Walter M. Robinson, also taken on commission, was then read to the Court. It confirmed General Middleton's evidence. In particular General Robinson testified that when the American troops entered Brest, there were numerous fires blazing caused by the phosphorous shells used in the bombardment which, in his opinion, were quite beyond the power of the garrison to master. The Court heard this unwelcome evidence in resentful silence.

The State Prosecutor, General Sabathier, however, remained unabashed. His concluding speech for the prosecution was certainly a remarkable achievement. Having dealt at length with French history, he reminded his hearers that France was fair land famed for its martial exploits: to the glory of France, French arms had at one time or another been carried to every corner of Europe. To this glory the doings of the members of 'La Résistance' had, in the gallant General's opinion, materially contributed. He then described in a burst of eloquence the virtues of the Partisan fighters against the German yoke, their courage, their self-sacrifice, their resolution and their patriotism. France, he declared, was at that moment looking to the Court to express by their verdict their gratitude, their pride and their thanks for this heroic struggle. For General Ramcke and his two officers he demanded severe punishment.

The most captious critic could at the most only complain that this speech had no bearing whatever on the facts at issue in the trial. But such an objection would be merely captious since the trial had disclosed no facts at issue. With a Napoleonic grasp of the situation, General Sabathier appealed to the Court to pass in the name of France a sort of vote of confidence testifying approval of "La Résistance".

In passing it may be remarked that if General Sabathier's gifts as a soldier equalled his gifts as an orator, it is a pity that in place of wasting his time on a political stunt in the Cherche-Midi, he was not directing the hard-pressed forces of France then engaged in a losing struggle with the Vietminh insurgents in French Indo-China. Some indeed may think it strange that if the gallant general's estimate of the martial virtues of the Partisans was not unduly flattering, so few of the heroes of 'La Résistance' enlisted to uphold the honour of France in the campaign in Indo-China and later in that in North Africa, with the result that these campaigns had to be carried on by foreign merceneries, three quarters of whom were German. Fortunately, however, it is not necessary to entertain the possibility that the general's eloquence led him to exaggeration. While patriotism and American dollars played their parts, the main driving force behind the 'La Résistance' was Communism. The most ardent of the Partisan fighters joined gladly in the struggle against "the forces of Fascism": they flatly declined to risk their lives for France in any colonial war, particularly as was the case in Indo-China, where the enemies of France were receiving the active support of the Soviet Government.

The trial concluded with speeches on behalf of the three defendants. These may be passed over without comment since of course they had no influence on the final result. The Court then withdrew to consider its verdict.

It is not the practice in a war-crimes trial for the adjudicating court to pronounce a reasoned judgement, disclosing what facts have been found proved, what evidence is accepted and the reasons for the decisions come to. Often when a number of charges have been made, the court does not even trouble to say upon what charges the defendant has been found guilty and upon what charges he has been found innocent. Generally the defendant is merely informed that he has been found guilty and what the sentence of the court is. Monsieur Ménéquaux and his six military colleagues followed this accepted practice and therefore we can only speculate as to what took place during their deliberations.

The violent campaign which had been raging in the Press for months against 'The Hangman of Brest' could have left the Court in no doubt as to what would be the consequences of an acquittal. Without question they themselves would be denounced throughout France as self-confessed collaborators. Only to German intrigue behind the scenes could so astonishing a result be ascribed. To every Communist in France a verdict of acquittal would be regarded as an insult to "La Résistance". All the parties of the left would support the Communist clamour in which would also join the factions of the extreme Right whose simple political creed was undying hatred of Germany and everything German. The downfall of the Government would inevitably follow: probably a coalition government of the Left would take office which would be dominated by its Communist supporters. The consequences of the establishment of such a regime in France on the international situation might well be incalculable.

It may seem that the Court could readily solve all its difficulties by bringing in a simple verdict of "Guilty". But the problem could not be solved quite so easily as that. The attitude of the United States had to be taken into account. To condemn General Ramcke in the face of the evidence given by General Roy H. Middleton would certainly be regarded in American military circles as an affront. Pride was felt in the story of the capture of Brest not only as an example of American prowess but of American chivalry. Americans could hardly be expected to welcome the addition of a footnote to that story recording that the defender of Brest was done to death by his French enemies five years after his surrender to the Americans. But most important of all, the execution of General Ramcke would certainly be received with the strongest disapproval by the American Government. Ever since the outbreak of the 'Cold War' with the Soviet Union, one of the chief aims of American foreign policy had been to win over German public opinion to the side of the Western Powers. The work had been hard but good progress had recently been made thanks to the support of the German Chancellor, Dr. Adenauer. This belated trial of General Ramcke would certainly be regarded in Washington as an adroit

Communist manoeuvre to re-awaken Franco-German hostility in order to bring about the downfall of Dr. Adenauer's pro-American regime. Ever since the War, France had depended on American financial and economic support. If an "agonizing re-appraisal" took place in Washington and the flow of dollars ceased, where could France turn for benevolent support? Would not the loss of the American pension be a high price to pay for the death of one more German general?

We may be sure that Monsieur Ménéquaux strove long and hard to implant a realization of the realities of the situation in the heads of his military colleagues. The outcome proves that he did not strive in vain.

The verdict of the Court was that General Ramcke and Captain Kamitschek were guilty of being accessories to murder, incendiarism and plundering. Both were sentenced to five years imprisonment. Lieutenant Marsteller was acquitted.

The Court did not specify what acts of murder, incendiarism, and plundering they had found had taken place. It is impossible therefore to comment on the connection of the two defendants, convicted of being accessories, with these acts. In regard to charge of plundering, no evidence had been given at the hearing, so that we may safely assume that with regard to murder and incendiarism also the Court used these words merely as convenient labels to describe conduct of which they disapproved.

Nevertheless the verdict was one of which King Solomon himself might well have felt proud. Both the convicted men had spent only three months short of five years in rigorous confinement awaiting trial as unconvicted convicts. Under French Law after serving another three months in exactly similar conditions, they were entitled to release.

Except for the Communists whose stunt had miscarried and General Ramcke who strongly resented being labelled a criminal, everyone was satisfied, or at least not seriously dissatisfied. Public opinion in France was gratified to hear that the Court had found the accusations against the "Hangman of Brest" and one of his confederates substantiated. In French legal circles Monsieur Ménéquaux received praise for convicting the two leading accused and so preventing the charge being made against French justice that innocent men had been kept in prison nearly five years without a trial: it was considered that Lieutenant Marsteller was too unimportant a person for such a slur to attach in his case: his acquittal was indeed praised as bestowing an air of verisimilitude on the findings of the Court. In Germany, public opinion remained entirely undisturbed at the news that General Ramcke would now

General Ramcke being welcomed
on his return from prison to his
home town of Schleswig.

The Nürnberg trial of Admiral Erich Raeder, hero of the battle of Jutland, who is being tried for the "crime" of invading Norway ahead of the British.

have to serve another three months imprisonment in a French prison. The verdict was considered unjust of course but it was felt that the General might well regard himself as fortunate in having become entitled to his freedom within so short a time as three months, in contrast at any rate with the tens of thousands of his comrades, convicted on equally fantastic charges, who without hope of release, were spending the remainder of their lives in the prison camps of the Soviet Union. In Washington relief was felt that the danger of a major political crisis had been adroitly averted. The negotiations with Dr. Adenauer proceeded as amiably as ever.

On the 23rd June 1951 General Ramcke was released from the grim Cherche-Midi Prison and was immediately driven by car to the German frontier. His long ordeal which had begun on the quay at Antwerp in March 1946 was over.

CHAPTER VII.

THE SUPER-ERSATZ CRIME

The President of the Tribunal was delivering the judgment of the Court.

Solemnly he pronounced, "The initiation of a war of aggression is not only an international crime, it is the supreme international crime, differing only from other war crimes in that it contains within itself the accumulated evil of the whole".

A hush fell on the assembled court. Three thousand, four hundred and thirty seven years before, according to the calculations of worthy Bishop Usher, Moses had descended from Sinai amid thunders and lightnings carrying under his arm two tables of stone with the Ten Commandments written thereon, according to the author of the Book of Exodus, by God himself. And now on the 30th day of September nineteen hundred and forty-six this mild-mannered aforetime scholar of Haileybury and member of the Inner Temple had formulated a new sin, an omnibus sin, which contained within itself, more or less, all the sins which it had taken Moses two tables of stone, writing on both sides, to set forth. But a single table of stone would have been sufficient for the new eleventh Commandment "Thou shalt not initiate a war of aggression".

A genuine shudder ran through the court. Indignant glances were cast at the bedraggled, weary-looking men in the dock. How could anyone, however desperately wicked, have the temerity, the presumption, the effrontery to commit so much evil by a single act! Some of the onlookers glanced upwards apprehensively as if expecting some manifestation of divine displeasure to crash through the roof. The grim-faced guards, posted menacingly behind each prisoner, fingered impatiently the clubs with which they maintained discipline among the prisoners once these unfortunates had been withdrawn from the public gaze. Beings capable of such enormity required stern and fearless handling in their cells.

The lawyers present glanced at each other expectantly. So the Tribunal had at last worked out a definition of 'aggressive war', a task which had completely baffled several international committees composed of some of the ablest lawyers in the world during the past three years. In legal circles it was well known that this task had at last been abandoned in despair. Every conceivable definition had been suggested and then promptly rejected on the ground that it was wounding to the susceptibilities of one or the other of the victorious nations. It was widely believed on good authority that several jurists of great eminence had turned their attention to the problem of squaring the circle or designing a perpetual motion machine as a relief from the hopeless task of finding an acceptable definition of aggressive war.

The President of the Tribunal gave a dignified cough—the unfailing dignity of Lord Justice Sir Geoffrey Lawrence throughout the trial had been the special pride of the foreign correspondents gathered at Nürnberg to report the trial of the twenty-one individuals who long before it commenced had been officially labelled "major war criminals".

Having coughed with dignity, the President of the Tribunal proceeded to deal with other matters. He made no further mention of the subject during the course of his judgment: aggressive war he left undefined. It has remained undefined to this day.

This, however, did not prevent the Tribunal from convicting certain of the prisoners in the dock of the crime of initiating and waging aggressive war. Among those so convicted was Admiral Raeder, referred to on the charge sheet and throughout the proceedings in accordance with the uncouth practice adopted at war-trials, as simply Erich Raeder.

Who was this Admiral Raeder? The readiest way of answering this question is to turn to Volume XI of the 1950 edition of that standard book of reference, Chambers Encyclopaedia: —

> RAEDER, Erich (1876-), German sailor, entered the German Navy in 1894 and became captain 1905. He was chief of staff to Admiral Hipper, commanding battle cruisers, 1912-1918, rear-admiral 1922, vice-admiral 1925 and commander-in-chief of the German Navy in 1939 and was responsible for the operations of the German Navy in the second world war until 1943 when he was succeeded by Admiral Dönitz. He was tried at Nuremberg by the international tribunal and sentenced on 1 Oct. 1946 to imprisonment for life.

If the reader has failed to note anything peculiar in the above passage, he should read it again—and again if necessary. The first sentences describe an honourable, distinguished and blameless career, the career of a naval officer who had risen to the head of his profession, a career which could be paralleled by many similar careers, equally honourable and distinguished, in the British, French, American and other foreign navies. The last sentence is in astonishing disharmony with the rest of the paragraph. It records tersely that this honourable, distinguished and presumably blameless career was ended by a sentence of life imprisonment.

The reader is left wondering the reason for this ferocious penalty. So far as Chambers Encyclopaedia is concerned he is left to wonder. Often, however, silence is most eloquent. The contributor of the naval sections of this encyclopaedia was Admiral Sir William Milbourne James, G.C.B., a British naval officer with a career as honourable and only a little less distinguished than that of Admiral Raeder. It would have been so easy to have made sense of the above paragraph by adding some non-committal and colourless words to the last sentence such as "for a war-crime". One is left to speculate how the paragraph was originally drafted and whether its final form might not be the result of an unsatisfactory compromise between an indignant British naval officer on the one hand and a harassed editor anxious not to incur official disapproval on the other.

It is unnecessary here to add much to the particulars given in the paragraph quoted above. The outstanding event of Erich Raeder's professional career was the battle of Jutland at which he served as Korvettenkapitän on the "Lützow", the flagship of Admiral Hipper's battle cruisers. The "Lützow" led the German line in that desperate thrust at the British fleet by which Admiral Scheer sought to prevent himself being cut off from his base. During this manoeuvre she received the most terrific battering of any capital ship taking part in the battle, being struck by no less than twenty shells of the largest calibre. Upon Raeder fell the responsibility of transferring Admiral Hipper from the crippled "Lützow" to another battle cruiser. Early the following morning, with 8,000 tons of water in her hold, and quite unmanageable, the "Lützow" was abandoned by her crew on Raeder's orders and then torpedoed to prevent capture.

The battle of Jutland was one of the last battles fought strictly in accordance with the old chivalrous traditions of European warfare. In accordance with these traditions, Admiral Jellicoe paid tribute to his opponents—and indirectly to himself and his men—with the comment, classical in its simplicity and brevity, "The enemy fought with the gallantry that was expected of him".

Only twenty-nine years separated the battle of Jutland in 1916 and the "war trials" at Nürnberg which began in 1945!

First of all, an effort should be made to get clear, so far as it is possible, of what crime or crimes was Admiral Raeder accused.

THE SUPER-ERSATZ CRIME

Admiral Raeder was charged under Count 1 of the Indictment of having participated in a common plan to wage aggressive war, under Count 2 of the Indictment of having committed a crime against peace by preparing and waging wars of aggression and under Count 3 of the Indictment, of having been responsible for war-crimes arising out of sea warfare. He was convicted on all three counts.

These may seem a formidable and complicated total but, in fact, the essential offence of which Admiral Raeder was convicted was very simple and related solely to the part he admittedly took in the German invasion of neutral Norway in 1940. So far as Admiral Raeder was concerned, Counts 1 and 2 were the same. If the invasion of Norway was a crime, he was clearly guilty under both counts. Count 3 in his case was only thrown in as a sort of make-weight. The Tribunal expressly acquitted him of the gravest item under Count 3, namely of having carried out unrestricted submarine warfare, because it was established that the British Admiralty on May 8, 1940 had issued an order that all ships in the Skaggerrak should be sunk at sight, and that the American Navy had carried out unrestricted submarine warfare in the Pacific from the first day the United States entered the war.

It should be stressed that whatever Admiral Raeder did, he did as a senior naval officer obeying the orders of his executive government. He was not an admiral-politician like, for example, Lord Charles Beresford. He was not one of the Nazi leaders. He was never a favourite of Hitler—who ultimately, using him as a scapegoat for the German disasters in Russia, dismissed him summarily on January 30, 1943 in favour of Admiral Dönitz—and he was on notoriously bad terms with Field Marshal Goering. Unlike Admiral Dönitz his interests were essentially naval. His achievements and crimes, if any, were entirely in connection with naval warfare.

Admiral Raeder's trial commenced at Nürnberg on the 20th November 1945: judgment was given on October 1st 1946. During this long and weary period of ten months he was compelled by his captors to sit in the dock with twenty other prisoners—a very uncomfortable dock as the foreign correspondents gleefully recorded—listening to evidence not one-tenth of which had the remotest connection with the charges brought against him personally. It has been hotly denied that this extraordinary procedure was adopted in order to inflict a sort of pre-conviction punishment on him and his co-defendants. The explanation generally put forward is that the London Agreement of the 8th August 1945 directed that the trial and punishment of "the major war criminals of the

European Axis" should be undertaken by a specially appointed tribunal to be known as the International Military Tribunal. Nothing in this Agreement, however, or in the so-called Charter attached to it, makes any provision that a mass-trial, on the model of the Soviet mass mock-trials, should take place. This decision was only reached later when agreement was reached, after much wrangling, as to which prisoners should be chosen to serve the role of 'major war criminals'. Admiral Raeder, it appears, was not included in the original list and was only added later, as the American prosecutor, Whitney R. Harris, cynically tells us, because he was "a not illogical defendant-counterpart to Field Marshal Keitel". Finally after much argument, twenty-one individuals were picked on and it was decided to make all twenty-one listen to all the evidence which could be alleged against all, some or any of them, and then at the end to decide who was guilty of what.

Only those who have sat through a long trial can know how inexpressibly tedious protracted legal proceedings can be. At Nürnberg the combined effect of boredom and acute nerve strain must have been terrific. Still it was agreed the defendants had no cause for complaint on this or any other ground since before the indictment had been read they had been labelled major war criminals. The Soviet representatives stressed this point of view with admirable frankness. Thus at a meeting, preparatory to the trial held on the 29th June 1945, General Nikitchenko urged, "We are dealing here with the chief war criminals who have already been convicted and whose conviction has already been announced at both the Moscow and Yalta conferences by the heads of the governments". At a later meeting on July 19th, General Nikitchenko declared, "The fact that the Nazi leaders are criminals has already been established. The task of the Tribunal is only to determine the measure of guilt of each particular person and to mete out the necessary punishment".*

In regard to the conviction of Admiral Raeder as a war criminal it is relevant to observe that one of his eight judges—the above mentioned Nikitchenko—expressed the following views on his duty as a judge at the trial: —"It has been decided that the prisoners should go through the process of a trial but the object of that trial is, of course, the punishment of the criminals. The role of the prosecutor should be merely the role of assisting the court: there is no question that the judge has the character of an impartial person".

As stated above, Admiral Raeder's "process of a trial" lasted ten months. In view of the simple nature of the charge made

* See the Report on the International Conference on Military Trials, published in 1949 by the Washington State Department, Pages 104-106, and Page 303.

against him, there is no reason why his case should not have been disposed of in a couple of days. The basic facts upon which this charge was based were not in dispute. It was not denied that Germany had invaded Norway in April 1940: it was not denied that Admiral Raeder had prepared the plans for this invasion and that as head of the German Navy at the time, he had directed this invasion: it was not claimed that Germany had any just cause for quarrel with Norway.

Taken by itself, without knowledge of the surrounding circumstances, the German invasion appears to be the result of a conspiracy to wage a senseless and wanton war of aggression, punishable as such under Count 1 of the indictment, and as a crime against peace, punishable as such under Count 2.

In a nutshell, Admiral Raeder's defence was that the German invasion of Norway was neither senseless nor wanton. It was undertaken, not as a result of any quarrel with Norway but to forestall a British invasion of Norway which was on the point of being launched. The German armament industry was mainly dependent on the import of iron ore from Sweden. If the British had been able by a sudden stroke to occupy Norway and then advance across northern Sweden to the port of Lulea on the Baltic, Germany's output of munitions would have received a paralysing, perhaps ultimately a fatal blow. It was, therefore, vital to Germany to prevent the British from occupying Norway.

It was common knowledge that the British Admiralty had had some such plan in contemplation. In fact, when in December 1939 the Soviet Union had started a most wanton war of aggression against Finland, the possibilities of sending troops across Norway and Sweden "to help the gallant Finns" had been openly discussed in the British Press. But how was the British plan to invade Norway to be proved at Admiral Raeder's trial? By Article 21 of the so-called Charter creating it, the Tribunal was expressly empowered to take judicial notice of facts of common knowledge. But the Tribunal insisted on wrapping itself in an impenetrable cloak of judicial ignorance and insisted that the allegations laid before it by the prosecution must be considered without regard to surrounding circumstances of which judicially they were ignorant. Thus in regard to charges of inhumanity, the Tribunal refused to take into account that while they deliberated thereon, the inhabitants of the eastern provinces of Germany, to the number of some twelve millions, were being expelled from their homes with indescribable brutality, leaving behind them everything except what they themselves could carry away: that in regard to charges of waging aggressive war the Tribunal refused to take into account that while Germany was waging her alleged war of aggression, one of the victorious Powers, the Soviet Union, had waged no less than six wars of flagrant aggression! The Tribunal insisted that the charges must be dealt with on the assumption that the world was a Garden of Eden in which no crime or violence of any kind existed—except, of course, the crime and violence for which, as General Nikitchenko had pointed out, the defendants had already been found guilty at the Moscow and Yalta conferences.

In regard to the case of Admiral Raeder, it was not disputed that he had planned and directed the invasion of Norway, a neutral state with whom Germany had no quarrel. This act was clearly "a crime against peace" and the Tribunal considered that it would be insulting to ask the British Government if they themselves had not planned a similar crime. Had not the Tribunal been expressly directed by Article 18 of the Charter "to take strict measures to rule out irrelevant issues"?

The result was the charge against Admiral Raeder was dealt with as concerning a single isolated act without regard to the surrounding circumstances. It was held that by planning and directing the invasion of Norway six years before, he had become retrospectively guilty of the newly created crime of initiating an aggressive war. He was sentenced to imprisonment for life.

Admiral Raeder's conviction aroused at the time neither interest nor concern. The man in the street had long since forgotten the little he had been told six years before concerning the facts which led up to the German invasion of Norway in 1940. The general opinion was that as a tribunal, two members of which were eminent English High Court judges, had found him guilty of "the supreme international crime", namely the planning and waging of an aggressive war, he was lucky to have escaped with his life. Only in legal circles was misgiving felt that until this newly created crime had been defined, a fatal flaw would exist in the conviction. It was hoped, however, that this flaw would soon be remedied.

To this day, however, this flaw had not been remedied. No definition has been found for "a war of aggression". In fact it is now claimed the concept is indefinable. In a recent book written to whitewash the memory of Mr. Justice Jackson, the chief American prosecutor at Nürnberg, his devoted assistant, Whitney R. Harris, writes, "Aggressive war has not been, and perhaps never will be, adequately defined and it has been contended that the very indefiniteness of the concept makes difficult its prohibition. But it does not follow that so elusive a concept may not afford an adequate judicial basis for criminal prosecution".

This contention is both contrary to fact and grossly mislead-ing. It is simply not true that the concept of "aggressive war" cannot be defined. Anyone who can speak English understands what these words mean and can suggest in thirty seconds a satis-factory definition.* Mr. Harris when he wrote the above lines knew perfectly well that the various committees of legal experts entrusted with the task of preparing for the Nürnberg trials had had no difficulty in finding a definition for "aggressive war". The task which they had been set and which had completely baffled them was to work out a definition of "aggressive war" which on the one hand would include the wars upon which Hitler had embarked and on the other hand would exclude the various wars undertaken at one time or another by the victorious Powers and in particular the recent wanton attacks by the Soviet Union on her neighbours, Poland, Finland, Estonia, Latvia, Lithuania and Japan.

The man in the street, however, was not troubled by legal definitions. He was prepared to take on trust that the apparent wars of aggression by so great and gallant an ally as the Soviet Union would be found to be justifiable if investigated in a charit-able frame of mind. Obviously a war in an unjust cause was an aggressive war and a war in a just cause was not. In his view, it would be pushing enquiry to unreasonable lengths to ask who was to decide whether a war was just or unjust, since no international court existed or ever had existed to decide the problem. Certainly enquiry along these lines would lead nowhere—if the opinion of the party attacked be accepted as the test, then every war that has ever taken place is an aggressive war, while if the view of the assailant be accepted as the test, no aggressive war has ever been fought.

Viewed in perspective, after the passage of over ten years, when the passions and prejudices of wartime have subsided, can the con-viction of Admiral Raeder by the International Military Tribunal at Nürnberg be justified?

Many lawyers would be disposed to dismiss as an obviously impossible task an attempt to justify this conviction since, in their view, it suffers from three fundamental defects. First of all, they deny that a prosecutor can appoint himself a judge of his own accusations. Secondly, they question whether it is possible to incur criminal guilt by committing an act, innocent at the time of its commission, but long afterwards declared a crime. Thirdly, they doubt whether a newly-created crime so nebulous that it utterly defies definition can be made the subject of a criminal charge.

* See the definition suggested by the present author on Page 59.

We are assured that these three objections raise abstract problems of jurisprudence so obtruse that they cannot be disposed of by reference to elementary principles of justice or to common sense. If reference to these be ruled out, we must rely upon authority—the authority of Lord Justice Sir Geoffrey Lawrence, now Lord Oaksey, and of Mr. Justice Birkett, now Lord Justice Birkett. As these eminent and learned judges concurred in the conviction of Admiral Raeder, we may feel assured that they considered that the three objections set out above, insurmountable as they may appear, were in fact, without foundation.

Relying on this weighty judicial authority we may assume that the so-called International Tribunal was a duly constituted court of law and that it adjudicated on the problems that came before it in accordance with normal judicial practice. We must resolutely reject the view, quoted above, of one of the judges composing the Tribunal, General Nikitchenko, that at this trial "there could be no question that a judge has the character of an impartial person".

In a normal criminal trial the first duty of the Court is to establish the facts of the case before it, that is to say, to decide whether the facts alleged by the prosecution are true. The second duty of the court is to decide whether the facts, so found, constitute an offence at law. Thirdly if the facts so found constitute an offence at law to impose the punishment prescribed by law.

Now the trial of Admiral Raeder at Nürnberg in 1945-46 was not a normal criminal trial. As we have seen, the facts alleged against him were substantially not in dispute. But it was impossible for the court to proceed in the normal manner by considering whether these admitted facts constituted an offence at law. No law existed on the subject. The International Military Tribunal, however, claimed the right—it unquestionably had the power—to make up the law guiding its decisions as it went along. It could declare any act a crime as it saw fit. Thus, if the charge had been brought, the Tribunal could have found that in sinking the "Lützow" at the battle of Jutland thirty years before Erich Raeder had committed a crime against peace by having prevented by violence Admiral Jellicoe's men from peacefully taking possession of the ship. The Tribunal saw fit to hold in law that in planning and directing the invasion of Norway six years before, Admiral Raeder had committed a crime, namely the newly-created crime of initiating and waging an aggressive war.

Viewed cold-bloodedly in this light, can more be said than that the International Military Tribunal exercised—arbitrarily and ruthlessly maybe—the powers and rights which it claimed to possess?

The problem is not, however, quite as simple as this. It is true that when it began its duties the Tribunal was unfettered by any existing law or by any rules of procedure. In theory the Tribunal claimed that the law on any subject was whatever the Tribunal declared it to be. But in practice the Tribunal acknowledged some limitation of its powers as a concession to common sense, and as time went on its omnipotence became gradually subject to its own declarations and rulings.

Now in one respect the Tribunal's omnipotence was strictly limited by the so-called Charter by which it had been created. It is a popular fallacy that the Tribunal was established to punish war crimes. It was not established to punish war crimes. Article 6 of the Charter expressly limited its jurisdiction to war crimes "committed in the interests of the European Axis countries". The Tribunal had thus no power to punish war crimes unless it could be proved that they were committed in the interests of Germany or Italy. The Tribunal interpreted this express limitation of its powers as imposing on it a duty to act on the assumption that the victorious Powers were, one and all, incapable of committing war crimes. From this assumption it followed logically that if one of the victorious Powers could be proved to have committed a certain act, the Tribunal had no power to declare that act a crime. The act in question received as it were a certificate of innocence. With remorseless logic the Tribunal decided that the same act which must be regarded as innocent as having been committed in the interests of the victors could not at the same time be pronounced a crime if committed in the interests of the vanquished.

Thus was laid down one of those so-called principles established at Nürnberg which Sir Hartley Shawcross has so often warned us must be preserved at all costs as a blessing for posterity. The Tribunal not only laid down this great principle but actually applied it. As we have seen, one of the charges under Count 3 of the Indictment against Admiral Raeder and his colleague, Admiral Dönitz, was that they had carried out unrestricted submarine warfare. This act was not denied: the prosecution demanded that the Tribunal should pronounce it a crime: the Tribunal would have been happy to oblige but unfortunately the legal defenders of the two admirals were able to prove that by an order of the British Admiralty dated the 8th May 1940 it was directed that all ships in the Skaggerrak should be sunk without warning. Unrestricted submarine warfare was therefore clearly

219

entitled to a certificate of innocence. Having pronounced unrestricted submarine warfare innocent, the Tribunal felt unable at the same time to declare it a crime. To the astonishment of everyone, the two admirals were acquitted on this charge.

The question whether Admiral Raeder's conviction for having initiated and waged a war of aggression can be justified resolves itself into whether the particular act of which he was accused was entitled to a certificate of innocence as having been also committed by one of the victorious Powers. The particular act of which Admiral Raeder was accused was that he planned and directed the invasion of Norway in 1940. If it can be proved that the British Government made similar plans which were forestalled in the initial stages by the German invasion, then clearly by the principle laid down by the Tribunal itself, Admiral Raeder was entitled to acquittal.

At the Nürnberg trials in 1946 the truth concerning the invasion of Norway was not fully known—or at least could not be proved. That Norwegian neutrality was first infringed by the laying of British and French minefields in Norwegian territorial waters in accordance with long contemplated plans, was frankly disclosed by Sir Winston Churchill to the House of Commons only a couple of days after the German invasion commenced. But the Tribunal insisted on being judicially ignorant of what it could have read in Hansard for April 11th 1940, although, as Lord Hankey has since written, "the whole story had long been a matter of public knowledge".

Judicial ignorance is within reasonable limits a necessary application of the principle that a court of law should reach its decisions without regard to anything but the sworn testimony laid before it. To prevent waste of time and money, however, under all legal systems facts of common knowledge are accepted without strict proof. What are facts of common knowledge is construed more strictly under some legal systems than under others. The Nürnberg Tribunal attached a most restricted meaning to the words in spite of the fact that Article 21 of the Charter expressly directed that it should "not require proof of facts of common knowledge", and Article 19 directed it should "apply to the greatest possible extent expeditious and non-technical procedure". In reliance upon Article 19 the Tribunal readily accepted hearsay and other inadmissable evidence against the accused.

It is the unshakeable conviction of the layman that judicial ignorance is a merry device of lawyers intended to enliven the tedium of legal proceedings. The Victorian judge could always be certain of raising laughter in court by asking, "Who is Dan

Leno?" and "What is a hansom?" just as his 20th century successors provided comic relief by enquiring "Who is George Robey?"
and "What is a taxi?" It would be interesting to know what the
Soviet judge, General Nikitchenko, and his colleague, Colonel Volch-
kov, thought of the judicial ignorance of their capitalist colleagues.
The personal relations between the eight judges appear to have been
excellent. Probably they regarded their non-Marxian colleagues as
genuine simpletons.

Since Admiral Raeder's conviction on October 1st 1946, the
full truth has gradually, very gradually, come to light. First of
all, in 1948, Sir Winston Churchill in his book, "The Gathering
Storm", amplified what he had told the Commons on April 11th,
1940. Next, in 1950, Lord Hankey in his book "Politics: Trials
and Errors", devoted a chapter to the events leading up to the German
invasion of Norway on April 9th, 1940, and dealt trenchantly with
the Tribunal's one-sided report on the matter and its wholesale
omission of vital facts. From these books it became clear that
as early as September 1939 the British Government began to consider ways and means of stopping the export of Swedish iron ore
to Germany. Sir Winston's Memoranda to the War Cabinet of the
29th September and the 16th December 1939 show that plans were
then in preparation to achieve this end and that the possibility of
using armed force against both Norway and Sweden was contemplated. In the latter Memorandum Sir Winston Churchill urged
that Britain was fighting the battle for the rights of small nations
and she must not allow these rights to tie her hands. Humanity, not
legality, should be the guide!

"By the beginning of April 1940", writes Lord Hankey,
"the preparations for the major offensive operation in Norway had
been completed both by the British and the Germans. Neither
side had given the other an easy excuse for launching their expedition, and by a coincidence the two operations were launched almost
simultaneously without any pretext having been found. The actual
German landing did not take place until April 9. Twenty-four
hours before that, namely between 4.30 and 5.0 a.m. on April 8,
the British minefields had been laid in the West Fjord near
Narvik".

Lord Hankey summarises the facts as follows: —
"From the start of planning to the German invasion, Great
Britain and Germany were keeping more or less level in
their plans and preparations. Britain actually started planning a little earlier, partly owing to Mr. Churchill's pre-
science, and partly perhaps because she had a better and more
experienced system of Higher Control of the War than

Germany. Throughout the period of preparations the planning continued normally. The essence of the British plan was to stop the German supplies of Gallivare ore during the winter. Both plans were executed almost simultaneously, Britain being twenty-four hours ahead in this so-called act of aggression, if the term is really applicable to either side."*

To those who desire to study in detail the facts relating to the invasion of Norway, there became available in 1952 an official record of the matter entitled "The Campaign in Norway", being the first volume of a series of military histories of the Second World War, published by Her Majesty's Stationery Office. Dr. T. K. Derry, the author, deals most frankly with the events leading up to the actual fighting in April 1940. He makes it clear that the British Admiralty began in November 1939 to push forward in earnest the preparation of plans for the occupation of Norway as a result of an enquiry by the War Cabinet to the Ministry of Economic Warfare as to what would happen if Germany was cut off from supplies of Swedish iron ore from the Baltic port of Lulea. The reply given by the Ministry of Economic Warfare was that Germany, after twelve months, would be unable from lack of munitions to wage active warfare.

By a coincidence, at this very time encouraging advice was received by the War Cabinet: Soviet Russia launched a war of aggression against Finland. Both in Great Britain and in the United States the greatest sympathy was expressed and even perhaps genuinely felt for the gallant Finns. In Britain the possibilities were openly discussed of sending help to Finland—an idea at that time not repugnant to British public opinion as Soviet Russia had just joined with Nazi Germany to partition Poland, to preserve the integrity of which country Britain was supposed to be at war. Thereafter, the two distinct plans, the one to cut off Germany's supplies of iron ore and the other to conduct a knightly crusade to defend brave little Finland, rightly struggling to be free, were muddled together. Ultimately on February 6, 1940 the Supreme War Council approved a plan to send an army to Norway which "on its way to rescue the Finns" as Dr. Derry demurely puts it, should seize the Swedish ore-fields and the Baltic port of Lulea. The possibility was entertained that this expedition would ultimately lead to a major campaign in southern Sweden which would distract the attention of the Germans, then massed along the French frontier.

The reader's attention is recommended to a remarkable re-

* "Politics: Trials and Errors" by Lord Hankey (Pen-in-Hand, Oxford, 1950). Page 78.

view of this official history of the Norwegian campaign which appeared in the *Times* of December 10, 1952 under the title, "A Gallant Fiasco". One passage which bears directly on the charge brought six years later against Admiral Raeder demands quotation in full: —

"Britain was dickering with a modified version of the original scheme for securing Narvik *and some troops had actually been embarked in warships* (italics supplied) when, in the early hours of April 9, Hitler struck.

With the exception of Oslo, which had never figured in our plans, the immediate German objectives in Norway were precisely (and inevitably) the same ports whose seizure the Allies had been assiduously plotting for several months".

The cynicism of this review certainly almost passes belief—the reader may well insist on checking the words "assiduously plotting for months" in the original text before accepting them as having been written in the "Times". It would almost appear that "Our Special Correspondent", the author of this review, had never read Lord Lawrence's solemn denunciation of "the supreme International Crime"! Rarely has so grave a matter been dealt with with such cheerful flippancy.

It would no doubt have been too much to expect that when the full facts relating to the charge against Admiral Raeder of having planned and directed an aggressive war were belatedly disclosed, angry crowds of lovers of justice would demonstrate in Downing Street or that the traffic in the Strand would be impeded by processions of legal luminaries connected with his trial proceeding to Temple Bar, there ceremoniously to commit hari-kari in expiation. Still some perceptible reaction in public opinion might reasonably have been expected. In Britain mention of the Norwegian campaign aroused no interest. It was merely, as the Special Correspondent of the "Times" called it, "a Gallant Fiasco", an unsuccessful prelude overshadowed by the far more important events which followed it so swiftly, a matter of interest only to military students, a closed chapter of history having no practical bearing on any current problem. Admiral Raeder himself had been long forgotten except by the few who remembered that he was one of those convicted and sentenced as a war criminal. The German public showed a similar indifference. Among his own countrymen, Admiral Raeder was remembered only as a leading figure in the Second World War and it was the sole desire of the average German to bury in oblivion all memory of that disastrous conflict and of everyone connected with it.

What was the fate endured by Admiral Raeder while the

truth concerning his fate was coming to light—and long afterwards? Was he condemned to honourable detention in the military custody of those to whom he had surrendered as a prisoner of war or was he dealt with in a manner similar to that meted out in civilised countries to convicts sentenced for major crimes to long terms of imprisonment?

As explained above, before their trials even began or before even they had been charged, one of the judges appointed to try them, the Russian General Nikitchenko, claimed that Admiral Raeder and his fellow defendants had already been adjudicated criminals by international agreement. Be this as it may, it is at least certain that the fate of Admiral Raeder and the six other defendants sentenced at Nürnberg to "imprisonment" was decided by international agreement. Months of wrangling took place, however, before this agreement was arrived at. The Soviet authorities urged that the prisoners should be kept in complete solitary confinement without visitors or books. The French vindictively supported this proposal. The British and Americans urged that if the Tribunal had intended solitary confinement they would have said so. The wrangling went on and became more and more acrimonious. Behind the scenes the victors were already bitterly at variance: even in public, politeness was beginning to wear thin. At last, probably through intervention from the highest political levels, it was decided to use the prisoners condemned at Nürnberg to stage a spectacular demonstration of allied unity, which it was only too clear no longer existed.

It was agreed that everything possible should be done to create the illusion that the seven survivors from the dock at Nürnberg constituted a standing menace to the happiness and security of the whole of mankind. Only by considering the stringency of the precautions taken against it, would the public be able to estimate the gravity of the peril. Therefore, everything possible must be done to make these precautions as stringent as possible. With the welfare of the whole world at stake, the responsibility of guarding these prisoners was too heavy to be entrusted to a single Power. It was therefore decided that this responsibility should be undertaken in turn by Great Britain, the United States, the Soviet Union and France, each for a period of three months. This arrangement to share responsibility had the additional advantage of demonstrating that these Powers could at least agree upon one subject.

Sentence was passed on Admiral Raeder on the 1st October, 1946 but it was not until the following 18th July that he set forth from Nürnberg, handcuffed to an American military policeman, to Spandau Prison, the place where it had been decided he should

(Wide World)

Admiral Raeder in his cell at the
City Jail in Nürnberg, during the
trial. Each of the defendants was
limited in dining gear to a spoon,
canteen cup without handle, and
meat can.

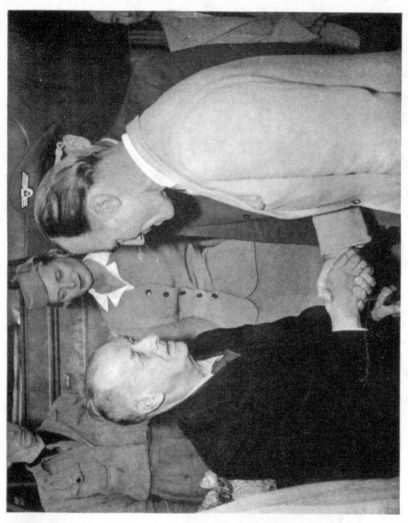

Admiral Raeder, in broken health, was released from bleak and massive Spandau Prison, in Berlin, on September 26, 1955. He had been sentenced to serve for life.

spend the remainder of his life. On arrival he was marched with the six other prisoners to the office of the chief warden. Here he was stripped and then marched, stark naked, to another office, where he underwent a rigorous medical examination intended to discover whether he had the means of suicide concealed on his person. He was then given prison clothes and told he would henceforth be known only as No. 4. Having been informed that he was strictly forbidden to speak either to his guards or to his fellow prisoners and that this Silence Rule would be rigidly enforced, he was taken away and locked in his cell.

This experience was only a foretaste of what lay before Admiral Raeder in the long dreary hopeless years which lay ahead of him. The strange Alice-in-Wonderland atmosphere of Nürnberg was transferred to Spandau, buffoonery and brutality remaining mixed in about the same proportions. It is less unpleasant to concentrate on the details of the buffoonery. The treatment of the seven elderly prisoners in Spandau was based on the assumption that they were desperate criminals of superhuman ferocity, audacity and strength: that if vigilance was relaxed for a single instance, they would overcome their unfortunate guards, tear their way through the stone walls which surrounded them and join the hordes of sympathisers that were ever waiting outside the prison for their appearance.

In accordance with this assumption, on the nine towers overlooking the prison and its surroundings, over a hundred soldiers armed with tommy-guns are kept scanning the scenery for signs of an assault, the outer wall of the prison, 30 feet high, is encircled with a fence of barbed wire 25 feet in width, and at night when the prisoners are locked in their cells, this fence is illuminated by search-lights and electrified by a high voltage cable. To guard against the alarming possibility that the normal Berlin supply of electricity might fail, Spandau Prison is equipped with a special power station.

The prisoners themselves are subjected to the strictest discipline, any infringements of which are ruthlessly punished. Elaborate precautions are taken to prevent suicide, it being assumed, no doubt rightly, that any prisoner subjected for long to such treatment, would commit suicide if given an opportunity. The health of the prisoners is the subject for ceaseless anxiety. On the one hand the authorities are instructed to do everything possible to keep the prisoners alive, and on the other hand they are instructed to inflict on them every possible deprivation and hardship and to supply them with the barest minimum of food. Concerning the latter question a difference of opinion early developed between the Russians and their allies. During the three months when the prisoners are in Russian custody, their normally meagre rations are cut to a point just insufficient to support life. Before however this regime has had time to lead to the inevitable and merciful result, one of the three gallant allies of the Soviet Union takes over and the wretched prisoners are restored by a just sufficient diet.

Night is allowed to bring no relief. Every quarter of an hour each prisoner must be inspected through the barred window in the door of the cell in order to make quite certain that since the previous inspection fifteen minutes before he had not slipped through the keyhole. For this purpose the light is turned on. It is said that when the British and Americans are in charge—it is not reported what the French do—the original regulations have been so far modified that this farcical performance is carried out with a darkened electric bulb: the Russians, however, insist on the eyes of the prisoners being dazzled every fifteen minutes throughout the night by an unshaded light.

One of the most important assumptions upon which the regulations are based is that each of the seven prisoners is possessed of vast and malignant political power. If, therefore, Admiral Raeder, for example, was permitted to write a single sentence in his monthly letter, strictly limited to 1200 words, the meaning of which had not been carefully considered from every conceivable angle, the whole world would be thrown into anarchy and the glorious work of 'liberation' would have to be undertaken all over again. On the 15th October 1950 "Die Strasse" published a photostatic copy of a letter written by Admiral Raeder to his wife. From this it would appear that the Mad Hatter himself had obtained employment in Spandau Prison: approximately half a short private communication had been carefully obliterated!

Every three months a solemn ceremony takes place at Spandau Prison when the troops of the Power having had custody of the seven prisoners hands them over to the troops of the Power whose duty it is to guard them for the next three months. To date this duty has been carried out successfully without anything alarming having to be reported. Not one of the prisoners has to date succeeded in fighting his way out of the prison and there have been no fatal casualties among the garrison—in fact the only casualties of any kind so far reported have been among persons trying to catch the rabbits who live in the danger zone surrounding the prison and who have been electrocuted by the high voltage cable above mentioned.

During the period of some eleven years which has passed since conviction, only one case of violence has been reported from

Spandau—violence, that is to say, by a prisoner to the guards, since, of course, violence by the guards to a prisoner would not be deemed worth reporting. This single incident concerned Walter Funk who one night at last became frantic as a result of the above mentioned regulation requiring that every fifteen minutes he should be awakened by a light flashed in his eyes. The warder on duty— a Frenchman—entered the cell to find out what the noise was about and was promptly seized and kicked into the passage. Fortunately no international crisis arose as a result of this resort to violence thanks to the prompt and resolute action of the other guards who quickly overpowered the frantic little man and dragged him away to the punishment cell for a period of solitary confinement.

One wishes that one could record the bestowal of one hearty kick on the backside of the person who framed these Alice-in-Wonderland regulations, but alas, no one person can be held responsible for framing them. As in everything connected with the Nürnberg trials, no single individual, no single group of individuals, no single nation can be held responsible. Responsibility is in fact so widely spread that no one feels any personal responsibility at all. The lawyers blame the cynicism and hypocrisy of the politicians who agreed at Yalta and elsewhere that when victory was achieved these so-called trials should take place: the politicians blame the pompous pettifogging stupidity of the lawyers: and those in charge of the prisoners plead that they are only carrying out instructions which they have no authority to alter or vary. Everyone is agreed that all blame rests on the Soviet Government which disclaims any blame whatever on the ground that all the prisoners are anti-Communists and therefore deserved death in any event. Certainly if Joe Stalin's proposal at Teheran that 50,000 German officers and technicians should be summarily massacred—a proposal which so aroused Sir Winston Churchill's indignation—the absurd farce of Spandau would never have taken place. No doubt Admiral Raeder as head of the German Navy and an unrepentant opponent of Communism, would have been one of the 50,000 victims of this proposed super-Katyn massacre.

While the conviction of Admiral Raeder has long failed to find defenders in legal circles, the rumour that discussions were in progress to mitigate the barbarity of his treatment aroused anxious alarm in certain political circles. On the 29th March 1954 appeared a letter in the "Evening Standard" urging that "the excuse of illness and old age of some of the prisoners in Spandau should be examined with extreme caution". At the time it was written Admiral Raeder was 78 and had recently undergone a major operation. The letter was illustrated by a portrait of a youngish, middle-aged man with a double chin, grinning cheerfully—certainly not the face of a man, one would say, who would begrudge a little extra food and a few minor comforts to a very old and dying man. Thereafter, the writer of this letter, Arthur Lewis, the Socialist M.P. for West Ham North proceeded to pester the Government for assurances that the regulations at Spandau were being strictly enforced. The information which had reached him, he told the Commons, was of an alarming nature. Was it not true that a bar of chocolate had been found in Baron von Neurath's cell? Had it not been providentially discovered by a Russian jailer, this sick old man of 84 might have been able to taste chocolate for the first time for ten years with consequences to world peace terrible to contemplate! Had not the wife of one of the prisoners written to the Prime Minister to enlist his sympathy for her husband? Dark influences, it was to be feared, were at work behind the scenes.

Sir Winston Churchill felt at last called upon to answer these questions himself. He replied tersely that he hoped his questioner had "not been devoting too much time to smelling out the details of private correspondence", and added, "for several years I have felt the conditions in Spandau were very hard and inhumane". It was true that the wife of one of the prisoners, Baron von Neurath, had written a letter urging that her husband should be transferred to a sanatorium, in his opinion a very natural act by a wife. As an old man himself—Sir Winston was then 80—he declared that Baron von Neurath had his sympathy. "We are dealing", he reminded the Commons, "with a sick man of 84 which I can tell you is quite a lot".

From the record in Hansard it would appear that the only result of Arthur Lewis' appeal was the administration to that person of a hearty snub by the Prime Minister. Certainly in the Commons the assurances for which he begged with such feeling were curtly refused. Nevertheless, it is possible that later Sir Winston found that he could not steel his heart indefinitely against the memory of that pleading face. Perhaps the reflection came to him that the public usefulness of the representative of the discriminating electors of West Ham North might become permanently impaired if an anxiety neurosis concerning Spandau was left implanted in his mind. Whatever the reason may have been, nothing was done following this debate to alleviate "the very hard and inhumane conditions" at Spandau apart from a few relaxations of the Alice-in-Wonderland regulations, such as a slightly increased diet and a recision of the imbecile rule forbidding a prisoner to lie down on his bed when locked in his cell except during specially authorised periods.

The intervention of the honourable member for West Ham North is mentioned here mainly because it demonstrates that the blunders of the Nürnberg Tribunal were preserved from rectification not entirely for the reason that these blunders had been allowed to slip into oblivion. Even nine years after the conclusion of hostilities, persons could still be found ready to uphold in public the perpetuation of these blunders. Concerning the episode itself many but only obvious comments can be made. Here it is sufficient to point out that this little footnote contributed to the Nürnberg-Spandau story by an obscure Socialist backbencher is exactly in keeping with its essential spirit of make-believe and fantasy. With no doubt complete sincerity, the representative of West Ham North professed to believe that behind the scenes was taking place an Edwardian melodrama in which ladies of title were directing the destinies of nations by influencing various puppet chancellors, prime ministers and ambassadors in that fictional world of Secret Diplomacy beloved by the romantic dramatists of fifty years ago.

It is, of course, possible that this appeal by the member for West Ham North had no influence whatever on the fate of the prisoners in Spandau. In fact there are good grounds for believing that several years before alarming rumours thereof reached anxious ears in West Ham North, the governments of the Western Powers had become heartily weary of the farce being played at Spandau and had begun surreptitiously to seek ways and means of putting an end to it. The realization had then dawned for the first time how unwise it had been to enter into a binding agreement with the Russian Government in regard to the fate of the surviving victims of the Nürnberg trials. The Spandau farce had been designed as a spectacular demonstration of the spiritual and political unity of the leading victors of the Second World War. Initiated by international agreement, this farce could only be terminated with the consent of all the high contracting parties, including of course, the Soviet Government. So the views of the Soviet Government were tentatively invited on the problem of how the barbaric treatment of the prisoners in Spandau could be ameliorated, and even whether those of the prisoners who had indisputably been wrongly convicted should be set free.

Once the 'cold war' had started and all pretence of unity had been abandoned, such suggestions could receive only one response. No doubt it afforded the rulers of the Kremlin much simple pleasure to point out that so far as the Soviet Union was concerned no problem existed. The regulations under which the prisoners in Spandau lived had been expressly framed to inflict on them the maximum suffering while keeping them alive as long as possible. When first drafted, these regulations had been enthusiastically acclaimed as near perfection not only in Moscow but in London, Washington and Paris. The Soviet Government regretted to find that the Western Powers were 'deviating' from the high standards which they had so recently affirmed: on principle the Soviet Government disapproved of 'deviation' in any shape or form. Perhaps in one sense some of the prisoners were innocent men: perhaps they were all innocent men. In that event it was to be feared that the learned British, American and French judges at Nürnberg had blundered badly. But in another sense all the prisoners were guilty men since they were all opponents of Communism. However barbarous their treatment, it was no worse than that to which many anti-Communists were at that moment being subjected in the prison camps for political prisoners in Siberia. There was therefore no problem to discuss.

To release any of the prisoners without the consent of the Soviet Government would be to repudiate an international agreement "by unilateral action", the very offence for which the Western Powers had so loudly denounced Hitler. So long as the Soviet Government maintained that there was no problem to discuss it seemed that nothing could be done, and so long as the 'cold war' continued it seemed certain the Soviet Government would maintain this uncompromising attitude merely for the satisfaction of obstructing and rebuffing the Western Powers. Great therefore was the general astonishment when the Soviet Government on its own initiative suddenly proposed that Baron von Neurath should be released on account of age and ill-health. Having been urging his release themselves for some years the Western Powers had no alternative but to consent. In the summer of 1955 Baron von Neurath was released from Spandau. It was realised with bitterness that the Communists as a manoeuvre in the 'cold war' had adroitly won the entire credit for a long overdue act of justice and humanity.

Shortly after the release of Baron von Neurath, it became widely known that discussions were proceeding to secure the release of Admiral Raeder. Rumours of these discussions naturally caused what in wartime parlance was termed alarm and despondency. No doubt these emotions were acutely felt in West Ham North but now, strange to say, they found most vehement expression from a member of the peerage. On September 11th, 1955 appeared an article on the main page of the "Sunday Dispatch" under the title "Would You Set These Villains Free?" Beneath this title printed in the largest type were published portraits of four of the Spandau prisoners, Speer, Admiral Dönitz, Admiral Raeder and von Schirach. Beneath the portrait of Admiral Raeder was the caption " 'Sink-at-Sight' Admiral".

At the first glance this headline with the accompanying portraits raised wild hopes that at last the alleged crimes for which these four villains had been condemned to life imprisonment were to be concisely and lucidly specified. In particular, what justification would the author of the article suggest for the continued detention of Admiral Raeder whose early release was then confidently expected? The author of this article was Lord Russell of Liverpool who has recently written a book on war-crimes and who therefore might reasonably be expected to know something about the subject. At long last, it seemed, the Iron Curtain of Discreet Silence was to be drawn aside and the crimes of this naval villain fearlessly disclosed by a member of the English Bar who had himself taken part in a number of war-crime prosecutions.

A perusal of Lord Russell of Liverpool's article quickly dashed these high hopes. Not a line in it referred even indirectly to a single one of the four "villains" whose portraits illustrated it. No authority was given for the caption attached to Admiral Raeder's portrait, " 'Sink-at-Sight Admiral". His name was not mentioned in the article nor any happening with which he had been even remotely connected. The first half of the article began with the denunciation of General MacArthur for having advocated a general amnesty for war criminals and was followed by a description of several alleged Japanese atrocities on the island of Aitape off New Guinea and in the Philippines: the second half consisted of airy references to the many crimes of "Hitler's instruments of tyranny, the Gestapo, the S.S. and the S.D."

We may feel sure that Lord Russell of Liverpool would have no difficulty in advising as to the position if he were consulted professionally by a client whose portrait had been published in a newspaper under the heading "Should This Villain Be At Liberty", with beneath an article describing the misdoings of some notorious criminal. Would he have any difficulty in reaching the conclusion that his client had been grossly libelled? At the least he would surely advise that some public explanation and retraction should be called for from the newspaper in question and from the author of the article.

The last two paragraphs of the article contained two glaring misstatements of fact. First it was stated that all war-criminals received "fair and patient trials, the proceedings of which were carefully reviewed". This is simply untrue so far as the four "war-criminals" whose portraits illustrated in the article were concerned. No court in any country existed with power to review the decisions of the International Military Tribunal of Nürnberg. By the international agreement creating it, this body was to be deemed infallible. No mere national court of law could presume to consider its doings, much less rectify its blunders.

Secondly the article stated that all war-criminals had recently been given an additional safeguard in the shape of Review Boards specially created "to revise and reconsider their sentences from time to time". That such review boards had belatedly been created was, of course, a fact, but these boards had been expressly debarred from jurisdiction in regard to the prisoners in Spandau. It was therefore a misstatement of fact to say that the sentences passed on Admiral Raeder and his fellow victims in Spandau were subject to revision and reconsideration from time to time.

A letter to the Editor of the "Sunday Dispatch", pointing out these errors of fact was acknowledged but not published. A letter of protest to the author received the explanation that he had not had Admiral Raeder in his mind when he wrote the article: the Editor had selected the four portraits to illustrate the article without consulting him.

Humanum est errare! No doubt to the Editor, the portrait of one war-criminal was as good as the portrait of another war-criminal for the purpose of illustrating an article on war-criminals. But surely, having in good faith made this mistake, both Lord Russell of Liverpool and the Editor were under an obligation to Admiral Raeder and to the readers of the "Sunday Dispatch" to put matters right by an explanation? To the average newspaper reader, glancing through the article, it would appear that somehow or other Admiral Raeder had been held responsible at Nürnberg both for the Japanese atrocities on Aitape Island and for the misdeeds of the Gestapo. It is certain that at least two readers of the "Sunday Dispatch" received this impression since this misleading article inspired them to write ecstatic letters of praise to the Editor, letters duly published by him in the following issue. What may be labelled the West Ham North mentality was by no means limited to the parliamentary constituency of that name. If as a result of this article delusions concerning the Admiral's alleged offences had become widespread, public opinion might have become so aroused that his release might have been delayed for further weary months or years.

Fortunately the article had no such evil consequences. On

the 26th September 1955, fifteen days after its publication, Admiral Raeder was released from Spandau Prison. Leaving out the period from May to November 1945 which he spent in custody awaiting trial as a person already included by international agreement in the list of "Major War-Criminals", and also leaving out of account the period from November 1945 to the 1st October 1946, during which time as "a Major War-Criminal" he underwent what was officially termed his trial, Admiral Raeder had spent almost exactly nine years in rigorous captivity in "very hard and inhumane conditions" (to quote Sir Winston Churchill) as an officially convicted criminal.

The news of Admiral Raeder's release nowhere aroused emotion of any kind. Even in West Ham North no indignant mobs disturbed the public peace in protest. As the release had taken place with the consent of the Soviet Government, it was secure from Leftist denunciation: throughout the world the Leftist Press in general passed over the subject without comment. In the new Germany, in that remnant of Germany left after defeat in two world wars, the majority of his countrymen felt little beyond a mild surprise to learn that a man who had been one of Admiral Tirpitz's most promising younger officers was still alive. The age in which Admiral Tirpitz had been a leading figure, the age of stability and apparent security which in Germany had found expression in the ambitions, follies and indiscretions of His Imperial Majesty, Kaiser Wilhelm II, seemed in 1955, as inconceivably remote as the age of the Emperor Frederick Barbarossa. The emergence of this very old man from Spandau Prison had of course no more political significance than would have had the salvaging from the sea bed at Scapa Flow of yet another of those great battleships which had served at Jutland against the Grand Fleet of Admiral Jellicoe, battleships which in the Atomic Age had become as obsolete as a Greek trireme. Admiral Raeder had become merely a link with the past and few in Germany desired to be reminded of the past since thoughts of the past inevitably caused reflection on the possibilities of the future. With two thirds of Germany lying exposed within a few hours to invasion and occupation by the Red Army, the majority of Germans preferred to devote their whole attention to the present and to make the most, while it lasted, of the wave of feverish material prosperity which had so unexpectedly followed the aftermath of the Second World War. The Admiral's so-called trial at Nürnberg was merely one of those episodes of the past which were best forgotten.

The death or release of a notorious criminal is invariably

treated by the British Press as an opportunity to publish an outline of his career, an account of his misdoings and a description of the trial at which he was finally brought to book. As we have seen, after a trial lasting nearly a year Admiral Raeder was solemnly pronounced guilty of "the supreme international crime, differing from other war crimes in that it contained within itself the accumulated evil of the whole". For this crime it had been decided that the normal treatment of a convict undergoing a sentence of penal servitude would not be a sufficiently severe punishment, and he was therefore condemned to spend the rest of his life in conditions as "hard and inhumane" as could possibly be contrived. For nearly a decade the most stringent precautions and the most rigorous censorship had effectively cut him off from all contact with the outside world. Then came the news that this presumably super-criminal had been set at liberty. Nothing was generally known about him except the unprecedented severity of his punishment. Full details of this monstrous crime, the exact nature of which was unknown, could not surely fail to be of interest to that wide section of the British public which devoured eagerly every detail of even the most commonplace offences, as well as to all serious students of contemporary history. We may be sure, therefore, that immediately the news of Admiral Raeder's release arrived, urgent instructions were given in a score of offices in Fleet Street that the old newspaper files should be turned up, the records searched and all available books of reference ransacked in order that as full and comprehensive an account as possible of the crime and of the criminal should appear next day on every British breakfast table.

It is to be feared that the result of all this feverish searching was equally disappointing to those avid for gruesome details and for those who desired exact information. Strict accuracy was achieved easily enough concerning Admiral Raeder's achievements as a naval officer in both world wars. But apparently all the records and reference books in Fleet Street failed to provide an answer regarding the crime which he was supposed to have committed. In a normal case a perusal of the verbatim report of the trial would have provided an answer. But a search for a needle in a haystack would be a hopeful undertaking compared with a search of the ponderous official white books recording the Nürnberg proceedings in order to find what exactly any one of the twenty-one defendants were supposed to have done. Seemingly no one thought of applying to one of the galaxy of legal luminaries who had taken part in the trial to clear up the mystery: perhaps application was made but no one could be found willing to revive what had become a distasteful memory. The result was only snippits of information were supplied to the British public, of which only the briefest achieved strict accuracy.

Thus "The Times" dismissed the whole subject with an airy wave in six words—"Raeder was sentenced for war-crimes"—while "The Daily Telegraph" was only a trifle more expansive—"Raeder was sentenced to life imprisonment for having prepared and conducted a war of aggression".

Both "The Daily Herald" and "The Evening Standard" attempted to achieve strict accuracy by the use of the colourless word "blamed". The former informed its readers, "The Allies blamed Admiral Raeder for the U boat atrocities and the Nazi invasion of Norway". The latter declared, "The Nürnberg Tribunal blamed Raeder for conceiving the Nazi invasion of Norway and for U boat atrocities". "The Daily Mail" scorned the use of the word "blamed" and explained, "Raeder was found guilty for crimes against peace, war crimes, and planning aggressive war". "The Manchester Guardian" devoted no less than twenty-six words to the subject and informed its readers that "Raeder was sentenced to life imprisonment for planning and waging aggressive war and carrying out unrestrictive submarine warfare, including the sinking of unarmed neutral shipping". As we have seen, the latter assertion is contrary to fact since the Nürnberg Tribunal expressly held that unrestrictive submarine warfare was not a crime on the ground that unrestrictive submarine warfare had been waged by both the British and American Admiralties.

The ending of this unique episode of modern history was thus in keeping with the whole shameful story. To the very last no one was sure what it was all about and what had been decided, if anything. The only fact upon which everyone was agreed was that a distinguished naval officer who had been on the losing side was kept by the victors in rigorous captivity for nine years.

The case of Admiral Raeder has been compared with the case of Captain Alfred Dreyfus of some fifty years before. The two cases have certainly some points in common. In the Dreyfus Case a horrible injustice was committed against an innocent man and yet no one person can be named as responsible: a burden of guilt certainly rests on a number of persons such as the forger, Major Henry, and the real traitor, Esterhazy, but the main burden of guilt rests on a wide and ill-defined section of Captain Dreyfus' own countrymen, who having been led to form a wrong view of the case in accordance with their political prejudices, obstinately refused to admit a miscarriage of justice had taken place. In short, the worst criminal in the case was the average French man-in-the-street who, hating the Germans and mistrusting the Jews, declined to admit an error could have taken place when an officer of Jewish birth was convicted by a French court martial of selling French military secrets to Germany. Proofs of Dreyfus' innocence made no impression on him because he refused to consider them and hotly condemned as unpatriotic everyone who demanded an examination of these proofs at a new trial.

But regarded simply as an example of a miscarriage of justice, the case of Admiral Raeder is in every respect far graver than the case of Captain Dreyfus. Firstly, the latter was charged with a real crime—Dreyfus was charged with selling his country's military secrets to a foreign Power. Had he been guilty, he would richly have deserved his fate. Admiral Raeder, on the other hand, was charged with a newly invented, indefinable crime which he was held to have committed retrospectively. Secondly, in the case of Captain Dreyfus the legal machinery existed for rectifying the wrong done him: the only problem for his defenders was how to set this legal machinery in motion. In the case of Admiral Raeder, on the other hand, no legal machinery existed to rectify the wrong done to him: the international Military Tribunal was created as an infallible court and so no court of appeal could put right its blunders. Finally, the penalty inflicted on Captain Dreyfus was no doubt a savage one, but compared with the incarceration in Spandau Prison endured by Admiral Raeder, his sojourn on the Ile du Diable seems an endurable fate, particularly as throughout he was cheered by the knowledge that some of the ablest and most powerful politicians and literary men in France were conducting a furious agitation to establish his innocence.

Undeniably the Dreyfus Case is a blot on French justice. Still against the stupidity of the various courts which repeatedly returned verdicts against him and the unscrupulous determination of his prosecutors to uphold his conviction regardless of facts, can be set the enthusiasm with which enlightened opinion in France rallied to his support once the truth had begun to come to light in spite of all attempts to suppress it. His sufferings aroused a wave of genuine enthusiasm for the cause of justice.

When however it became undeniable that an even greater injustice had been inflicted on Erich Raeder, the truth was received with complete apathy. Those responsible for the conviction of Alfred Dreyfus were driven to uphold his conviction by forging documents. It was unnecessary to forge documents to uphold the conviction of Erich Raeder: the popular phrase, so characteristic of that period, "I could not care less", exactly expresses the universal attitude to the question whether his conviction could be upheld or not. No revelations of the truth disturbed the public indifference. Erich Raeder would have been left to die in his cell in Spandau Prison but for the chance that a change in the political situation made it expedient for the Soviet Government to consent to his release as an adroit manoeuvre in the 'Cold War'.

Only a year after Admiral Raeder's release from Spandau Prison an epilogue was provided to what the players in *Hamlet* would probably have classified as a comical-historical-tragedy. Great Britain and France, two of the Powers which had so solemnly condemned him at Nürnberg, invaded Egypt and pleaded in justification the same plea put forward by Germany to justify the invasion of Norway in 1940, namely, that vital national interests were at stake.

It is quite open to the reader to hold the view that this plea in the case of the invasion of Egypt was entirely justified. But the General Assembly of the United Nations rejected it and ordered the invaders to withdraw. Can it be doubted that if the distinguished admirals, generals and air marshals who directed the invasion of Egypt in 1956 had subsequently found themselves before an Egyptian War-crimes Tribunal, they would have been condemned for obeying the orders of their executive government just as Admiral Raeder was condemned at Nürnberg? It is even likely that the Egyptian Tribunal would have accepted the dictum of General Nikitchenko and held that the question of their guilt had already been decided by the General Assembly of the United Nations so that the only duty of the court was "to mete out the necessary punishment."*

* See page 214.

INDEX

Aggressive Warfare, Definition of: 58, 210-211, 216-217.
Alexander, Field Marshal Lord: 52, 66, 92, quoted 148, 153.
Algeria, The War in: 140, 142, 168, 186.
Ashmead-Bartlett: quoted, 15.
Audisio, Walter (alias 'Colonel Valerio): 27, 74, 76-84.
Azzano: 75, 78, 80.

Badoglio, General: 63-64, 141, 142, 144, 153, 172.
Barnes, Dr. Harry Elmer: 35.
Bologna: 138, 140, The Trial of Major Reder at: 160-162.
Bonzanigo: 75.
Brest, The siege of: 189-193, 203-204.

Caneva, General: 172, 173.
Chambers Encyclopaedia: cited, 54, 211, 212.
Churchill, Sir Winston: 18, 19, 26, 47, 52, 57, 63, 86, 90, 167, 220, 221, 228, 233.
Como: 68, 70, 71.

Derry, Dr. T. K.: quoted, 222.
Dombrowski, Roman: quoted, 29, 79.
Dongo, Mussolini's capture at: 73-75.
Dongo Treasure, The: 85.
Dönitz, Admiral: 211, 213, 219, 231.
Dreyfus Case, The: 235-236.

EOKA: 137, 140, 167, 168, 170.
Epopea Partigiana: quoted, 143, 146-147, 152.

Fort Clinton Prison Camp: 194, 196, 197.
France: Conditions in after Liberation: 30-31, 129-130.

Goebbels, Dr. Joseph: 25, 39.
Goering, Marshal Hermann: 213.
Gordeaux, Paul: quoted, 99, 133.
Gorrieri, Dante, 87, 88, 89.
Grivas, George: 137, 170.

Hampden Jackson: quoted, 97-98, 130.
Hankey, Lord: Foreword, VII-XIII, Views on Invasion of Norway, 221-222.
Harding, Field Marshal Sir John: 135, 138, 142, 170,171.
Harris, Whitney R.: quoted, 36, 58, 214, 216.

Hitler, Adolf: 18, 22, 107, 108, 111, 213, 230.
Huxley, Professor Julian: quoted, 16.

International Military Tribunal, The: 48, 49-51, 155, 186, 214-221, 232.

Judicial Ignorance: 220.
Jutland, The Battle of: 212, 218.

Katyn Forest Massacre, The: 25-27, 38-51.
Kershaw, Alister: quoted, 103-104, 110.
Kesselring, Field Marshal: 159, 170, 175.
Khrushchev, Nikita: Views on Stalin: 24-25.

Lawrence, Lord Justice: 50, 58, 155, 211, 218, 223.
Legoli, Julien: 153-157, 165, 171, 174.
Lewis, M.P., Arthur: quoted, 228-229.
London, The Treaty of, (1915): 61.
London Agreement, The, (1945): 213-214.
Lupo, 'Major',—see Mosolesi, Mario.

Mackiewicz, Joseph: quoted, 42-43.
Marzabotto: 31, 32, 138, 143, 151, 165.
Marzabotto Massacre, The: 31-32, 138-139..
Matteotti, Giacomo: 55.
Menaggio: 70, 71, 72, 73.
Ménéquaux, Monsieur: 177, 180, 182, 188, 201, 202, 203, 204, 207, 208.
Middleton, General Troy H.: 33, 192, 205, 207.
Mihailovitch, General: 22, 77.
Milan: 65-68, 75, 91-92.
Milton Bracker: quoted, 91-92.
Molotov, Vyacheslav: 40, 41, 42, 45, 46, 109.
Monelli, Paolo: quoted, 56-58, 80, 84, 93-94.
Moretti, Michele, (alias Pietro Gatti): 80, 87.
Mosolesi, Bruna: 143, 146-147, 152.
Mosolesi, Mario, (alias 'Major' Lupo): 140-141, 145, 151-153, 165, 167.
Mussolini, Benito: 27-29, 58-94.

Naville, Professor: 39, 48.
Neri, Captain: 75, 78, 86-87, 90.
Neurath, Baron von: 228, 230.
Nikitchenko, Major-General: 49-50, 179, 214, 216, 218, 221, 224.
Norway, The invasion of: 215-216, 220-223.

Oradour sur Glane: 140, 164, 165, 174.